The Political Dramaturgy
of Nicodemus Frischlin

University of North Carolina
Studies in the Germanic Languages and Literatures

Initiated by RICHARD JENTE (1949–1952), *established by* F. E. COENEN (1952–1968), *continued by* SIEGFRIED MEWS (1968–1980) *and* RICHARD H. LAWSON (1980–1985)

PAUL T. ROBERGE, Editor

Publication Committee: Department of Germanic Languages

For other volumes in the "Studies" see pages 154–55.

Number One Hundred and Eleven

University of
North Carolina
Studies in the
Germanic Languages
and Literatures

The Political Dramaturgy
of Nicodemus Frischlin
Essays on Humanist Drama in Germany

David Price

The University of North Carolina Press
Chapel Hill and London 1990

Library of Congress Cataloging-in-Publication Data

Price, David, 1957–
    The political dramaturgy of Nicodemus Frischlin : essays on
humanist drama in Germany / David Price.
        p.   cm.—(University of North Carolina studies in the
Germanic languages and literatures; no. 111)
    Includes bibliographical references.
    ISBN 0-8078-8111-2 (alk. paper)
    1. Frischlin, Nicodemus, 1547–1590—Criticism and interpretation.
2. Latin drama, Medieval and modern—Germany—History and criticism.
3. Political plays, Latin (Medieval and modern)—Germany—History
and criticism.   4. Humanists—Germany.   I. Title.   II. Series.
PA8520.F85Z87   1990   89-16733
872'.04—dc20   CIP

The paper in this book meets the guidelines for
permanence and durability of the Committee on
Production Guidelines for Book Longevity of the
Council on Library Resources.

Manufactured in the United States of America

94 93 92 91 90   5 4 3 2 1

For
Valerie Hotchkiss

Contents

Acknowledgments

I could not have written this book, nor could I have pursued an academic career without the generous support, both in intellectual and personal matters, of the Department of Germanic Languages and Literatures at Yale University. In particular, I owe an enormous debt to Professor George Schoolfield and Professor Ingeborg Glier for their encouragement, criticism, and, moreover, the example of excellence they have set in their own scholarship. I am also mindful of my obligation to the many librarians who helped me at virtually every turn in my studies, though I am especially grateful to Christa Sammons, Curator of the Collection of German Literature in the Beinecke Library, Yale University, and John Bollier, Assistant Divinity Librarian, Yale Divinity School. I also wish to thank Professor Richard Schade of the University of Cincinnati, who first whetted my interest in German literature, for his lively introductions to Renaissance and baroque literature, and for his abiding interest in my scholarship.

Many of the ideas as well as the organization of this book hark back to my dissertation, "Nicodemus Frischlin and Sixteenth-Century Drama" (Yale University, 1985). Over a period of two years, I revised my arguments and rewrote every chapter, with the result that this is, in virtually every respect, a new study of Frischlin and Renaissance drama, one that supersedes my earlier, somewhat hastily formulated views. Postdoctoral research on this project was supported by a generous grant from the German Academic Exchange Service; with this assistance, I was able to undertake a research trip to the Federal Republic of Germany in 1986.

Special thanks are due to Professor Paul Roberge, the editor of this series, for his prudent and expert review of my manuscript. In every respect, both professional and personal, it has been a pleasure to work with Professor Roberge. I should also mention that I am indebted to two anonymous referees who read my manuscript with great care and, drawing on their formidable competence in Renaissance literature, offered numerous corrections and suggestions.

Valerie Hotchkiss criticized this work, with rigor and expertise, at every stage of its development. I dedicate this book to her in recognition of her sacrifice of time and energy, and also in the hope that someday, should she become involved in such a project, I might be able to return the favor.

Austin, May 1989

1. An Introduction

Nicodemus Frischlin (1547–90) is now remembered more for his tragic fate than for his artistic accomplishments. Throughout his life, Frischlin was constantly involved in conflicts with those, mostly academics and noblemen, who had been offended by his critical and sometimes caustic writings. Eventually he was imprisoned by Duke Ludwig of Württemberg (1554–93), his erstwhile patron, and perished in a desperate escape attempt. However, his colorful biography aside, Frischlin was unquestionably one of the most important German writers of the late Renaissance, perhaps the most gifted playwright in Germany before Andreas Gryphius. If he is now largely ignored as an author, it is, as I hope to persuade, an undeserved fate, though one that he shares with most writers of the German Renaissance.

Frischlin's vicissitudes and struggles are so intriguing that, in retrospect, it appears that interest in his unusual life has detracted from study of his poetic works. In itself, the biographical trend in scholarship is neither amazing nor regrettable since, after all, his life makes for a remarkable story and also provides a glimpse into the political and academic conditions of the sixteenth century. While there is, relatively speaking, a dearth of research on Frischlin as an author, we have an *embarras de richesses* as far as biography goes. Carl Heinrich Lange, Carl Philipp Conz, Wilhelm Scherer, Reinhold Stahlecker, Gustav Bebermeyer, Klaus Schreiner, and Samuel Wheelis are several scholars who, to varying degrees of comprehensiveness, have attempted to depict the circumstances of his life.[1] All of their work, however, pales in comparison to the exhaustive biography David Friedrich Strauß published in 1856.[2] Some have quibbled with Strauß's pronounced tendency to sympathize with his subject's plight; Strauß apparently saw in Frischlin a fellow Swabian who, like himself, was undeservedly excluded from the upper echelons of academe. Nonetheless, his portrait of Frischlin is not only the richest and most poignant, but also, as even Strauß's critics have admitted, authoritative.

One might say that Frischlin, who was born on 22 September 1547, was destined for a professorial career from early childhood. At the age of thirteen he composed a translation of Psalm 23, most precociously, in Greek distiches. After entering the University of Tübingen in 1563, he expeditiously completed the requirements for the bachelor of arts (1564) as well as the master of arts (1565). As a beneficiary of the

Tübingen *Stift*, a foundation established by Duke Ulrich of Württemberg to educate Protestant clergy, Frischlin then embarked on an obligatory curriculum in theology that, in his case, lasted two years. In 1568, after having performed well in some minor capacities, he was named *Professor Poetices et Historiarum* at Tübingen, a post he would hold until 1582.[3]

Frischlin's ambitions, however, outpaced his academic successes. Not content merely to publish several impressive scholarly works, he expended considerable energy currying the favor of Duke Ludwig of Württemberg as well as the imperial Hapsburg court. He became something of an unofficial court poet to Ludwig and eventually composed several panegyrics to him, the most notable of which are lengthy poetic commemorations of Ludwig's two weddings.[4] Rudolf II (1552–1612) crowned him *poeta laureatus* in 1576 and, as recompense for Frischlin's *Panegyrici tres de laudibus Maxaemyliani II et Rodolphi II*,[5] even raised him into the lower nobility as a *comes palatinus* in 1577.[6]

Despite these preferments, he found it impossible to advance to the rank of *ordinarius* at Tübingen. It appears that some at Tübingen genuinely worried about Frischlin's propensity for getting into trouble, and others were perhaps jealous of his accomplishments. As even Strauß makes clear, Frischlin was a man entirely lacking in modesty; this trait, coupled with his early successes, seems to have irked many of his colleagues. Whatever the ultimate causes for it may have been, before long he had earned the enmity of nearly the entire faculty senate at Tübingen, with the result that he was passed over several times for promotion. A serious weakness, one that plagued him throughout his life, was his utter inability to ignore a slight of any kind, be it professional or social. Due to this pathologically exaggerated sense of pride as well as a proclivity to displays of drunken foolishness,[7] he eventually found himself embroiled in several minor conflicts with Tübingen nobility, all of which set the stage for an altercation with very grave consequences.

To a certain extent, his hour of fate struck in 1580, a full decade before his actual death. His troubles grew out of an attempt to publish a speech concerning peasant life in Germany with the unassuming title of *Oratio de vita rustica*. While it had been composed, harmlessly enough, as an introduction to academic lectures on Virgil's *Georgics* delivered in 1578–79, parts of *Oratio de vita rustica* were critical of corruption in the nobility, one might say stridently so. Already ill-disposed toward Frischlin, some of the local nobility got wind of the work's unflattering depiction of their class before it had been released for sale. In the ensuing scandal, the nobility of Württemberg and several other parts of Germany demanded that Frischlin be severely punished; some of his detractors even attributed to him the revolutionary spirit of Thomas Münzer, a leader of the Peasants' War.[8] Despite the tremendous pressure applied by the nobility, Ludwig initially supported Frischlin's cause. However, Frischlin, unquestionably his own worst enemy, lost much of the duke's support through a series of foolhardy moves, most importantly an attempt to go over Ludwig's head to gain Emperor Rudolf's permission to publish a response to one of his detractors. After this had been discovered, Frischlin was placed under house arrest and Ludwig forbade him to publish or write anything further on the matter without authorization. The affair was never actually resolved, and it remained a miasma that hung over the poet for the remainder of his life.

Because his career in Tübingen had essentially collapsed as a consequence of *Oratio de vita rustica*, he left Swabia in 1582 to assume a position as schoolmaster in Laibach (present-day Ljubljana), a city at the southeastern extremity of the German Empire. It seems that he performed quite well in that capacity, but to everyone's astonishment Frischlin resurfaced in Tübingen after less than two years, hoping against all odds to reestablish himself there. That not only did not happen, but his actions also led to further estrangement from Ludwig. At first Ludwig did in fact try to work out something at the university. But ultimately he turned against Frischlin, mainly as a result of a clearly substantiated charge of adultery that Frischlin's numerous enemies brought against him on this occasion. Instead of facing a trial, he accepted the alternative of perpetual banishment from Württemberg and also promised not to publish works that defamed Tübingen faculty. Frischlin did not abide by this agreement but issued pamphlet upon pamphlet excoriating his former colleagues, especially Martin Crusius (1526–1607), a professor of Greek at Tübingen.[9]

His final departure from Tübingen in 1587 was the beginning of a genuinely pathetic life as gypsy academic. Prague, Wittenberg, Braunschweig, and Helmstedt were the principal stops in his ultimately vain search for a suitable position. His demise came in 1590 as the result of an attempt to raise capital to establish his own printing press. Frischlin had written to relatives in 1589 requesting that his wife's patrimony, a tidy sum of one thousand florins, be turned over to her from the trusteeship that controlled it. Now he asked Ludwig to intercede on his behalf so that he could invest in a press as well as a saltworks. In an incredible lapse of judgment, Frischlin also threatened in the same petition to continue his pamphlet-war against Crusius. Ludwig's advisors, it appears, were flabbergasted and, instead of answering Frischlin's request concerning his wife's patrimony, admonished him in their reply to abide by his promise not to publish defamatory writings without ducal permission. The tone of the response was quite harsh, and it concluded with the ominous verse by Ovid: "An nescis, longas regibus esse manus?"[10] Upon receipt of this letter, Frischlin apparently lost self-control and immediately returned an insulting letter directly to the Stuttgart chancellery, threatening in most explicit terms to lambast members of the Stuttgart court in subsequent writings.

At this point, Ludwig issued a writ for the poet's arrest, and, because rulers indeed had long arms (*longae manus*) in the sixteenth century, Frischlin was promptly apprehended in Mainz. Eventually he was imprisoned at Hohen Urach under punitively harsh conditions, for the court had decided, rather cold-heartedly, that Frischlin should learn to rue his arrogance. Despite some improvements in the conditions of his incarceration, the poet's despair increased steadily until he ended his life on 29 November 1590, falling from the steep bluffs of Hohen Urach in a suicidal escape attempt.

His conduct and writings were controversial in many respects, but not even his worst enemy would have questioned Frischlin's brilliance as professor and poet. During his short life he published a prodigious amount of scholarship and poetry. Among his scholarly works are a lexicon, Latin grammar, and handbook on classical rhetoric.[11] He translated works by Callimachus, Aristophanes, and Tryphiodorus into Latin[12] and also composed paraphrases of works by Virgil, Horace, and Persius.[13] An unusually prolific lyricist, Frischlin published twenty-two books of elegies, three of odes, and one of anagrams.[14] And undeterred at the end of his life by the misery of his prison cell, he composed the *Hebraeis*, a massive biblical epic in imitation of Virgil's *Aeneid*.[15]

Despite the importance of these many works, it was his dramas that earned Frischlin a place among the foremost German authors of the sixteenth century. His beautiful latinity and the fascinating scope of his plays probably accounted for his success in the late Renaissance, though the modern reader might admire most of all Frischlin's instinct for dramatic character and situation as well as his detached sense of humor. His satiric nimiety and occasional burlesque remind one of Aristophanes, as does the preponderance of social and political subjects. While his satire engendered some enmity and occasionally even hostility, the plays rapidly became popular in schools and stages throughout Germany.[16] The Latin plays were frequently reprinted until the outbreak of the Thirty Years' War; the collected edition of his plays, as far as I can determine, went through at least seventeen printings between 1585 and 1636,[17] while the plays, counting originals and translations, were printed separately about thirty times. All of the major Latin plays were translated, most of them several times. As a consequence of his broad popularity, Frischlin strongly influenced subsequent Lutheran dramatists[18] and, perhaps due to the absence of confessional polemic in most of his plays, also contributed to the development of Jesuit drama.[19]

Frischlin used common biblical themes for his first two comedies, *Rebecca* (1575) and *Susanna* (1577), but soon progressed to less conventional subjects in his *Priscianus Vapulans* (1578), *Hildegardis Magna* (1579), *Frau Wendelgard* (1579), *Phasma* (1580), and *Julius Redivivus* (1585). He also published three minor plays, *Dido* (1581), *Venus* (1584), and *Helvetiogermani* (1589), which, as almost verbatim paraphrases of Virgil and Caesar, are primarily notable as examples of a pedagogically inspired use of Renaissance imitation. Some consideration will be accorded his minor works, but the major plays will for obvious reasons be the focus of the following study.[20] Moreover, I have endeavored throughout to widen my perspective as much as possible to include general consideration of humanist drama and literary theory. Frischlin's plays and theoretical writings, though distinctive in many respects, proceed from important trends such as biblical, historical, and confessional dramaturgy, making it not only desirable but also obligatory to consider them in the larger framework of German humanism. Indeed, though allowance must be made for idiosyncrasy in writers like Frischlin, one of the principal values in a study of his plays is the opportunity to explore humanist techniques for several important kinds of drama. Though it remains my wish to write an extensive work on humanist drama, it seemed premature, given the paucity of studies on individual authors, to undertake such a Herculean task. Yet the choice of Frischlin as a subject permits me to pursue larger questions while attempting to assess the work of a relatively neglected author.

Apart from substantial biographical interest, most literary scholarship on Frischlin has concerned his dramas, in particular a single play, *Julius Redivivus*.[21] Though one of Frischlin's best, the relatively high level of attention it has attracted is due, at least in part, to the excellent edition of it prepared by Walther Janell.[22] I shall have more to say of this in the appropriate place, but a curious feature of the scholarship on *Julius Redivivus* is the resistance on the part of scholars to observe its critical undertones; instead, most read it inappropriately as an unqualified encomium to German humanism. Of the earlier Frischlin studies, I should like to single out two which, like my own, surveyed the dramas comprehensively. In 1924, Erich Neumeyer wrote a lengthy dissertation on Frischlin's dramas that, while offering much useful information, failed to move beyond summarizing the plays to the task of interpreting them.[23] Another general work is Josef Kohl's study of the social satire in Frischlin's plays.[24] Kohl, however, was not interested in literary questions of form or the interpretation of individual plays; rather, he dissected the dramas with the exclusive goal of documenting what Frischlin said about members of various social classes. Other studies on Frischlin's writings, though important, are of a much smaller scale, and I shall mention them later as they relate to my interpretations of the individual plays.

In the following essays, I have studied Frischlin's dramaturgy from several perspectives. As a complex and versatile writer, he not only engaged several literary traditions and political interests but also composed several different kinds of drama. A professor of poetics and history, Frischlin was steeped in the traditions of Renaissance literature and theory, and he drew heavily upon these conventions in his theoretical treatises. As was the case with humanists in general, imitative theory formed an important basis for his writing. In several of the works I discuss, he articulated an approach to imitation that legitimated the peculiar symbiosis of Christianity and classical culture now called Christian humanism. Frischlin imitated Roman drama in all of his plays, though especially in *Rebecca*, *Susanna*, and *Hildegardis Magna*. His concept of imitative drama, as I shall demonstrate, was paradoxical; while it proceeded from conscious and sometimes rigorous conformity to the Terentian-Plautine canon, it also entailed extensive modification, one might even say subversion, of the Roman paradigm.

With remarkable frequency, Frischlin integrated sociopolitical themes and commentary into his plays and other writings. Although understanding of Frischlin as a political playwright must depend primarily on close reading of the dramas, I have found that consideration of his political theory of comedy can be elucidating. Frischlin's dramaturgy was strongly influenced by his study of Aristophanes and Roman concepts of rhetoric, especially the Roman focus on the political application of the language arts. Political rhetoric is a new but important subject for interpretation of Frischlin, one which, I believe, also has relevance for other humanist playwrights. In general, it was his political concept of drama that resulted in significant modifications of the model of Roman comedy and therefore constitutes the most salient element of his dramaturgy.

Of equal importance to the question of theoretical backgrounds is the task of interpreting the individual plays. My goal is ultimately to illustrate, by using the example of Frischlin, some of the different ways in which imitation, rhetoric, theology, and humanist pedagogy shaped sixteenth-century drama. Consequently, I have striven in the following essays to achieve a flexible balance between close readings of individual plays and broad discussions of trends in Renaissance literature.

I proceed in the following chapters through consideration of several topics, testing assumptions about Renaissance literature and putting forth descriptions of several kinds of German humanist drama. The organization is, I hope, fairly organic, one in which subsequent discussions grow out of previous ones. In chapter 2 as a prelude to analysis of the individual plays, I consider the implications that the act of playwrighting had for Frischlin and humanists. Like most humanists, Frischlin felt compelled to validate his literary interests. Consideration of the ways humanists justified their dramas situates Frischlin's dramaturgy within the humanist movement of Germany while forgoing an annalistic survey of his forebears. Imitation, the subject of chapter 3, is considered generally as an introduction to humanist literature and then more specifically in terms of the relationship between biblical and Roman drama. Renaissance imitation is the pervasive force of mediation between classicism and humanism; it was particularly important as an underpinning for humanist biblical drama. The impact of Renaissance rhetoric on drama is the topic of chapter 4, though I place emphasis on the role of rhetoric in the development of a political form of comedy. While political rhetoric also has bearing on the biblical comedies, it, along with Frischlin's politicized theory of comedy, serves as the basis for my discussion of *Hildegardis Magna* and *Julius Redivivus*. Pedagogic drama and the role of drama in humanist education are the subject of chapter 5. Consideration of several plays, but in particular *Priscianus Vapulans*, reveals that humanists consistently linked educational reforms to theological and political issues. The theological and political foci of humanist dramaturgy, a subject briefly addressed in the discussion of imitation and biblical drama, emerge as a single issue in the final essay, an interpretation of confessional dramaturgy and Frischlin's *Phasma*. I have tried to compose each discussion symmetrically, counterpoising description of a general issue or characteristic with detailed analysis of appropriate plays. The close readings of the dramas do not hide the fact that these categories overlap and that the general divisions into imitation and biblical drama, rhetoric and historical-political drama, pedagogic drama, and confessional drama are more of a practical, rather than strictly generic, nature.

Drawing on theological, political, and pedagogic interests, German humanists had a proclivity for didacticism. On the one hand, this occasionally resulted in a pernicious inability to grant any ambiguity whatsoever in political, moral, or theological matters; on the other hand, it should be noted that Renaissance German poets, taken as a group, evince an unusual degree of sociopolitical engagement, frequently in the face of personal danger. Either way, politics and theology, areas of intense concern to humanists, determined the selection of subject matter and also informed dramatic compositions in various ways.[25] Consequently, it is by studying literary technique in the context of these topics that we can further our understanding of humanist drama in general and the plays of Frischlin in particular.

2. Frischlin in the Apologetic Context of Humanist Drama

Why were humanists interested in drama, and, moreover, what importance did the act of composing drama have for them? While these questions would elicit slightly different answers for every individual author, it is possible to isolate some of the general reasons humanists advanced for writing and presenting dramas. On the whole, humanists were given to defending their literary activities, so much so that the apology for poetry is an important background to Renaissance literature. The explicit apology, both in theoretical musings and in literary texts, is partially a consequence of the controversiality of humanism; as such, consideration of humanist apologetics provides an initial glimpse into the issues that shaped humanist drama. Few, if any, Renaissance authors were in a position to write about politics or theology without fear of possible recriminations. It should therefore come as no surprise that, despite eclecticism and relative liberality in matters of form, little was published in the sixteenth century without some kind of justification. The pressures from those with authoritarian views of politics and theology affected literature in two ways: the apology, either explicit or implicit, became a constitutive element of poetry; and, more importantly, concepts of morality and politics began to determine what literature should be. As writers fully knew, dramas were judged according to political, theological, or moral merits, perhaps least of all on artistic criteria. The correlative to usefulness as a gauge for literary quality was, naturally enough, the prominence of moral and political ideologies in concepts of literature. Although there is room for argument over which was the cause and which the effect, it appears the expectation that literature should have didactic value led to the development of literary forms that propagated social and political ideologies. Specifically for humanist drama, this meant that the nonpolitical dramaturgy of New Comedy underwent certain mutations before it could serve as a model. Therefore, even though it partially exceeds the boundaries of an inquiry into drama, an account of the arguments generated to vouch for the usefulness of literature provides a convenient grounding for humanist drama.

Virtually always in the position of defending their programs, humanists encouraged the production of ancient drama for the simple reason that fluency in Latin could thereby be improved. From its inception through the propaganda of Italian humanists, northern European humanism enthusiastically embraced Roman comedy. In the first decade of the century, Germans began producing Roman comedy; the first recorded performances were organized by Conrad Celtis (1459–1508) and Laurentius Corvinus (ca. 1465–1527), and before long the practice became widespread.[1] Philipp Melanchthon (1497–1560) took up the torch from the early humanists and abetted the institutionalization of ancient drama in schools.[2] In a significant document, the School Ordinance of Saxony (1528), Melanchthon advocated Terentian comedy on moral and academic grounds. His arguments proved so persuasive that soon the requirement to learn Roman comedies proliferated in school ordinances throughout Germany.[3]

With virtual unanimity, the humanists considered drama an integral aspect of their attempts to alter the curricula in German schools and universities. Accordingly, it is important to remember that the phenomenon of humanist drama embraced performance in addition to composition. It is worth noting that the emphasis among many Protestant humanists until after the mid-century was on producing ancient drama. Melanchthon, for instance, did not write a single play, though he organized many productions of ancient drama in Wittenberg. Johannes Sturm (1507–89), the great schoolman of Strasbourg, has received much attention for institutionalizing dramatic performances in standard curricula, but he rarely permitted production of nonclassical drama in the Strasbourg gymnasium.[4] Only in the 1580s, after Sturm's decline, did sixteenth-century pieces become quantitatively significant in the repertoire of the Strasbourg school theater. In the second half of the century, the Jesuits institutionalized the composition and production of original neo-Latin comedy; professors of rhetoric at Jesuit institutions were required ex officio to write and produce a play with their students every year.[5]

The late institutionalized combination of rhetoric and drama had its roots in the early phases of the humanist movement. *Eloquentia*, as illustrated by Celtis's famous speech at Ingolstadt, became a buzzword for humanists seeking to increase the importance of the study of rhetoric at universities.[6] The humanists also generally held that the study of ancient poetry, especially Virgil and Terence, engendered the attainment of rhetorical eloquence. Strongly influenced by Italian practices, humanists advocated the production of Roman comedies in schools as a medium for improving students' elocution and fluency in a refined kind of colloquial Latin. In the imprint of his Ingolstadt speech under the marginal rubric of "quare comoediae et tragediae actae sint," Celtis says that the Romans instituted "publica spectacula" to help their youth learn both *sapientia* and *eloquentia*.[7] The inseparable combination of philosophy and eloquence, with its political benefits, forms the leitmotif of the oration.[8] With the Reformation the accents shifted slightly to emphasize the moral, in addition to the rhetorical, value of the production of Roman comedy in schools. Because the humanists, following Cicero, made the combination of *eloquentia* and *sapientia* indivisible, eloquence was never completely overshadowed by the Reformation's increasing interest in morality.

Nonetheless, the pedagogic value of reading Terence, a justification that could be used for virtually any classical author or genre, was usually tied to moralistic apologies. According to Melanchthon, Terence represented an ideal teacher not only of eloquence but also of morality: "et orationis et vitae magister."[9] Martin Luther (1483–1546), who was probably well read in the subject, also recommended performing classical comedy in schools.[10] As recorded in the *Tischreden*, he based his approbation largely on moral and pedagogic considerations. Using the ever popular Ciceronian topos of theater as a *speculum vitae*, Luther affirmed the commonly held, though disputed, notion that students could learn about the ethics of life from Terentian drama.[11] Although Terence and Plautus were shunned by many, Luther himself countered moral objections with a comparison to the Bible, observing that, like Roman comedy, it does not eschew obscenity or examples of adultery: "Und Christen sollen Comödien nicht ganz und gar fliehen, drum, daß bisweilen grobe Zoten und Bühlerey darinnen seyen, da man doch um derselben willen auch die Bibel nicht dürfte lesen."[12]

Moral defense of scurrility in fiction was germane to the study of ancient comedy, as well as to satirical writing. This was of concern to Frischlin, because, like many didactic authors, he portrayed the unsavory and immoral, sometimes rather extravagantly. His first play, *Rebecca*, elicited complaints about the characterization of Ismael as a debauched, abusive nobleman, though it was performed apparently without alteration during festivities celebrating Duke Ludwig's first marriage.[13] In his second drama, *Susanna*, he referred to the earlier controversy only to redouble his determination to continue portraying and satirizing reprehensible characters. Frischlin's justification for this, as spoken by the archangel Raphael in the prologue, was that the shock of seeing evil would deter youth from immorality.[14]

Many, including some humanists, were not inclined to see a moral agenda behind the bawdiness of Plautus and Terence. This, of course, was not a new attitude. Hrotsvitha of Gandersheim (tenth century), whose plays were first published by Celtis in 1501, asserted that Terence's indecency induced her to write moral comedies as substitutes for the *palliata*:

> Plures inveniuntur catholici, cuius nos penitus expurgare nequimus facti, qui pro cultioris facundia sermonis gentilium vanitatem librorum utilitate praeferunt sacrarum scripturarum. Sunt etiam alii, sacris inhaerentes paginis, qui licet alia gentilium spernant, Terentii tamen figmenta frequentius lectitant et, dum dulcedine sermonis delectantur, nefandarum notitia rerum maculantur. Unde ego, Clamor Validus Gandeshemensis, non recusavi illum imitari dictando, dum alii colunt legendo, quo eodem dictationis genere, quo turpia lascivarum incesta feminarum recitabantur, laudabilis sacrarum castimonia virginum iuxta mei facultatem ingenioli celebraretur.[15]
>
> [On account of the eloquence of the more highly polished Latin, many Catholics prefer the vanity of pagan books to the usefulness of Holy Scripture, a practice from which we cannot cleanse ourselves entirely. There are others who, while clinging to the Bible, scorn other pagan writings, but frequently read Terence's fictions; though delighted by his eloquence, they are nonetheless tainted by his blasphemies. Therefore I, the strong voice of Gandersheim, did not refrain from imitating him in the same manner of speech (i.e., same genre) in my poetry, since others value reading him; and while he retold the wantonness of lewd women, I have glorified the praiseworthy chastity of holy virgins, as much as my feeble wit was able.]

Obviously, moral considerations sometimes resulted in restrictive views of what constituted suitable dramatic form. Whereas Carnival provided playwrights with an excuse for writing secular dramas,[16] others composed "serious" plays explicitly to castigate the license and alleged immorality of *Fastnachtspiele*.[17] This illustrates not only how important Carnival was for theater but also that pressures from moralists definitely had an impact on drama. Burkard Waldis's *De Parabell vam vorlorn Szohn* was performed during Shrovetide in 1527, but its prologue devolved into a vitriolic attack on the depravity of *Fastnachtspiele*.[18] In the same vein, the Jesuit dramatist Jakob Gretser (1562–1625) characterized his *Dialogus de Udone Archiepiscopo* (first ed., 1587; rev. ed., 1598) as an antidote to what he perceived as the godlessness of Carnival.[19] According to its prologue, the play was composed with the specific goal of distracting audiences for one hour from the frivolity that was tolerated before Lent. Though Gretser expressed general concern about Carnival celebrations, *Udo* illustrates that the specific need to legitimate theater as a morally acceptable institution did not diminish, even as humanism spread and became established.

Expanding into the realm of political morality, many writers, such as Sixtus Birck (1501–54) and Frischlin, asserted that their dramas contributed to political education.[20] Like many others, most prominently Erasmus (1466/69–1536) and Melanchthon,[21] Frischlin believed that, by reviving the political philosophy of antiquity, humanist education fostered a healthy state. Humanists not only developed theories of political education, they also claimed that humanist studies in general provided the nobility (and others) with grounding in both political rhetoric and the ethics of their social responsibilities. Late in his career, Frischlin published several essays (to be discussed in chapter 4) in which he used the example of Aristophanes to support a theory of political comedy. Ultimately, this development of a political approach to comedy resulted in even greater incongruity with the *palliata* than did the attempt to foist moral didacticism onto Terence.

In his own plays, Frischlin frequently focused on the subject of proper conduct at court as well as the political responsibilities of the nobility. Because they were performed at court, his comedies were part of the larger enterprise of political education. Though Frischlin's emphasis was often on political morality of the nobility, social responsibilities of many classes concerned him. Some political figures were intended to be exemplary, but Frischlin also depicted injustices perpetrated by the nobility and the concomitant suffering of lower classes. His interest in social injustice is consistently reflected in his plays, and it is also the major theme of his controversial *Oratio de vita rustica*.[22] The speech entails an encomium of ancient peasants to whom sixteenth-century townsmen, courtiers, peasants, and, above all, noblemen are contrasted. The comparison of country and city life, as well as the criticism of corruption at court, was, as Frischlin pointed out, topical; new and important was the contrast of good peasants and corrupt noblemen, coupled with the strident condemnation of the latter. At various points Frischlin claimed that from an ethical point of view good peasants are actually noble, whereas corrupt noblemen are "peasantlike": "Quod si mores et vitia hodie facerent hominem rusticum, nihil per immortalem Deum rusticius, nihilque agrestius esset, eo genere hominum, qui quod revera non sunt, volunt esse Iunckeri et nobiles."[23] [But if today morals and vices would make a man peasantlike, by God, nothing could be more peasantlike, more barbarous than the sort of men who claim to be *Junker* and noble, but in actuality are not.] Although, strictly speaking, *Oratio de vita rustica* should be seen in the context of critical writings about courtiers and princes that flourished in the sixteenth century,[24] its political sensibilities are essentially the same ones we encounter in Frischlin's plays.

In addition to pedagogic, moral, and political justification, humanists sought theological grounding for the study and propagation of classical literary techniques. Luther's testimonies to the moral and pedagogic usefulness of drama, tucked away as they are in the *Tischreden*, pale in significance before the impact of his assertion that parts of the Holy Scriptures are actually dramas. He formulated this idea in his famous prefaces to Tobit and Judith. Obviously, he perpetuated the moralistic argument by claiming that the Jews probably produced such "dramas" in order to provide their youth with moral education. But in essence Luther argued that the art of writing comedy and tragedy originated with the Jews, whence it passed to the Greeks: "Und Gott gebe, das die Griechen ire weise, Comedien und Tragedien zu spielen, von den Jüden genomen haben, Wie auch viel ander Weisheit und Gottesdienst etc. Denn Judith gibt eine gute, ernste, dapffere Tragedien, So gibt Tobias eine feine liebliche, Gottselige Comedien."[25]

Luther's concept of the literary connection linking the Bible to the Greeks touches on a basic issue of Renaissance culture: the need to justify revival of ancient practices in a Christian world.[26] In addition to considerations of practical morality, two related theories were used to legitimate the revival of the pagan literary past: 1) many claimed that rhetoric and poetics originated in the Bible or were at least divine gifts to man; and 2) the presence of rhetorical and poetic conventions in the Bible justified the study of classical rhetoric and poetics by Bible exegetes. Naturally, theological legitimation of the study of classical poetics and rhetoric extends beyond the domain of humanist drama, but theoretical discussions of humanist drama can be understood only in light of these concepts.

Theological justification for the study and emulation of the classics was derived in large part from church fathers who had written extensively on the relationship of the Bible and Latin literary culture.[27] Early Christian writers educated in the Roman arts of rhetoric and poetics faced the intellectual problem of harmonizing two diverse traditions. In a sense, fifteenth- and sixteenth-century authors faced the same problem, but from the opposite perspective: they had to apologize for their study of classical literature, whereas the early fathers found themselves compelled to defend the simple, some said artless, language of the Bible. An important approach to appraising the Bible began with Jerome (ca. 347–419/420), who claimed not only that it was artistic but also that its achievement could be appreciated using the standards of classical poetics. Augustine (354–430) made an even stronger weld between Christian theology and Roman literary theory. Shying away from many of Jerome's erroneous claims for the metrical art of the Bible, Augustine expanded upon Jerome's observation that the Bible employs rhetorical tropes, going so far as to suggest that God invented the rhetorical arts. Based on such a view of the divine origin of rhetoric, he claimed that the interpreter of the Bible must fully comprehend the meanings and qualities created by the use of figurative language.[28] Thus knowledge of formal classical rhetoric and poetics came to be viewed as indispensable to Christian theologians.

Bede (672/673–735), the prolific theologian and historian, also drew on Augustinian concepts of exegesis but used them to revise the classical system of rhetoric and poetics.[29] His two works on rhetoric and poetics, *De Schematibus et Tropis* and *De Arte Metrica*, probably served as handbooks for instruction in monastery schools. In them, Bede used a new strategy that enabled him to sidestep the issue of the obviously different formal aspects of Greek and Hebrew poetry while still claiming that classical genres such as drama were derived from the Bible.[30] Following the grammarian Diomedes, Bede asserted that the mode of address was the determining characteristic of classical genres. This system reduced the number of poetic genres to three: *dramaticon*, *narrativum*, and *micton* (i.e., a mixture of drama and narrative). From this perspective, the forerunner of the *micton*, in Bede's view, was not Homer but Job; many of the Psalms were the first examples of *narrativum*, and the Song of Solomon was the first *dramaticon*. Such a tradition of blending the classics and the Bible was extremely important for the Renaissance. In a sense, Bede's *De Schematibus et Tropis* prefigures Renaissance rhetoric because it adopted classical categories and organization while expunging non-Christian content. Similarly, the idea that the Bible contained drama, as Luther contended, was supported by the intellectual tradition of late antiquity; Bede and Luther both found the genre represented, if not invented, in the Bible.

Bible exegesis of late antiquity had repercussions for the development of literature and formal rhetoric in the Renaissance. Melanchthon, one of the foremost humanist rhetoricians, invoked Augustine's argument in his own defense of the study of classical rhetoric. In *Elementa Rhetorices*, Melanchthon attacked medieval methods of Bible interpretation, asserting, however, that classical rhetoric was essential for Bible exegesis:

> Et sine discrimine omnes versus totius scripturae quadrifariam interpretati sunt. . . . Sed has nugas commenti sunt homines illiterati, qui cum nullam dicendi rationem tenerent, et tamen viderent scripturam plenam esse figurarum, non potuerunt apte de figuris iudicare.[31]

> [Without distinction they (i.e., medieval theologians) interpreted every verse of the Bible in four ways. . . . But illiterate men who have no concept of language invented this nonsense, and although they saw that the Bible was full of rhetorical figures, they were still unable to understand these figures correctly.]

Interpretation of the Bible, according to Melanchthon, proceeded from application of modified classical literary theory. But viewing the classics as derivatives of biblical literature also had an apologetic function. Study of classical literature, it could be argued, was valuable because it sharpened interpretative abilities for use in Bible exegesis. Many defended study of the classics on such a basis. For example, Valentin Boltz (died 1560), a playwright and early translator of Terence, cited the goal of comprehending the Bible as justification for avid interest in ancient literature. According to his own account, Boltz learned to understand the Bible through study of pagan writers, *sacra ex profanis*:

> Darab werden sich onzweifel auch etliche ungelerte verwänte Teologi streüssen/ das ich als ein kirchendiener/ mich solcher weltfreydiger/ schimpffiger/ fleischlicher matery undernimm. Denen gib ich dise antwort/ Das ich auß Virgilio/ Terentio/ Plauto und andern heiden/ hab das Lateinische Evangelium lernen verstan/ sacra ex profanis, und drumb nit jren glauben unnd leichtfertigkeit angenommen. Nun hat uns ye gott die freyen künst durch die heiden geben/ unnd welcher die künst verachtet/ der verachtet und verschmächt Gott selbs/ dann durch dise/ werden Gottes wunderwerck erkent/ [32]

In general, humanists had to develop a theologically oriented apology for their literary programs, and drama was not unique in this regard. Fortunately, they were able to cite the authority of the church fathers to support their cause. By searching for ways to find literary merits in the Scriptures, the church fathers eventually had developed a system that made classical theory essential to Bible exegesis. The humanists in turn could argue for the need to move away from medieval scholasticism and back to the classical approaches to literature used, as they claimed, so effectively by the church fathers. Thus defenses of humanist poetry in northern Europe often contained ex-

plicit references to the patristic tradition. In *Codrus* (1485), an early
humanist drama, Johannes Kerckmeister pleaded a long defense of
humanism based on Bible exegesis and the authority of the church
fathers. To lend authority to his position, Kerckmeister invoked Bede
specifically and allied himself with the patristic method of approach-
ing the Bible from the perspective of classical theory:

> Nonne primum carminibus oracula vaticina et Sibyllina et pro-
> phetarum data fuere? Num non prophetarum monarcha rex Da-
> vid lyrico carmine psalmos suos cecinit? Testis est venerabilis
> Beda presbyter in opere suo de arte metrica, qui ipse etiam tracta-
> tum nonnullum scripserit de scematibus, tropis et figuris, quibus
> nomen inscribens sacrarum litterarum claves voluit appellari.
> Tam sunt sacre littere poetice rhetoriceque dulcedinis plene, ut
> eas intelligere sine harum rerum peritia plene possit nemo.[33]

> [Were not the prophetic oracles, both the Sibylline and those of
> the Prophets, first given in poetic form? Did not King David, the
> monarch of the Prophets, sing his Psalms in verse? The Venerable
> Bede, a presbyter, proves this in his work on metrics. He also
> wrote a treatise on schemes, tropes, and figures, which he enti-
> tled the keys to the Bible. The Bible is so full of poetic and rhetori-
> cal sweetness that no one can understand it adequately without
> knowledge of these things (i.e., rhetoric and poetics).]

Even after humanism had become established, this type of defense
endured because there remained some visceral opposition to the
study or imitation of non-Christian literature. In an extensive oration
on imitation,[34] one of his major theoretical works, Frischlin also vali-
dated dependence on classical literary forms on the basis of the church
fathers' respect for Latin culture. At one point, Frischlin invoked
Jerome to sanction the continued use of the classics, provided, of
course, that the classical traditions be used to the advantage of the
church:

> Quanto magis nos merebimur laudem: si aurea veterum dicta
> nobis propria fecerimus? Divus certe Hieronymus alibi nos horta-
> tur, ut sequamur Israelitas: qui spoliarunt Aegyptios, et ex auro
> illorum fecerunt vasa ad Templum Domini. Nam et nos decere ait:
> ut profanorum Rhetorum, et Poetarum insignes sententias, ab
> iniquis possessoribus auferamus, et in Ecclesiam Dei, atque ad
> laudem et decus Domini conferamus.[35]

> [How much more praise we will earn, if we make the golden
> words of the ancients our own. Indeed, St. Jerome in one place
> admonishes us to follow the example of the Israelites who plun-

dered the Egyptians and made implements for the temple of God from Egyptian gold. And he said we should steal the excellent thoughts of pagan orators and poets from these unjust owners and carry them to God's church and transform them for the praise and honor of the Lord.]

To Frischlin's mind, the issue was neither the origin of classical literature in the Bible nor the use of classical rhetoric and poetics for exegesis but rather adaptation of the classics to create art with relevance to his culture.

Nonetheless, Frischlin also appropriated the concept that drama originated in the Bible. In his inaugural lecture at the University of Tübingen (1568), he restated the Lutheran argument that the stories of Tobit and Judith were scriptural dramas and asserted that many found a holy *soccus* (i.e., the sock, or light shoe of Roman comedy) in the Bible. At the very outset of his literary career, Frischlin contended that such a view of the literariness of the Bible was widely held in order to give his own study of classical literature the necessary apologetic underpinning. Frischlin's *soccus sacer*, however, represents a widening of the argument that drama is present in the Bible into an advocation of new biblical drama composed in imitation of Roman comedy.[36] The view that the Bible was the fount of playwrighting had sanctioned and nurtured the development of biblical drama in both German and Latin.[37] In the Latin tradition, as can be seen in Frischlin's earliest plays, biblical drama lent itself to the praxis of humanist imitation because of the obvious opportunity it offered to combine classical technique and Christian subjects.

Many dramatists had cause to worry about objections from theologians because drama was frequently used as a medium for confessional propaganda. Unfortunately perhaps, dramatists were always under the scrutiny of theological and political authorities. Gulielmus Gnapheus (1493–1568), the brilliant author of *Acolastus*, had to flee from The Hague because of his unorthodox ideas.[38] The council of Nuremberg also vigilantly regulated the dramas produced in its city. Nuremberg dramatists such as Hans Folz (ca. 1440–1513) and Hans Sachs (1494–1576) had to secure official approval in order to produce their works. During the 1520s Sachs was explicitly forbidden to compose works containing ideas that supported the Reformation.[39] Censorship was widespread and practically unchallenged. Authority for censuring publications, though resting ultimately with the emperor and territorial princes, was frequently delegated to theologians. Given this background, as well as the inveterate intolerance of many theologians, authors wrote confessional dramas at considerable risk to themselves.

Thomas Naogeorgus (ca. 1506–63), a leading Protestant dramatist, staunchly defended the use of drama as a medium for propagating theological as well as moral doctrine. In the introduction to *Iudas Iscariotes* (1552), a play that addressed the dilemma of not being able to detect false doctrine, Naogeorgus claimed that the theologian's office is not incompatible with that of the dramatist:

> Si Theologiae officium est docere pietatem verumque Dei cultum, et vitam Deo placentem bonaque opera tradere, atque e regione reprehendere impietatem, falsosque cultus vitamque pravam, haec omnia quoque nostris insunt Tragoediis, et efficacius quodammodo docentur. Nam, / Segnius irritant animos demissa per aurem. / Quam quae sunt oculis subiecta fidelibus. / ut Flaccus ait.[40]

> [If it is the duty of theology to teach piety and the true worship of God and to advocate a lifestyle that pleases God and works that are good, and consequently to rebuke impiety, incorrect worship of God, and depraved behavior, all of these things are also in our tragedies, and in a certain way they are taught there more effectively; for, as Horace said, "things heard incite the mind much less than those things our trusting eyes see."]

In *Phasma*, a comedy about confessional disunity, Frischlin addressed a major part of the German apologetic epilogue to theologians likely to resent poetic treatment of theological issues.[41] Disapproval of churchmen had to be feared particularly in Württemberg, where theological censorship was active.[42] Frischlin himself had been instructed on several occasions to avoid theological issues in his *Streitschriften*,[43] though in *Phasma* he obviously did not accede to such wishes. According to Frischlin, poets had a broad domain that not only gave them high social status but also empowered them to write about theological and political matters. For the theological issues raised in *Phasma*, he cited Luther's familiar claim that drama originated in the Bible, but he altered the argument into a defense of playwrights who use biblical or religious material:

> Ich will dir nit viel sagen hie/
>   Wie Geistlich sein die Comedi/
> Nemlich Susanna und Judith/
>   Tobias/ Lehren gute Sitt/
> So in der Bibel werden gelesen/

Daß lauter gedicht Spil seind gewesen.
Darumb es gar nicht unrecht ist/
    Ein Geistlich Spiel so zu gericht/
Und nimpt des Kirchendieners Ampt
    Gar nichts/ [44]

As was perhaps inevitable, political, moral, and theological apologies melded; Frischlin combined these elements by asserting that the poet functioned as an arbiter of Christian society. Such a definition had political implications that may have run counter to the wishes of Frischlin's censors, for the theologians at Tübingen claimed such a domain exclusively for themselves.[45] Frischlin cited precedent for his view in an impressive invocation of secular authors from the sixteenth century who wrote critically on theological and political topics:

Nam si Ecclesiastica et Christiana vitiorum taxatio, ad solos pertinet Theologos, et concionatores populi: tum sane omnes Iurisconsulti, omnes Medici, omnes Philosophi, omnes Oratores, omnes Poetae, qui praeterito hoc seculo, contra mores et flagitia humana vel in Scholis declamarunt, vel literis, ad posteritatis memoriam transmissis, aliquid in eam sententiam scripserunt: omnes hi inquam, sui officii limites excesserunt. . . . Damnandus igitur Erasmus Roterodamus, qui in omnibus suis scriptis, pessimos quosque homines insectatur: damnandus Ludovicus Vives, qui cum vocatus esset ad Regem Hispaniarum instituendum, multis libris in lucem emissis, flagitia ac scelera hominum liberrime et acerbissime taxavit; damnandus Sebastianus Brandus et Thomas Murnerus, ambo Iurisconsulti, qui argumentum suscepere Theologicum: et Satyrica libertate, in omnes ordines, in omnia vitae genera invecti sunt; damnandus Euricius Cordus medicus, qui patrum nostrorum memoria, in adversarios suae religionis, pro Luthero arma Poetica induit; damnandus Ulricus Huttenus: qui cum unus esset ex ordine equestri, ingenii sui vires, pro gloria DEI adversus malorum hominum conatus, pro defendendo Luthero convertit: damnandus Eobanus Hessus, Stigelius, Fabricius, Siberus: qui non modo verbum DEI carminibus suis explicuerunt et illustrarunt: sed etiam in flagitia et scelera hominum passim invecti sunt.[46]

[But if the ecclesiastical and Christian criticism of immorality pertains solely to theologians and preachers, then indeed all the lawyers, doctors, philosophers, orators, and poets who, during the past century, either declaimed in schools or wrote their opinions for posterity against morals and human failings, all of these,

I say, exceeded the domain of their office. . . . Therefore Erasmus of Rotterdam must be condemned because he inveighed against evil men in all of his works; Ludovicus Vives, who was summoned to educate the King of Spain, must be condemned because in many published books he sharply and bitterly criticized the sins and immorality of men; Sebastian Brant and Thomas Murner, both lawyers, must be condemned because they took up theological matters and they inveighed with satirical outspokenness against every social class and type of lifestyle; Euricius Cordus, a doctor, must be condemned because within the memory of our parents he donned poetic arms for Luther's sake against the enemies of his religion; though a knight, Ulrich Hutten must be condemned because for the glory of God he applied himself to defend Luther against the efforts of evil men; Eobanus Hessus, Stigelius, Fabricius, Siberus must be condemned, not only because they explained and illustrated the word of God in their poetry, but also because they inveighed everywhere against men's sins and offenses.]

Like so many others, Frischlin tautologically construed subject and apology; he had to defend taking his poetic subjects from politics and theology, while at the same time arguing for the worth of his poetry on political and theological grounds. From this apologetic stance, it is clear that an important, if not peculiar, theological role accrues to literature, because, as Frischlin asserts, it embodies a new weapon (*arma poetica*) in the battle for salvation. While political morality, especially that of Vives and Erasmus, figured prominently in Frischlin's defense of satirical writing, it was incumbent upon him to cite theological sanctification, here by listing the examples of Brant, Murner, Cordus, and Hutten. Theology, emerging with undiminished or perhaps increased importance after the religious schisms, retained its binding power, making it impossible to defend literature without invoking its endorsement. Drawing on diverse traditions, literary apologetics in the sixteenth century usually relied on citation of authorities, sometimes in the manner of an academic game. Yet it often happened, as in Frischlin's case, that dramatists were indeed controversial and therefore needed such convenient ways to justify the pungency of their art.

3. Renaissance Imitation and Biblical Dramaturgy

A recurrent theme in the literature has been, and probably will remain, the impact of Roman comedy on the development of drama in early modern Germany. Extrapolating from the prominent role of Roman comedy in Renaissance education, scholars have maintained that Terence dominated Renaissance comedy; as Marvin Herrick put it, "it is well known that Renaissance comedy was modeled principally on the plays of Terence."[1] Though it is, in my opinion, unquestionable that Terence was the most important model, such an observation does not by itself reveal a great deal about Renaissance comedy. Beyond establishing that Terence was an authority, it is instructive to consider the extent and nature of his influence. Furthermore, assuming that Renaissance comedies are not replications of New Comedy, we should try to account for the ways humanists differed from Terence even when imitating him. The general tendency has been to assess the impact of New Comedy in Renaissance Germany from a positive view, looking diligently for scraps and pieces of Terence in humanist drama. Though much has been unearthed and some similarities such as characterizations, diction, and the five-act structure were always patently obvious, preoccupation with borrowings from Roman comedy can obfuscate important characteristics of humanist drama. Consequently, it is necessary to pay close attention to fundamental differences in addition to the similarities between German humanist drama and Roman comedy.

Early humanists assigned enormous value to the study of Roman comedy, though virtually all their reasons for doing so coincided with run-of-the-mill defenses of the *studia humanitatis*. As we have seen, humanists claimed that Terence taught eloquence and moral lessons; he was even supposed to sharpen one's ability to interpret the Bible. But these arguments, which do not depend on qualities specific to Roman comedy, were also adduced to promote the study of Virgil, Cicero, and others. That Terence was prominent in humanist education is indisputable, but, despite widespread knowledge of his plays, the degree of his influence on early dramatists in Germany varied greatly. Jakob Wimpheling (died 1528), Heinrich Bebel (1472–1518), and Conrad Celtis included little more than occasional flourishes of

Roman comedy in their plays, while Jakob Locher's *Ludicrum Drama de sene amatore* (ca. 1505) and Johannes Reuchlin's *Henno* (1497) conform a great deal more to Roman comedy.[2] The early plays embrace religious satire (Reuchlin's *Sergius*), political panegyric (Celtis's *Ludus Dianae* and *Rhapsodia*, Locher's *Tragedia de Thurcis et Suldano* and *Spectaculum more tragico effigiatum*), or advocations of humanist education (Wimpheling's *Stylpho*, Bebel's *Comoedia*).[3] The political and religious interests of the humanists, particularly as evident in the satirical and panegyric plays, often precluded imitation of New Comedy.

Humanists imitated Roman conventions with remarkable resoluteness in biblical drama, a genre that attained importance after the advent of the Reformation.[4] But even in the case of humanist biblical drama, it is important to observe that in the process of assimilation classical dramatic forms were modified, distorted, and ultimately superseded. It has long been noted that Gulielmus Gnapheus achieved a breakthrough in humanist comedy with his unusually popular prodigal son play, *Acolastus*.[5] In addition to successful imitation of Terentian Latin and versification, he eschewed the simultaneous stage of medieval religious drama and tailored *Acolastus* instead for the Terentian stage-type.[6] Borrowings from Roman comedy are eclectic, but it appears that in particular Terence's *Heautontimorumenos* inspired his composition.[7] However, as he asserted in a prefatory letter, Gnapheus did not intend to confine himself to the conventions of New Comedy. The incongruity at hand was inclusion of lofty rhetoric as one would find in tragedy, but his justification for departure from Roman convention is to be understood in a very broad sense:

> Argumentum delegi ex sacris, quod in comoediae formam cogi posse iudicarem, praeterquam quod hic res subinde in nimis Tragicas exeat exclamationes idque praeter comicas illas leges, quas nobis tradidit Flaccus. Quod quidem crimen levius esse duxi quam a sensu et rei dignitate recedere. Malui enim pietatis respectui quam litteraturae decoro alicubi servire.[8]

> [I selected a story from the Bible that I thought could be put into the form of comedy, except that the material sometimes leads to rather tragic exclamations, which breaks the rules for comedy that Horace gave us. But I considered this flaw less serious than a departure from the meaning and dignity of the story. I sometimes preferred to respect piety rather than literary decorum.]

While moral didacticism and faithfulness to the Bible necessitated deviation from models,[9] the combination of dependence on, and divergence from, classical techniques was typical. Other important humanist dramatists, such as Birck and Naogeorgus, not to mention some Catholic humanists such as Georg Macropedius (ca. 1475–1558), Hieronymus Ziegler (died 1562), and Jakob Schöpper (died 1554), composed consciously under the influence of ancient drama, but all of them developed individual styles and deviated from conventions in various ways. Going well beyond the pale of New Comedy, these playwrights moralized and proselytized; they wrote about confessional and political subjects and more often than not drew their plots from the Bible.

Sixtus Birck's plays illustrate the important, but limited, influence of Roman dramaturgy. Initially, he wrote in German for performances in Klein-Basel and defended his use of the vernacular on the authority of Terence, who wrote in Latin, after all, and not in Attic Greek.[10] After having moved to Augsburg to direct the St. Anna Gymnasium, Birck continued composing dramas but began using Latin. While it is little more than an expansion of his three-part German version of 1532 into five acts, Birck's Latin *Susanna* (1537) represents an attempt to replicate Terentian diction and metrics. Nonetheless, Birck retained the choruses of the original, a practice never found in the *palliata*; he merely translated these metrical German versions of the Psalms in imitation of Horace's odes, thinking perhaps that two types of imitation were better than one. While the latinity of his play, some comic devices, the scenic organization, and some characterizations drew heavily upon Terence, Birck did not feel constrained by New Comedy; instead, he pursued a gamut of moral, theological, and sociopolitical agenda.[11]

The basis for this apparently contradictory practice of imitating and rejecting Terentian conventions can be explained in terms of the theory of imitation as it evolved during the Renaissance. Imitation became a complicated and controversial issue because it lay at the heart of all efforts to span the cultures of antiquity and the Renaissance. Eventually the scope of imitation became so broad that it not only encompassed consideration of basic questions of pedagogy and literary criticism but also addressed the relationship of literature to social criticism and theology.

Imitation took several shapes during the Renaissance. Beginning with Celtis's rediscovery and edition of Hrotsvitha of Gandersheim's plays,[12] extending over Frischlin and culminating in the dramas of Cornelius Schonaeus (1540–1611), the aspiration of biblical dramatists was to achieve the symbiosis of classical and Christian culture expressed in the popular epithet "Terentius Christianus." Though German has a strong claim to being the first,[13] and was perhaps the numerically dominant, language for biblical drama, this genre gained significance in the Latin tradition precisely because humanists could validate the technique of imitating Roman drama by taking their subject matter from Holy Scripture. Humanist study of ancient literature left its mark on many German plays, but it was the latinists who adopted imitation of classical practices and dramatic idiom as an overarching goal. However, most Renaissance theorizing about imitation concerned nondramatic genres; imitation's salience transcends a limited study of drama, but without understanding imitation it is virtually impossible to appreciate Renaissance literature of any genre.

Although it is difficult, probably impossible, to locate the beginning of the Renaissance, for practical purposes Petrarch (1304–74) can be taken as a starting point for a discussion of humanist imitation. Unfortunately, scholars have not taken stock of the polarity in imitative theory, namely, that imitation, even according to the earliest theories, entails dissimilation. In Petrarch's view, dissimilation is not only presupposed in imitation but also essential to it because divergences from models provide room for achieving originality.[14] Petrarch's flexible approach was both elaborated and challenged in the ensuing generations. The battles of the so-called Ciceronians against those with a more Petrarchan view of imitation raged until Erasmus's time.[15] Pietro Bembo (1470–1547), for example, took the extreme position that Latin could be learned only through imitation; because the best Latin author was deemed to be Cicero, he alone, according to Bembo, should be imitated.

Erasmus sported lightheartedly with the issue of imitation in his dialogue *Ciceronianus* (1528), a controversial work that had a strong impact on the attitudes of northern humanists.[16] Ciceronians were dismissed with the argument that Cicero's style, as even Quintilian noted, was not perfect, does not suit the temperament of all writers, and, furthermore, has been surpassed in many ways by other authors whose works also deserve attention. Although intending above all to widen the purview of Ciceronian imitation, Erasmus also opposed imitative literature that smacked of neopaganism. He did not limit his guidelines for good style to pedantic tests of grammaticality but instead linked them to the basic problem of using classical Latin to write for sixteenth-century audiences. Christianity took precedence over classicism, but Erasmus cleverly observed that Cicero, should he be resurrected in the sixteenth century, would not be a Ciceronian because, following the ground rules of Roman rhetoric, he would have to adapt his style to the new culture. In Erasmus's view, strict Ciceronians contradicted the classical dictum, one to which Cicero himself subscribed, that style must be appropriate to subject matter. There-fore, somewhat paradoxically, abidance in classical norms legitimated Christianization of the Latin language.[17] Erasmus was obviously influ-enced by the apologetic argument of early patristic writers that the style of the Bible, though naturally not classical, was nonetheless fitting for its rhetorical purpose of revealing the path to salvation in simple, readily comprehensible language.[18] From such a premise, he deduced that imitative literature must extend beyond imitation into dissimilation: "Porro, cum undequaque tota rerum humanarum scena inversa sit, quis hodie potest apte dicere nisi multum Ciceroni dissimi-lis?"[19] [Since the stage of human life has been altered completely, who could speak nowadays in an appropriate style without saying many things unlike Cicero?] Thus patristic defense of the simple language of the Bible surfaced in the sixteenth century as a caveat for parochialism in humanist culture. As if to plead for a pluralistic canon for Latin literature, Erasmus concluded that an imitation should not be incon-gruous with the temperament of an author and, most importantly, that Christian authors should study the Scriptures and the church fathers to find models. Using a humorous analogy, Erasmus stressed that the Bible itself legitimates rhetoric which differs from that of Cicero: "Habet divina sapientia suam quandam eloquentiam, nec mirum si nonnihil diversam a Demosthenica seu Ciceroniana, cum alius cultus deceat summi regis uxorem, alius gloriosi militis ami-cam."[20] [Divine wisdom has its own sort of eloquence; nor should we be annoyed if it is quite different from the eloquence of Demosthenes or Cicero. After all, one type of dress befits the wife of a king, while another befits the girlfriend of a braggart soldier.]

In *Elementa Rhetorices* (1532) Melanchthon included an essay on imi-tation, a significant contribution which, as far as I can determine, scholars have overlooked. Of general importance in *Elementa Rheto-rices* is the frequent use of the Bible and church fathers in addition to classical authors to illustrate rhetorical devices. Instead of caviling about the neopaganism of orthodox Ciceronians, Melanchthon strove to defend classical rhetoric; he feared that the study of rhetoric was becoming increasingly vulnerable to attack because of its pagan roots. The Bible had been misinterpreted, in his opinion, by those with a faulty grasp of rhetoric. Such a view reveals that Melanchthon was treading the narrow path of defending the language of the Bible while remaining aligned with efforts to promote humanist study of classical poetics and rhetorical theory. In part, his goal was to expand the applicability of ancient rhetoric for theological studies. He sided with humanist trends in education by fiercely attacking the allegedly obscure style of scholastic theologians, rather than their dependence on dialectics: "quis enim intelligit istos, qui genuerunt novum quoddam sermonis genus, quales sunt Thomas, Scotus, et similes?"[21] [Who can understand those people who invented a new type of language, examples of whom are Thomas Aquinas, Duns Scotus, and the like?] He touched on the Ciceronian controversy rather gingerly by calling this genuine crux of the humanists a special kind of imitation: "Sed praeter hanc generalem imitationem inventionis, dispositionis, verborum, phrasis, et figurarum, specialis quaedam est imitatio Ciceronianae compositionis, de qua inter doctos quaedam controversia est."[22] [But in addition to this general type of imitation of invention, disposition, words, phrases, and figures, there is a specialized imitation of Ciceronian composition; about this there is great controversy among scholars.] By thus stating that the Ciceronian is but one possible form of imitation—a misrepresentation of Bembo's view—Melanchthon was able to give his blessing to the practice of imitating Cicero.

As a basic principle of imitation, Melanchthon insisted that literature expand its scope beyond Ciceronian imitation in order to facilitate writing about contemporary life and institutions: "alia forma nunc est imperii, religio alia est, quam Ciceronis temporibus. Quare propter rerum novitatem interdum verbis novis uti convenit."[23] [Now the form of the empire and religion are not the same as they were in Cicero's time. Owing to the newness of things it is proper to use new words now and then.] Thus it is evident that Melanchthon, like Erasmus and many other humanists, held a flexible view of the refinement of latinity. Naturally, he felt that the would-be *orator absolutus* should consult Cicero, but he also recommended close study of the style of the Bible, church fathers, and even Renaissance authors.[24]

Frischlin developed his approach to imitative theory in several works, though most completely in an oration he delivered at the University of Wittenberg in 1587: *Oratio de exercitationibus oratoriis et poeticis ad imitationem veterum.*[25] Despite a strong orientation toward classical literature, Frischlin also concerned himself with the problem of using classical traditions for Christian literature. Although his tendency to Christianize the Latin heritage is most apparent in his approach to composing biblical drama, imitation is a pervasive element in his poetics. His favorite illustration of it was a parody of the Ennian extolment of Quintus Fabius Maximus Cunctator, "unus homo nobis cunctando restituit rem" [one man saved the state for us by delaying], as "unus homo nobis moriendo restituit rem" [one man saved everything by dying for us].[26] In a simple way, this example demonstrates the theological dissimilation at the root of much imitative literature.

Always displaying a strong historical consciousness, Frischlin made a point of advocating imitation for Renaissance authors on the grounds that it was integral to Roman literary practices.[27] He documented the ancients' penchant for imitation with many examples, sometimes showing that the model for an imitation was an imitation itself. In sorting out the layers of imitation, Frischlin tried to illustrate that writers, by recognizing the strengths and weaknesses of models, are able to make literary progress. Thus, in Frischlin's scheme, the craft of the philologist is theoretically subsumed in that of the poet.

An exemplary author in this respect is Virgil, whose critical skills enabled him to improve upon his precursors. To illustrate Virgil's use of imitation, Frischlin cited Donatus's pronouncement: "aurum collegit e sterquilinio Ennii."[28] [He collected the gold from Ennius's refuse]. Frischlin was a great admirer of Virgil and often imitated his works. He delivered a speech on the value of studying Virgil, *Oratio de praestantia et dignitate Virgilii Aeneidos*,[29] and also prepared editions and paraphrases of Virgil's *Eclogues* and *Georgics* as well as the first two books of the *Aeneid*.[30] Further, he recast books I and IV of the *Aeneid* into dramatic dialogue,[31] and his last major work, *Hebraeis*, was an imitation of the *Aeneid*. This infatuation with Virgil is particularly interesting because of the striking similarity between Renaissance approaches to literature and the traditions of Virgilian scholarship. Since the first century, literary scholars had viewed Virgil as an author who was deeply conscious of his literary predecessors. Virgil, after all, quoted other authors with astonishing frequency and often modeled his poetry on the works of earlier Greek and Roman poets. The view of late antiquity and the Renaissance was largely that Virgil had surpassed Homer with his imitation of the *Iliad* (*Aeneid*, books VII–XII) and the *Odyssey* (*Aeneid*, books I–VI). The comparative tendency in Virgilian scholarship, as well as the preeminence of Virgil in schools, served to legitimate imitative approaches to literary theory. Because scholarship indicated that Virgil attained his greatness through imitation, that technique, it could be argued, was valuable for other aspiring Latin authors.

Although Erasmus and Melanchthon laid down important principles for imitation, they did not produce a comprehensive treatise on the topic, either from a philosophical or practical perspective. The major accomplishment of Frischlin's *Oratio de imitatione* and *Methodus declamandi* was the expansion of general guidelines, such as those advanced by Erasmus and Melanchthon, into a rhetorical system.

Like others, Frischlin rejected slavish imitations of models[32] but still accorded imitation the central role in his literary theory: "Ut vero sententias et animi conceptus eloqui possimus sive verbis propriis, sive figuratis, requiritur Imitatio."[33] [In order to be able to express our opinions or concepts either literally or figuratively, we need to use imitation.] To a certain extent, Frischlin had a fairly puritanical attitude toward neologisms; in contrast to Melanchthon, he felt that new inventions and contemporary institutions should be described with classical vocabulary. To demonstrate how this could be done, he cited his own *Julius Redivivus* where characters discussed the new political system, modern weaponry, printing presses, and the manufacture of paper, using, as Frischlin claimed, Pliny and Vitruvius as models. This relative purism in comparison to Erasmus and Melanchthon bears an affinity to certain Italian theoreticians. According to Frischlin, Erasmus took too many liberties in his diction,[34] and Melanchthon, the *praeceptor Germaniae*, was guilty of over three hundred barbarisms and solecisms.

In his Wittenberg oration, Frischlin succinctly delineated the process of creating original compositions through imitation. According to his essentially pedagogic system, a student should exercise simple techniques of verbal imitation as an initial stage before proceeding to more ambitious imitations in which entire speeches were to be constructed following classical models. Frischlin codified three traditional types of imitation: *heterosis*, *parodia*, and *paraphrasis*. *Heterosis* is the easiest and consequently the least important exercise. With this method an imitation is rendered as prose or poetry in accordance with the model but executed in a slightly different genre. Examples of it, as Frischlin suggested, include rewriting an ode as an elegy and making a dialogue out of two letters.

Parody represented the linchpin in Frischlin's practical theory of imitation. Adopting a definition from Julius Caesar Scaliger (1484–1558),[35] Frischlin described parody in simple terms as the expression of an idea different from that of the model, executed, however, with identical or similar words. As the foundation of his system, Frischlin posited that humanists should parody ancient models from a Christian perspective. For example, Horace's poetry deserves diligent study since his piety, though pagan, is transferable to Christianity: "Et quid religiosius possit dici de Christo quam quod Horatius dicit de Phoebo: Nil desperandum Christo duce, et auspice Christo?"[36] [What more religious thing can be said about Christ than that which Horace said about Apollo: With Christ as our leader and under his auspices, we must never despair.] The concept that Christians could transmogrify pagan poetry into hymns for the worship of God would be enough, in Frischlin's view, to justify study of the classics.[37]

Parody was obviously a crucial technique for Christianizing the classical heritage, but Frischlin also considered *paraphrasis* a necessary exercise for the aspiring Latin poet. In a paraphrase the *sententiae* of the model, while remaining unchanged, are expressed in the language and style of a different genre; prose is transformed into a form of poetry and vice versa. In his view, *paraphrasis* inculcated basic understanding of the words, figures, and forms appropriate to different classical genres and also sharpened interpretative skills. Consequently, this exercise became the cornerstone for the *lectiones poetices* he conducted at Tübingen between 1568 and 1582.[38] In addition to his recastings of Virgil, Frischlin paraphrased Horace's *Epistolae* and Persius's *Satyrae*. As stated in his Wittenberg speech and elsewhere, had he not found himself in such straits at Tübingen, he would have composed even more paraphrases.[39] Of course, the paraphrases of Latin literature were executed in the style of other Roman authors: Persius and Horace, for example, were paraphrased in imitation of Ciceronian invective. According to Frischlin's taxonomy, his translations from the Greek also constituted paraphrases because they were composed in imitation of Roman works.

These are the paraphrases of classical literature, but works from other literatures could also be paraphrased in the style of classical models. Such an expansion of imitation marks a boundary between philological exercises and humanist literature. Because of its theological focus, the concept of imitation assumed special importance for Frischlin's biblical plays. Had his life taken a more prosperous turn, he would have written more biblical drama in imitation of the *palliata*. In the dedication of the first edition of *Julius Redivivus* to the city of Strasbourg (dedicatory letter dated 1584), he announced his intention of composing a trilogy based on the story of Joseph and a fourth biblical drama about Ruth. He planned to model his Joseph comedies on Terence's *Eunuchus*, *Heautontimorumenos*, and *Adelphi*, whereas *Hecyra* was to provide the basis for the Ruth drama.[40] Although, while incarcerated in 1590, Frischlin began composing the four Terentian biblical plays he had mentioned, the project was never completed. The drafts for these dramas are in German, but Frischlin most certainly had intended to write them in Latin as complementary plays to his very Terentian *Rebecca* and *Susanna*.[41]

Rebecca was Frischlin's first play. In the preface to the 1585 edition of his collected works, Frischlin referred to *Rebecca* as his child, the first one that "tied on the light shoe of Roman comedy": "Prima Rebecca venit, socco devincta Latino."[42] Such a characterization fits the play well because in it Frischlin imitated Terentian-Plautine Latin with unusual persistence; in fact, both *Rebecca* and *Susanna* contain over one hundred borrowings from Roman comedy.[43] Although Terence's *Andria* was arguably the most important model for *Rebecca*, the scope of imitation was eclectic; language, scenes, and characters were taken from various comedies. His particular keenness for using Terence and Plautus in biblical drama becomes clear when these two plays are compared to his secular dramas. The nonbiblical plays were also cast in the idiom and meters of Terence and Plautus, but, with the exception of *Hildegardis Magna*, they have far fewer direct borrowings.[44]

Rebecca begins with the following exchange between Abraham and Eleazar; it is important primarily because it corresponds almost exactly to the beginning of Terence's *Andria*:

> AB[rahamus]. Vos caeteri rus hinc abite, Eleasare
> Adesdum: paucis te volo. EL[easarus]. Dictum puta:
> Nempe ut curentur recte haec. AB. Imo aliud. EL. Quid est,
> Quod tibi mea ars efficere hoc possit amplius?
> AB. Nihil isthac opus est arte, ad hanc rem, quam paro:
> Sed his, quas semper in te intellexi sitas,
> Fide et sedulitate. EL. expecto quidnam velis.[45]

> [Abraham: You others, go to the fields; Eleazar, wait a minute. I'd
>   like to speak with you briefly.
> Eleazar: Save your breath. I suppose you want these things taken
>   care of.
> Abraham: No it's something else.
> Eleazar: What else is there that my expertise could accomplish for
>   you?
> Abraham: There's no need of your expertise for what I want done;
>   the faithfulness and industry I have observed in you are needed.
> Eleazar: I'm waiting to hear what you want.]

In Terence's play, Simo and Sosia speak these very words as they begin to discuss a scheme to force Pamphilus, Simo's son, to marry the daughter of a wealthy Athenian. Although it proceeds without the shenanigans and vicissitudes of *Andria*, *Rebecca* was also configured as a play about a father arranging his son's marriage. The opening scene and the same general subject indicate that *Rebecca*, according to Frischlin's intention, was to be a Christian equivalent of *Andria*. Not surprisingly, Jakob Frischlin, Nicodemus's brother, expressed precisely this view in his introduction to a translation of *Rebecca*:

> Jedoch weil diese sacrae Comoediae auß heiliger Göttlicher Schrifft
> und Biblischer Historia genommen/ und zumal auß dem Terentio

und Plauto, als dem Brunnen der Lateinischen Sprach herfliessen/ unnd nichts anders seyn/ dann eben der Terentius selber in phrasibus, und aber zu dem/ unnd uber das auch Gottselige Gespräch unnd H. Schrifft Historiae unnd Geschichten seyn/ acht ich das für nützlich/ löblich und gut/ wann man ein Comoediam Terentianam, als Andriam, absolviert und außgelesen hat/ daß man Rebeccam darauff oder darzwischen/ horis privatis et succisivis, tractiere unnd außwendig lehrne/ dann die schön Rebecca sich aller Dings mit jener Terentianischen vergleichet.[46]

Rebecca, however, is by no means solely indebted to *Andria*. Frischlin used other Roman comedies to prop up several scenes. The play's subplot, which concerns Abraham's other son Ismael, illustrates this eclecticism. Its first scene, a portrayal of Ismael tormenting the peasants in his realm, draws on Plautus's *Pseudolus*, act I, scene 2. In *Pseudolus*, the pimp Ballio enters the stage flogging a train of slaves, screaming, "Exite, agite exite, ignavi, male habiti et male conciliati."[47] [Get going! Move! Get going, you bums. It's stupid to keep you, and it was stupid of me to buy you.] Accompanied by his henchman Chamus, Ismael enters the stage doing the same thing, though peasants take the place of Ballio's slaves; Ismael also quotes Ballio practically verbatim, "Exite, agite, ite ignavi: vos male conciliati, male habiti,"[48] and his tirade is peppered with additional borrowings from Ballio's speech. This introduction is so powerful that it provides the direction for the entire subplot at Ismael's home in Pharan, the portion of the play most independent of the Bible. The influence of Plautus is also evident in Gastrodes, a figure who seems to be a composite of the braggart soldier and parasite. The tall tales he tells in act IV, scene 6 are a tour de force of Frischlin's ability to lift and splice together Plautine material. In the course of this scene, Gastrodes uses lines taken from the cook in *Pseudolus* (act III, scene 2) and the soldier Antamonides in *Poenulus* (act II, scene 1), as well as the parasite Artotrogus and the braggart soldier Pyrgopolinices in *Miles Gloriosus* (act I, scene 1). It is likely that Frischlin used Roman comedy in his depiction of Gastrodes, Chamus, and Ismael as a kind of rearguard action to protect himself against objections to the negative portrayal of these characters. As he actually did in other cases,[49] Frischlin could have claimed that they were not figurations of the Württemberg nobility but merely stock characters appropriated from Roman comedy. From this perspective, we see that a critical poet could use imitation as a defensive tactic, making it possible to cite a source should social criticism elicit too much controversy.

Frischlin, however, did not compose *Rebecca* merely to demonstrate how a biblical drama could be cast in the style of Roman comedy. The religious goal of imitation was significant, but Frischlin also heightened the political aspect of *Rebecca* in both general and fairly specific ways.

Frischlin dedicated the first edition (1576) to Emperor Maximilian II with the ostensible purpose of procuring patronage,[50] though his immediate desire was to be crowned *poeta laureatus*, a distinction he soon received from Rudolf II.[51] The connection to Maximilian is also consonant with the close ties which Ludwig's court maintained with the emperor; from the Treaty of Kaaden (1534) until 1599, the dukes of Württemberg held their duchy as a mesne-fief from the emperor. And perhaps because he in no way wanted to offend the Hapsburgs, Frischlin exercised great caution in the matter of religion. *Vera religio* is a central theme in the play, but, probably in deference to the Hapsburgs, it contains not a single overt reference to Lutheranism. The homage to Maximilian even suggests the kind of political register Frischlin intended for the interpretation of the play; in the dedicatory elegy he equated the emperor with Abraham, exclaiming: "Tu pater Abrahamus nostros defende penates: / Sisque Rebeccae huius cum pietate memor. / Sic toto vincas hostes super orbe rebelles: / Sic eat ante tuas Turcia capta rotas."[52] [You, father Abraham, defend our penates, and piously remember this *Rebecca*. Thus may you conquer your rebellious enemies throughout the world, and thus may Turkey go before your chariot in captivity.]

Frischlin's ambition for the laurels notwithstanding, the play was written primarily for reception at the Stuttgart court, a fact of some consequence for the interpretation. It was first performed at the wedding of Duke Ludwig and Dorothea Ursula, daughter of Markgraf Karl of Baden, in November 1575, and a subsequent performance marked Ludwig's birthday on 1 January 1576.[53] Ludwig's wedding kept Frischlin busy for a while. In a manner reminiscent of Ovid's *Heroides*, he wrote two elegiac love letters which the bride and groom supposedly exchanged.[54] After the festivities were over, Frischlin commemorated them in a full-length epic.[55] In addition to its general appropriateness, *Rebecca* has bearing specifically on the marriage of Ludwig and Dorothea. Abraham recounts at length that he is deeply worried about the prospect of Isaac marrying a Canaanite not of his faith because such a woman could be ruinous. Instead of risking an interreligious marriage in Canaan, he decides to send an envoy to Charra to ask for Rebecca's hand. Although he makes the larger claim that matchmakers are interested solely in political and financial qualifications, he laments in particular that the *fides* and *religio* of a prospective bride are no longer properly considered. He even attributes Ismael's godlessness to the influence of a foreign wife. By analogy, then, the play is a warning against a ducal match with a non-Lutheran and, as such, a commendation of the marriage of Ludwig and Dorothea Ursula. In the elegy to Maximilian, Frischlin made such a correlation to Ludwig and his bride explicit: "At neque Ludvico mea, Dorotheaeque Rebecca / Displicet: ille Isacus, illa Rebecca mihi. / Hunc Isacum commendo tibi, commendo Rebeccam."[56] [Ludwig and Dorothea enjoyed my *Rebecca*. He is my Isaac, she my Rebecca. I commend this Isaac to you, as well as Rebecca.] In spite of this, *Rebecca* represents Ludwig's court for the most part by loose analogy; Frischlin met any laudatory needs of the audience with a certain measure of modesty by avoiding explicit references to Ludwig and Dorothea in the text proper.

In one respect, however, the text alludes rather strongly to the situation at the Stuttgart court. Since Ludwig succeeded his father Christoph as a minor, he was entrusted to the guardianship of his mother, Anna Maria of Braunschweig-Ansbach, Markgraf Karl of Baden, and a few other noblemen. It is interesting to note in the play that, although Abraham is still alive, he has entrusted his servant Eleazar with Isaac's education and upbringing. Eleazar's extrabiblical role as tutor and guardian also gave Frischlin room for pontificating on the value of humanist education, as Abraham's encomium shows:

Tum filium meum, fidei, ac fiduciae
Tuae mandatum, curasti probe et bene:
Pudiceque educasti ingenium illius, in
Artibus, in honestis literis, et moribus.
Nam caeteri, quod faciunt plaerunque aulici
Magistri, ut principes suae concreditos
Fidei, a studiis ac literis ad otium
Retrahant, et philosophos contemnere, et viros
Doctos ridere assuefaciant: quasi principe
Indignum esset, vacare literis bonis:
Et satius, ut corpus venando exerceat,
Quam animum, praecipuam partem hominis, studio artium,
Et literarum expoliat. Horum tu nihil
Eum docuisti: sed ea tantum, quae pium,
Sapientem, laudandumque principem decent.[57]

[My son was committed to your trust and faith, and you took good care of him. With modesty you educated him in the liberal arts, literature, and morality. Other teachers—many courtiers act this way, too—are in the habit of scorning philosophers and mocking learned men so that they can divert the princes entrusted to their care from literature, leading them instead to leisure, as if it were unworthy of a prince to devote himself to literature, and as if it were better for him to exercise his body by hunting, rather than to sharpen his mind, the distinctive part of man, by studying literature and the liberal arts. You taught him none of that, but rather those things which befit a pious, wise, and praiseworthy prince.]

When Abraham vouches for the importance of education for noblemen and rulers, he is, to a certain extent, speaking in Frischlin's voice. But his expression of gratitude for the education of his son is also a thinly veiled homage to Ludwig's guardians.

Another political element of the play concerns widespread addiction among the nobility to the sport of hunting. In praising Isaac's virtues, Frischlin meticulously notes that he studied and worked hard but did not overindulge in the hunt. In this positive image of Isaac, one would suspect that Frischlin presented a model to the duke. Despite other similarities to Isaac, Ludwig seemed on occasion to have been more devoted to hunting than to ruling. By characterizing the raving mad figure of Ismael predominately by his preoccupation with hunting, the hunt becomes the basis for social injustice in the play. Still, this device has a general valence because hunting, after all, was the exclusive privilege of the nobility. The deprivations suffered by the peasants in *Rebecca* on account of this vice represent emblematically the disastrous consequences of an irresponsible nobility.

The structural principle of the drama is juxtaposition of societal order and malaise. Because there could be no suspense in the plot (and there was no dramatic plight such as one finds in *Susanna*), Frischlin introduced dramatic antithesis with the subplot. Before Frischlin's, no fewer than five plays about the marriage of Isaac and Rebecca had appeared in German.[58] To a man, the earlier German dramatists compensated for the absence of an intrigue structure, as one finds in Roman comedy, by introducing disruptive devils into the plot. Frischlin added the contrastive story of Ismael, which begins with Ismael and Chamus flogging a band of peasants (act II, scene 1) and ends with several of the same peasants beating Chamus (act V, scene 4). However, the subplot is completely distinct from the main action; it runs, spliced harshly between stages of the wooing plot, as a thematic opposition. As is common in Protestant drama, marriage symbolizes

the ordered regiment on earth, and the achievement of marriage constitutes a happy closure. The closure of the subplot is, however, distinct. The beating of Chamus serves to relieve the sense of injustice
that hung as a pall over the subplot, but it leaves the social problems
unresolved.

Generally speaking, the characters themselves embody good and
evil. Abraham, Isaac, Eleazar, and Rebecca represent wisdom, loyalty,
and piety, whereas Ismael and Chamus, who are both tinged with
characteristics of the stereotypical braggart soldier, are the negative
examples. Because it appears that he exercises power only over peasants, Ismael seems to represent a member of the rural nobility, a
favorite target in Frischlin's writings. Frischlin also included some
rather impassioned outcries over the plight of peasants who are
abused by noblemen. These crude noblemen are, at one point, called
Satyri, and their deplorable actions are even challenged by Syrus, one
of the victimized peasants:

> Deum immortalem, quae huius venatoris est
> Iniquitas? quae iniuria in hos innoxios
> Et immerentes agricolas? Itan' homines
> Pecudum ritu tractare istis Satyris licet?
> Quasi vero miseri in hoc nati sint rustici,
> Venaticos ut alant canes: quibus domi,
> Quod ipsi edant, nihil est. Nam liberos fame
> Experiuntur non raro contabescere.[59]

> [Oh immortal God, how unjust is this hunter? What injuries does
> he inflict on these harmless, undeserving peasants? Are these
> monsters ("Satyri") allowed to treat men like cattle? It is as if those
> wretched peasants were born to feed these hunting dogs, though
> they have nothing at home to eat. And frequently their own
> children waste away from starvation.]

This was not to be the last time Frischlin excoriated the brutishness
of the lesser nobility. As we have seen, in the course of the uproar over
the searing criticism in his *Oratio de vita rustica*, the nobility in most of
Germany called out stridently for his arrest and punishment. Ludwig
defended Frischlin in that affair and probably was largely in agreement with Frischlin's criticism. Perhaps more than elsewhere, Württemberg was characterized by a rift between ducal power and that of
the lesser nobility. The scandal prompted William of Hesse to write to
Ludwig, chastening him for allowing Frischlin to affront the nobility
with satirical dramas.[60] During the same period, Frischlin wrote to

Ludwig to remind him of the banishment of Duke Ulrich, Ludwig's grandfather, from Württemberg during the revolt of the Swabian League. Frischlin emphasized that one of his current detractors descended from a nobleman who had deserted Ulrich.[61] Given the sixteenth-century history of the house of Württemberg, it seems likely that this emphasis in Frischlin's satire was not discordant with ducal policy of consolidating its power over the nobility.

Frischlin devoted some scenes in *Rebecca* to courtly ethics and politics. Much of the didacticism is couched in antithetical terms, as in Abraham's praise of Eleazar to whom he contrasted the typical courtier.[62] Furthermore, the repartee between Abraham and Eleazar (act I, scene 1) demonstrates how a model relationship between ruler and minister functions. The other perspective, that of the bad minister, is embodied in Chamus. In act V, scene 4, Chamus, who to that point had been designated a hunter, is called an *aulicus* (minister or courtier). Pointing to the drunken Chamus as an example of a debauched courtier, Syrus complains to the audience: "Exemplum vide. / Isti, dum sanitati principum student, / In morbos incidunt, podagram, cheragram, hydropem, / Dolorem colicum, et similes febres."[63] [Look at this specimen, while they are concerned about the health of princes, they get diseases such as gout (in their feet and hands), dropsy, colic, and similar fevers.] Frischlin, however, exercised caution in this subject. For example, Abraham's claim that most courtiers act on their own behalf probably had special poignancy during the period of Ludwig's minority, though the substance of the criticism, cast as it is in broad terms, would have found general approbation at virtually any court.

Frischlin obviously felt that a biblical comedy must be more than a reconstitution of biblical material set in the language and style of Terence. He achieved his aim very deftly by shaping the biblical story in such a way that the action in *Rebecca* reflected elements of importance to German courts, especially the Stuttgart court. The gravity of religion in a political marriage, courtly conduct and misconduct, the education of a prince, and even the guardianship of a ruler during his minority were important political issues in general, but ones of particular interest to a Württemberg audience of 1575.

Although it has attracted little scholarly attention, *Susanna* (1577) was Frischlin's masterpiece in the medium of biblical drama.[64] In writing a play on this subject, Frischlin did nothing out of the ordinary; Birck, Sebastian Brant (1457–1521), and Paul Rebhun (ca. 1500–1546) number among the several authors who dramatized the apocryphal story of Susanna.[65] After Frischlin, and partially in imitation of him, authors such as Heinrich Julius of Braunschweig (1564–1613), Schonaeus, and Samuel Israel (died 1633) composed Susanna dramas.[66]

Susanna should also be considered in light of its relationship to Roman comedy. In contrast to *Rebecca* and the plans Frischlin made for other biblical dramas, it is not possible to claim that *Susanna* was composed as an alternative to a particular Terentian play.[67] Frischlin's style in *Susanna*, however, corresponds generally to that in *Rebecca*. It too employs the metrics and diction of Plautus and Terence and abounds with reminiscences of scenes and characters of the *palliata*.

Like *Rebecca*, *Susanna* represents an eristic composition vis-à-vis Terence. In the school ordinance he composed for Laibach, Frischlin recommended that *Primaner* be required to read his *Susanna* in addition to a play by Terence.[68] Georg Pflüger, who edited Frischlin's dramas in order to document the compatibility of Frischlin and Roman comedy, also suggested that Frischlin's comedies be read in addition to, not instead of, Terence.[69] Pflüger belabored this point because there were movements afoot calling for the replacement of Terence in the schools with the pious comedies of Christian authors. In his first two dramas Frischlin pursued the goal of composing *sacrae comoediae* in the manner of Terence, running the risk, as it were, of ultimately replacing Terence as a school author. But despite his success, Frischlin resolutely opposed the notion of banning pagan authors from the classroom.

Frischlin quoted copiously from Roman comedy in the prologue and opening scenes of *Susanna*. The dialogue between Midian and Simeon, the two offending judges, suggests the opening scene in *Heautontimorumenos*. As Pflüger observed, Midian echoes the role of Chremes, while Simeon evokes the inquisitive Menedemus. Like Terence, Frischlin used the dialogue to establish setting, but the tenor of Frischlin's scene differs starkly from that in *Heautontimorumenos*. Terence depicted the essential good-heartedness of Chremes and Menedemus in this dialogic exchange, whereas Frischlin's scene exposes the utter depravity of his judges.

While it is hard to prove every argument for a specific influence, Frischlin's play evinces some similarities to Birck's *Susanna* (1532 and 1537) and Rebhun's *Susanna* (1536). In comparison to both of these, however, Frischlin conformed somewhat more strictly to the conventions of Roman comedy. Unlike the two earlier dramatists, he included neither chorus nor epilogue in his play. Perhaps in reliance on Birck, Frischlin began the action with the attempted seduction. Birck ended his first act with an uproar among Susanna, her servants, and the judges. Frischlin's judges leave the stage briefly at the end of act I in order to attract the attention of Susanna's servants; act II begins with a prayer in soliloquy by Susanna, followed by the judges' denunciation before Susanna's servant Philergus (act II, scene 2). The sequence of action is identical in the two versions: 1) meeting of lecherous judges; 2) Susanna and servants; 3) Susanna and the judges. Although it probably influenced Frischlin, Birck's version is rather flat in comparison; his text and characterizations pale next to Frischlin's. Furthermore, while Frischlin wrote a deeply disturbing subplot, Birck expanded the biblical narrative with a laborious enactment of the trial.

Frischlin drew his characters skillfully. In *Susanna* he adeptly cast lecherous villains, pathetic matrons, noble judges, common criminals, and idealistic peasants. This is a result not only of his sense for the dramatic and ludicrous but also of Frischlin's verbal artistry, for the subtle fluency of his Latin enabled him to breathe life into the various characters of his plays. The two dissolute judges are a good illustration of this. Frischlin cast one, Midian, as a timid offender, the other, Simeon, as a brazen scoundrel. Unlike most moralists of the century, he portrayed the seaminess of both in a comic, one might say Aristophanic, manner. He highlighted the comic elements at considerable risk to the drama's coherence, because the judges eventually turn out to be wholly despicable creatures instead of merely lecherous fools. Of the two, Midian is the more comic figure. He cowers meekly before the forceful Simeon, and, at the crucial point, falls flat on his face trying to seduce Susanna with flattery. Simeon, the mastermind of the plot, is evil through and through. His language is subtle and possessed of rare colloquial eloquence, enabling him to formulate his schemes and desires in ingenious ways.

In his attempts at levity, Frischlin interjected humor in scenes where it is unexpected, perhaps even inappropriate. An example of this is act I, scene 2, the overture to the attempted seduction. There, Susanna discusses preparations for the welcome of her husband Joachim, only to be overheard by Simeon and Midian. As she says with too much emphasis, Susanna wants to bathe and perfume herself in anticipation of Joachim's arrival. Thamar, her maid, insists that such preparations are not necessary because Susanna is naturally charming. With exaggerated prescience, Thamar and Susanna expatiate on the harm which can result from such prodigious beauty, as had happened, they point out, to Sarah and Rebecca. Because Frischlin adopted in this instance the New Comedy technique of staging two conversations simultaneously, the scene contrasts the judges' crude palaver with Susanna's espousals of fidelity. As the judges' conversation gets seamy, Frischlin

undercuts its grotesqueness with some funny, albeit somewhat soph-
omoric, touches. For example, Simeon, who enjoys mocking his col-
league's ineptitude, outdoes Midian in articulating the intensity of his
lust:

> MI[dian]. Dii immortales, omnipotentes, quid apud vos pulchrius?
> Nam prae hac, Iuno non est Iuno, Venus non est Venus.
> Hanc equidem Venerem venerabor, me ut amet, ac sit propitia.
> SI[meon]. Ita me dii ament, ut illa me amet malim, quam alii
>   coelites.
> MI. Scin tu quid fieri nunc optem? SI. quid? MI. Iuppiter. SI.
>   quamobrem? MI. ut hac
> Cum Iunone accubem illico. SI. at ego te alium hic fieri mavelim.
> MI. Quem nam? SI. Vulcanum: ut me cum hac Venere catena nec-
>   tas ferrea.[70]

> [Midian: Immortal, omnipotent gods! Do you have anything so
>   beautiful? In comparison to this woman (i.e., Susanna) Juno is
>   not Juno, Venus is not Venus. Indeed, I will adore this Venus so
>   that she will love me and be willing.
> Simeon: May the gods love me, but I'd prefer that she, more than
>   any other gods, would love me.
> Midian: Do you know what I'd like to turn into?
> Simeon: What?
> Midian: Jupiter.
> Simeon: Why?
> Midian: So I could make love with that Juno immediately.
> Simeon: I'd rather you became someone else.
> Midian: Who?
> Simeon: Vulcan, so that you could bind me in iron chains to that
>   Venus.]

Act II, scene 3 begins an extensive subplot about the dealings of the
peasants Sichar and Hiram with the salacious judges. Although subplots occur frequently in Frischlin's dramas, it should be noted that
Rebhun had also used this technique in his *Susanna*. In the second act
of Rebhun's drama, one of the judges cheats a widow out of her
husband's legacy. Frischlin's subplot also focuses on the judges. Sichar, a rambling talker, complains about Midian's refusal to hear a case
Sichar wants to bring, unless a fee of three shekels is paid. Hiram, one
of Sichar's neighbors, also happens onto the scene and begins lament-
ing the treatment he has received from the judges. Hiram's problems
are, however, much more serious; he is dealing with the two judges
over a case of rape involving Simeon's son, who, it turns out, had

assaulted the daughter of another neighbor. Midian refused to prosecute the case on the grounds that Simeon's son, as a nobleman, was immune to a charge brought by a peasant. Intensifying the horror of the story, Hiram discloses that Midian, on the pretext of interrogating the girl, also raped her. Naturally, the peasants are keen for revenge, but unfortunately they are at a loss as to what action they should take. While the rapes are the dark reflection of the Susanna story and meant to represent just that, Frischlin also used the subplot to place the sexual intimidation in a second social context. Unlike Susanna, who is at least entitled to a hearing, the peasants struggle in vain to find any avenue of recourse; their state of affairs is even more threatening than that of Susanna because class distinction, so it appears, sanctions the blatant injustice perpetrated by the judges.

The social dimension differentiates Frischlin's from Rebhun's *Susanna*. Whereas for Frischlin the potential for injustice in a rigid class-society was cause for concern, Rebhun sought to demonstrate in his play that the lower classes should have faith in the justice of God in the face of social injustice on earth. According to Rebhun's epilogue, the abused widow in his play is an example to the impoverished that they should endure their lot in life and not disobey social superiors, no matter how corrupt noblemen may be.[71] Rebhun was obviously writing in the aftermath of Luther's and Melanchthon's calls for the peasant class to obey the nobility unconditionally. However, at no time do the characters of Frischlin's play show the slightest sign of resignation, passivity, or acceptance of fate. Susanna, Joachim, and the peasants are all resolutely engaged in their opposition to the magistrates. In the denouement—with Daniel functioning as prosecutor (act V, scene 3)—all of the crimes, taken together, result in the conviction of the judges. In fact, the peasants' testimony about the rapes issues directly in the condemnation of the judges. In his summation of the case, Daniel emphasizes the pervasiveness of social injustice, remonstrating the crimes against Sichar, the peasant girl, and Susanna: "leges pretio fixas, refixisti pretio: / Torsisti iura, extorsisti pecunias: quin insuper / Vitiasti virgines: probis matronis insidiatus es."[72] [For a price, you posted laws. For a price, you rescinded laws. You twisted the laws, you extorted money. Worse than that, you raped maidens and plotted against honest women.]

Frischlin and Birck focused sharply on the legal proceedings in the story of Susanna. Whereas Birck devoted over half of his play to the trial, Frischlin concentrated it neatly into equal parts: Susanna's trial and initial conviction (act IV), and the cross-examination of the two judges by Daniel and their subsequent conviction (act V). Frischlin's trial scenes emphasize rhetoric. When Cleophas, the presiding judge, summons the plaintiff to make a statement, he asks Simeon to use simple oratorical style: "Dic tu ergo prior, Simeon, et dic omissis vocum ambagibus / More Attico."[73] [You speak first, Simeon, and speak in the Attic style (i.e., unadorned style) without any circumlocutions.] Obligingly, Simeon delivers a tight, plain narration of the fabricated events of the crime, though only after disavowing any personal interest in the case: "dicam. sed hoc primum mihi credatis velim, / Nihil a me cuiusquam odio, nihil invidia, sed studio rei, / Et veritatis omnia dici."[74] [I will speak. But first I want you to believe that I will say nothing because I dislike or envy anyone, but rather everything is said out of a concern to clear up this matter and find the truth.] After this auspicious beginning, the jury, it would seem, is putty in his hands. Simeon continues his account with consummate Ciceronian eloquence, concluding with a request that capital punishment be meted out in this case.

Susanna, though bareheaded as a mark of disgrace, delivers her own impassioned defense. After opening with a plea that the jury hear her with the same level of attention accorded the judges, she describes herself as a woman without place, a person without refuge, now that she has been robbed of trust and virtue. In the *narratio*, she explains in measured but forceful cadence that the prosecution's charges depart widely from the truth. To this reasoned and dignified statement, Frischlin counterposed a bitter complaint, delivered by Susanna herself after her conviction. To be sure, she utters a lament, bursting with pathos, of injustice on earth, but she never submits to the yoke of such tyranny. Ultimately, however, the different rhetorical approaches matter little. In Frischlin's play, rhetoric emerges as being utterly ineffectual, for again, as in Rebhun, the case turns on the reputations of the accusing judges; Susanna is convicted solely on the strength of their perjured oaths. This, of course, is an unusually pessimistic outlook, one that is perhaps unexpected in a humanist. Despite humanist claims for the power of rhetoric, Frischlin portrays it, even when perfectly executed, as being either inefficacious or tragically deceptive.

In addition to the focus on rhetoric, Frischlin stressed procedural ethics in his courtroom scenes. In act IV, Cleophas raises the issue of justice and juridical ethics by trying to counteract the unprofessional tendencies of the jury of judges, who are inclined to believe their colleagues Midian and Simeon without considering the facts of the case. To avoid a miscarriage of justice, Cleophas urges the judges to overcome their biases in order to evaluate the case properly: "praeiudicia mihi haud placent. / Nam pars altera ut itidem audiatur, ipsa ratio postulat: / Et aequitas iubet."[75] [I do not like these prejudgments. Reason (or law), as well as a concept of equality, requires that the other side be heard in the same way.] Yet, as a result of Frischlin's goal of interpreting the near tragedy in social terms, the prejudices cannot be dislodged, and only divine intervention can rectify the mistrial.

As is frequently the case in Renaissance literature, we can best appreciate Frischlin's originality by looking at the imitative qualities of *Susanna*. For the popular genre of biblical drama, this play embodies the fruition of the cultural program of Christian classicism. Dramaturgically, Frischlin profited from earlier experiments with the material, but he was also able to give his own distinctive stamp to the techniques of sixteenth-century dramatists and those of Roman comedy. His use of language, orchestration of particular scenes, and occasional characterizations need to be viewed in comparison to Terence, but Frischlin maintained enough distance from his models to write a coherent and fluent script. Not at all a cento of Terentian comedy, *Susanna* attests the ease with which Frischlin shaped traditional material and techniques to create original dramas. He strayed farthest from his sources in the composition of subplots. But the peasant subplots in both *Rebecca* and *Susanna* were essential because they provided the context for sharply focused social criticism that corroborated Frischlin's political interpretations of the scriptural stories.

The topic of biblical drama invites consideration of an aspect of cultural incongruence in the Renaissance: the dichotomy of Latin and German literature. Biblical drama constituted one of the most popular and complex vernacular genres. Birck composed his first version of *Susanna* in German, and the first dramatization of the subject was, as far as I can determine, an anonymous German play of the late fifteenth century.[76] Both Rebecca and Susanna were popular subjects for German dramatists before Frischlin. Frischlin definitely drew upon the vernacular versions, though he shaped his plays in accordance with the demanding principles of imitation. This, however, did not exhaust the confluence of the frequently bifurcated traditions of Latin and German literature. Frischlin's two Latin biblical dramas, in turn, were translated seven times into German.[77] The moral as well as sociopolitical thematics of Frischlin's biblical dramas enabled them to enjoy considerable popularity outside the Latin schools, though it proved impossible to translate the elegance of Frischlin's Latin.

While incarcerated at the end of his life under abhorrent conditions, Frischlin eked out two biblical dramas in German: *Ruth* and *Die Hoch-*

zeit zu Kana. Because both plays remained unprinted until the mid-nineteenth century, they had absolutely no impact on German letters. In them, Frischlin again demonstrated his ability to amplify biblical stories into complete dramas, though his facility in German was rather uneven, especially in the use of imperfect rhymes, line-fillers, and syncope. These two plays are rather disappointing from a political perspective because of the sharply limited scope of their plots, although both plays quote New Testament formulations concerning the nobility of the poor and corruptness of the wealthy. Nonetheless, Frischlin's German biblical dramas reveal that the efficacy of imitation was quite restricted by the use of the vernacular. Although Luther's German had an impact, German literary models appeared slowly. It was actually only in the seventeenth century, in the aftermath of Opitz and the *Sprachgesellschaften*, that some German poetry could be viewed as exemplary of verbal artistry. In Frischlin's time, German literature could provide an important stimulus to Latin writers, but the poetic and rhetorical complexity of Latin literature and theory could not yet be transported into the realm of German letters.

In conclusion, I should stress that practical and theoretical approaches to imitation fostered the growth of Renaissance literature in general and biblical comedy in particular. *Paraphrasis* and *parodia* were important techniques for Latin composition, especially for combating a drift toward cultural irrelevance. Gradually, Renaissance playwrights mastered the language and versification of the *palliata* but in other respects felt free to ignore Roman practices. Due to the preeminence of theology in humanist concepts of imitation, biblical drama, more than other genres, took shape under strong influence of Roman comedy. But even in the case of biblical drama, dissimilation of Roman technique was an inevitable result of imitation. The fictional mimesis of New Comedy was replaced in the process of rhetorical imitation by comedy that claimed to reenact the truth of its source. Consequently, didacticism supplanted the intrigue structure, and, as we have seen in the case of Frischlin, humanist dramatists used biblical drama to propagate theological and political concepts.

Imitation was the theoretical grounding for Frischlin's writings; to him it represented nothing short of the means to achieve a cultural unity of the present and the past. Frischlin expressed his concept of cultural syncretism with particular eloquence in a commemoration of his alma mater, the Tübingen *Stift*. The *Stift* had been established as a theological seminary for Württemberg, and it eventually became an important institution in German intellectual history; in the ensuing centuries it provided support to such eminent writers and thinkers as

Hölderlin, Mörike, and Hegel. Forecasting its importance, Frischlin invoked the *Stift* as "the grove of Christ and the Muses": "O Christi Pieridumque nemus!"[78] This epithet captures the ideal of Christian humanism, the essence of the imitative culture of the Renaissance. Although political relevance was a prominent issue in theories of imitation, such considerations were typically predicated on an advocacy of theological pertinence in literature. Perhaps as a consequence of this, Frischlin concluded his *Oratio de imitatione* with an appeal to Christ to promote the study of classical rhetoric so that it might be used against the forces of Satan. In this plea, Christ becomes the incarnation of the cultural symbiosis that Erasmus, Melanchthon, and Frischlin advocated: "Orator summe, et eloquentissime, quo nemo inter mortales locutus est perfectius et eloquentius."[79] [Greatest and most eloquent orator, no mortal has ever spoken more eloquently or consummately than you.] This metamorphosis of Christ into a classical *orator summus* symbolizes the principles of imitation Frischlin used in his Latin biblical dramas, although it must be remembered that the *orator summus*, even when wearing the *soccus sacer* of biblical drama, retained the political thrust of his Ciceronian ancestry.

4. Rhetoric and Political Drama

Renaissance literary theory, though acutely dependent on ancient rhetoric and poetics, was not divorced from theological and political developments of the sixteenth century. As we have seen, an important aspect of Renaissance Latin literary theory was Christianization of classical, especially Roman, theories of poetics and rhetoric. But the close attention theorists paid to formal aspects of writing and composition can be misleading. In a strongly worded article, Erich Trunz argues that literature in this period became an aesthetic game, devoid of political referentiality:

> In ihrem äußeren Leben gute deutsche Bürger der Zeit, schufen sie sich daneben ein eigenes literarisches Ich und schmückten es mit allen Mitteln ihrer Wissenschaft und Kunst. Nur der Zunftgenosse konnte das würdigen, und er besang es und ehrte es und wurde ebenso wieder besungen und geehrt. Man hatte eine selbstgeschaffene Seite des Lebens, um die niemand als der Gelehrte wußte, und man baute sie aus mit viel feinem ästhetischem Egoismus und Freude am literarischen Spiel.[1]

Although he justifiably stresses the poetic erudition of the *litteraria nobilitas*, Trunz's ascription of isolated societal egotism to humanists is an evaluation that, in my opinion, needs modification. To my mind, Trunz overestimates the formal complexity of Latin literature. Although learned literature of this kind places great demands on readers, it does not necessarily exclude from its practitioners those who are concerned about larger social issues. Indeed, German humanists emphasized Roman formalism to engender the refinement of Latin, but they did not put pen to paper merely to display a technical or academic kind of virtuosity. On the contrary, they frequently dealt with political and religious issues, sometimes even in works addressed to political leaders. Furthermore, not only were many humanist works translated into vernacular languages for general audiences, but many authors also wrote in Latin assuming that their works would soon appear in German. Frischlin, for example, was frequently translated, and he even arranged to have several of his works translated into German.[2]

Sixteenth-century academics and poets were attuned to the socio-political ramifications of their writings. We have already seen that many theorists counteracted potential epigonism by prescribing cultural relevance as a fundamental principle of imitative literature; it is possible, especially in the case of Frischlin, to demonstrate how concepts of literature became intensely political. Owing to the bulk of pertinent material on this subject, I have focused the following discussion on Frischlin, though, I should add, Frischlin's theories were far from maverick; apart from some details and nuances, they represent mainstream views.

The importance of Roman rhetoric on the formal development of Renaissance poetics is generally known. What is not sufficiently appreciated is that Roman rhetoric had evolved as a branch of political science, and its purview, even when revived in the Renaissance, encompassed the political role of literature. According to most ancient and Renaissance accounts, rhetoric divides into three genres, *genus demonstrativum, genus deliberativum,* and *genus iudiciale.*[3] The three distinctions were made largely on the basis of subject matter, as Frischlin's description shows:

> Una est materia Popularis, ut sunt laudes et vituperia personarum, rerum et factorum. . . . Altera est civilis materia, ut sunt deliberationes et consultationes de Republica: et de commodis vel incommodis Reipublicae ac civitatis. . . . Tertia est forensis seu iudicialis; ut sunt res, quae ad iudicia, ad leges, ad ius, ad forum spectant.[4]

> [One is subject matter for the general public, such as laudations and vituperations of people, issues, and deeds. . . . The second is political subject matter, such as deliberations and consultations about the state, or about advantages and disadvantages for the state or city. . . . The third is forensic or judicial subject matter, such as pertains to trials, laws, justice, and the courts.]

Obviously, "materia popularis" (which refers to the *genus demonstrativum*) is the most general category, one that could impinge upon "civilis materia" and "iudicialis materia." In contrast to deliberative (also called conciliar) and juridical rhetoric, both of which can be defined strictly by context, demonstrative rhetoric is a general structure for the opposing modes of panegyric and vituperation. Guidelines for it are not limited to fixed prescriptions for the constituents of a speech but actually focus on aspects to be considered when arguing the merits of an issue. Generally speaking, rhetoric figured prominently in humanist concepts of political education. By exercising skills essential for conducting juridical business, the rhetoric of the *genus iudiciale* provided a basis for subsequent study of law; the *genus deliberativum* also served as a propaedeutic curriculum for future civil servants and governmental ministers. Demonstrative rhetoric, on the other hand, constitutes not only a practical theory for composing persuasive arguments, it is also a method for dissertating on issues of any kind from affirmative or negative perspectives.

The Renaissance mind-set was, in a word, synthetic, and Frischlin's was no exception. In his *Oratio de imitatione*, Frischlin devised a system for showing the relatedness of all types of writing. For the sake of completeness, I have transcribed a diagram Frischlin used to depict the entire scheme (see Figure 1); of primary concern for this discussion, however, is the connection it documents between poetics and rhetoric.

This taxonomy of writing relies in part on imitation. According to Renaissance and ancient theories, imitation made it possible to transform genres; such transformations, in turn, revealed generic relationships. In particular, imitative theory fostered a syncretic view of rhetoric and poetics. *Paraphrasis*, an exercise that even Quintilian advocated, basically entailed recasting prose works as poetry and vice versa. Among Frischlin's most carefully composed works are his paraphrases of Horaces's *Epistolae* and Persius's *Satyrae* executed substantially as Ciceronian invectives. Frischlin even labeled rhetorical divisions in his paraphrases of Persius. The Ciceronian recastings illustrate a significant concept: the poetic genre of satire and the rhetorical *genus demonstrativum* can be refracted through imitation in such a way that they become cognate genres. For drama specifically, it is worth mentioning that in *Methodus declamandi*, a practical handbook on demonstrative rhetoric, Frischlin devoted most of his discussion to a lengthy explanation of how to write a *laudatio muliebris*. The impact of such a rhetorical exercise on Frischlin's dramas is self-evident; the "praise of women" is, at least in part, a basis for *Rebecca, Susanna, Hildegardis Magna, Frau Wendelgard*, and *Ruth*.

According to Frischlin's chart, demonstrative rhetoric is a general classification for several poetic genres (ode, elegy, satire, epigram). Owing to its use of dialogue, drama does not fall under the heading of *genus demonstrativum*. Ultimately, however, drama and demonstrative rhetoric are linked because both branch off from the category of those genres which address an actual, contemporaneous audience ("omnis oratio . . . ad praesentes ac vivos"). The poetic basis provided by the *genus demonstrativum* suggests that poetry, in Frischlin's view, consists largely of praise and criticism. Because a poet is compelled to take a

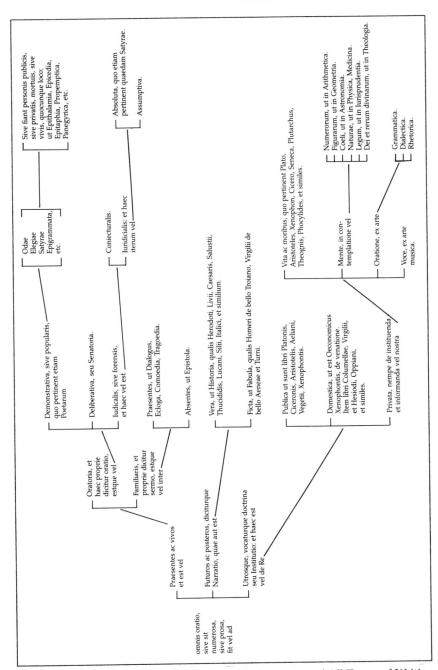

Figure 1. Frischlin's Diagram Showing the Relatedness of All Types of Writing

judgmental stance on subject matter, one would not expect to find descriptions of intimate experiences or consciously subjective poetry in such literature. To Frischlin's mind, the subject matter of the *genus demonstrativum*, though potentially limitless, embraces above all "materia popularis"—subjects with general social relevance. Thus, we should expect to find that the poet's perspective is outward; his goal is to censure or affirm aspects of society.

Just as demonstrative rhetoric, according to all definitions, consists of both *laudes* and *vituperationes*, it is evident that Frischlin did not limit political poetry to encomiastic verse. Indeed, the combination of *laudatio* and *vituperatio* neatly characterizes much of his nondramatic poetry, for he composed major panegyrics as well as numerous satires. The techniques of the two subtypes of the genre are the same; for example, the *loci inventionis* of the genre are applicable to both *laudatio* and *vituperatio*.[5] In each case, the same criteria are relevant to the poet; the goals differ only in that virtue is praised in panegyric, whereas evil is castigated in vituperation. A special form of demonstrative rhetoric that illustrated the kinship of praise and censure was the *encomion paradoxon*, the best-known example of which is perhaps Erasmus's *Praise of Folly* (1511). In view of the predominance of both satiric and panegyric literature in the sixteenth century, an examination of the impact of demonstrative rhetoric would appear to be a worthwhile undertaking. Such a study might shed light on the proliferation of satiric and panegyric literature from a literary perspective to complement the historical approach usually taken. The intellectual turmoil of the century not only provided the impetus for the primacy of these two forms but also abetted the development of a literary theory geared to epideictic poetry.

Taken as a group, humanists tended to connect rhetorical and dramatic studies. Because rhetoric and drama were major elements of the humanist program, the attempt to view the two genres as related phenomena heightened the coherence of humanist pedagogy. These two forms were easily construed in terms of pedagogy because humanist study of rhetoric and drama held the common goal of developing communicative skills. Formal rhetoric, humanists claimed, offered an argumentative framework for generating persuasive arguments on various issues. Likewise, performing drama in schools was thought to enhance verbal skills by increasing vocabulary, improving elocution, and fostering the development of a good memory. Delivering speeches before an audience or role playing in dialogic exchanges exercised rhetorical skills necessary for eventual legal, governmental, or ecclesiastical careers. Such a goal of performing drama resulted in a pronounced tendency to rhetoricize dramatic composition.

Sixteenth-century views of Roman comedy strengthened this bond between drama and rhetoric. Renaissance commentaries on Terence usually labeled rhetorical devices used in the plays and located points where Terence, according to scholars, used the genres of Roman political rhetoric. Following Donatus's commentary, Melanchthon interpreted the language of Terence's plays in terms of deliberative, juridical, and demonstrative rhetoric. He claimed, for example, that *Andria* consisted entirely of deliberative rhetoric.[6] To a limited extent, Terentian comedy admits of such rhetorical classification, but the political focus of the Roman system of rhetoric is, of course, wholly irrelevant to it. Furthermore, humanists dissected Terentian plays using two structural schemata: the dramatic scheme of *protasis, epitasis,* and *catastrophe;* and the rhetorical scheme of *exordium, narratio, confirmatio,* and *peroratio.*[7] The dogged efforts of humanist scholars, especially the Germans such as Melanchthon and Iodocus Willichius (1501–52),[8] to account for the organization of individual scenes in accord with rhetorical divisions suggest that they believed a comedy and its parts should prove or demonstrate something. Yet, whereas there is much wheedling and cajoling in Roman comedy, there is little of the rhetorical didacticism that abounds in humanist drama. Thus, the increasing importance of rhetoric in Latin imitative comedy, be it conciliar, epideictic, or judicial, and the growth of political and theological comedy are perhaps more directly related to sixteenth-century interpretation than to the Roman comedies themselves. Biblical and historical comedy reveal not only a strong interest in politics but also familiarity with the genres of Roman political rhetoric. This represents a departure from the nonpolitical content of Terentian comedy, but not a break with the rhetorical formalism ascribed to it by Renaissance commentators.

In his own essays on comedy, Frischlin continued Melanchthon's tendency to rhetoricize dramatic interpretation, but he seems to have noticed the one glaring problem with the method: the sociopolitical function of classical Latin rhetoric could not be documented in interpretations of New Comedy. Frischlin remedied this incompatibility by shifting his focus to the plays of Aristophanes, where indeed the political aspect of rhetoric could be applied to dramatic theory.[9]

The extensive introductory essays to his *Aristophanes* make it possible, at least in part, to reconstruct Frischlin's theory of comedy.[10] In the essays dealing with the structure of comedy, Frischlin drew heavily on Julius Caesar Scaliger's *Poetices Libri Septem,* especially the chapter "Comoediae et Tragoediae Partes."[11] Frischlin valued this work primarily because in it Scaliger offered a structural analysis of comedy general enough to encompass both Old and New Comedy. In order to formulate a comprehensive definition of drama, Scaliger established a hierarchy of elements: *primariae partes, accessoriae partes,* and *attinentes partes.*[12] According to Scaliger's scheme, the stages of dramatic action are the primary parts of a play; in conscious disagreement with Aristotle's tripartite division of drama,[13] he claimed that four stages of action were necessary, namely, *protasis, epitasis, catastasis,* and *catastrophe.*

In his own theory, Frischlin adopted the *catastasis,* Scaliger's addition to the Aristotelean scheme, but also made a slight modification; unlike Scaliger, Frischlin ascribed a pronouncedly rhetorical quality to this stage by claiming that it frequently included disputation on the events of the plot.[14] Furthermore, while Frischlin concurred with Scaliger that the *catastrophe* should be unexpected, he diverged from the then popular assumption that a comedy should issue in a happy ending. On the basis of Aristophanes' example, Frischlin asserted that comedy could result in a complex closure which was joyous for some characters and disastrous for others.[15] Another important structural element was the relegation of the chorus to a nonessential component. De-emphasis of the chorus, which is an extremely important element of Old Comedy, coincided with Frischlin's desire to square Old and New Comedy. Failure to appreciate the chorus gave Frischlin the basis to divide Old Comedy into the five-act structure of New Comedy. We might justifiably find such tampering with the original odd, but the scholars of the Renaissance and Baroque did not; Frischlin's division of Aristophanes' plays into five acts persisted in subsequent editions until the late eighteenth century.[16]

Although Frischlin generally tried to illuminate points of similarity between both Old and New Comedy, he did not pass over the profound difference in the subject matter of the two forms. In contrast to New Comedy, Frischlin emphasized the politics of Aristophanes' plays:

> Materia vero discrepant, quod vetus Comoedia, res veras et gestas, verasque personas in theatrum producit: nova autem personas fingit, sed in speciem veras, et ad vitae humanae similitudinem ac speculum, in quo homines vitam moresque suos contemplentur.[17]

> [The subject matter differs very much since Old Comedy brings real affairs and deeds as well as real people onto the stage; New Comedy, however, creates characters, though they are realistic, similar to human life, or like a mirror in which men can contemplate their life and customs.]

Frischlin was able to advance the observations of Melanchthon and Scaliger on the importance of political satire in Aristophanes into a balanced view of the differences and similarities of the two ancient forms of comedy. While Melanchthon associated Aristophanic comedy with tragedy because both focused on human flaws,[18] Frischlin emphasized the historical references and the portrayal of actual people in Old Comedy, as opposed to the fictitious plots and characters of New Comedy.[19]

Frischlin also invoked Aristophanes as an authority who, by his example, legitimated political engagement of the comic poet. He claimed that the political nature of the comedies induced him to dedicate his Aristophanes translations to Emperor Rudolf II. In his letter to Rudolf, which laments the corrupt exemplars of the text and culminates in a plea for patronage, Frischlin stressed the political satire in Old Comedy and characterized Aristophanes as a responsible critic of politics: "Nam is auctor est Aristophanes, qui magna cum libertate homines seditiosos ac turbulentos in scenam producit, eosque nominatim perstringit: qui principum in Republica virorum dissensiones acerbe insectatur."[20] [Aristophanes is an author who, taking great liberty, introduced seditious and troublesome men onto the stage, criticizing them by name; and he inveighed vehemently against the dissensions of the leading men of the state.]

Aristophanes, however, was not as popular in the sixteenth century as New Comedy was, and his plays were generally held to be inferior to those of his successors. To counteract these prejudices, Frischlin composed a detailed refutation of the sweeping condemnation of Aristophanic comedy in Plutarch's *Moralia*.[21] Plutarch's comparison of Old and New Comedy in the *Moralia* enjoyed considerable circulation in the Renaissance, in part because it provided some information about the lost plays of Menander. Furthermore, Plutarch's opinion that New Comedy was superior to Aristophanic comedy seems to have been largely unquestioned in the sixteenth century.[22] Frischlin, however, opposed this view and defended Aristophanes on the basis of the political didacticism of Old Comedy:

> Idem ergo finis nostro poetae fuit propositus, ut spectatores in risum solutos excitaret, et de sapientibus dictis, atque occultis in Comoedia consiliis admoneret, ipsosque de corrigenda Republica et emendandis moribus quasi praepararet.[23]

> [Our poet had the goal of rousing the spectators to a good laugh, and of admonishing them concerning wise ideas and advice hidden in the comedy. He prepared them, as it were, for improving the state as well as their own practices.]

Aristophanes thus represents the political comic poet who shouldered the responsibility, as Frischlin might conceive it, for criticizing political leaders and policy. Though both forms of comedy, according to Frischlin, served a didactic function, the distinctly political focus of Old Comedy increased its value. As if to create a symbol for his view of Aristophanes as politicized New Comedy, Frischlin transformed the popular Ciceronian mirror simile used to describe the didacticism of Roman comedy. In his new simile it is a political body, not an individual, which looks on the play as if into a mirror. By seeing a reflection of societal ills in the comedies of Aristophanes, a political body, in this case the city of Athens, could mend its affairs: "Sed voluit Poeta, ut populus Atheniensis, sua suorumque Magistratuum turpitudine, in scena, tanquam in speculo conspecta, malum Reipublicae statum emendaret, et ad meliorem frugem, ac saniora consilia animum revocaret."[24] [But the poet wanted the people of Athens, after they had seen, as if in a mirror, their own faults as well as those of their magistrates on the stage, to improve the problems of the state, and he wanted to direct them to reforms and wiser policies.] Because it evoked pedagogic defenses of New Comedy, Frischlin used the modified *speculum vitae* topos to promote inclusion of Aristophanes in school curricula.

Frischlin's concept of comedy and those ideas he absorbed from Scaliger's monumental work resulted in a syncretic theory that encompassed both Old and New Comedy. Frischlin attempted to hypostatize the recombinant form by translating Aristophanes into Terentian-Plautine Latin and using the five-act structure of New Comedy. On the one hand, Frischlin sought to render Aristophanes more palatable to those schooled on Terentian comedy. But more important in Frischlin's merger of Old and New Comedy is its appreciation of the political themes and satiric techniques of Aristophanic comedy; both aspects could be imitated in Renaissance comedy and also used to defend political forms of comedy.

In 1579, after his success with politicized biblical drama and after his experimentation with *Priscianus Vapulans*, a satiric pedagogical comedy, Frischlin turned to historical drama. The new subjects suited his affinity for political drama, but they also reflect the avid interest of humanists in German and Greco-Roman history. Frischlin's own humanist lectures were not limited to rhetoric and poetics; he also delivered lectures on ancient and contemporary history. Thus the composition of historical drama was natural for him because it combined the two fields of his academic post as *Professor Poetices et Historiarum*.

Frischlin was not the first to use historical materials for political drama. The politically charged stories of Lucretia and Virginia, especially as recorded in Livy, became the subjects of several plays in the

sixteenth century.[25] Perhaps the most successful adaptation of historical material was Heinrich Bullinger's *Ein schön spil von der Edlen Rö-
merin Lucretiae* (1533).[26] This work, which attracted interest in Strasbourg and Basel in addition to Bullinger's native Zürich, concerned
the solidification of political stability in the aftermath of the formation
of the Swiss Federation. Before Bullinger, Switzerland had a substantial tradition of political drama, examples of which are *Das Urner
Tellenspiel* (1512/13) and *Das Spiel von den alten und jungen Eidgenossen*
(ca. 1514), as well as the plays of Pamphilus Gengenbach (ca. 1480–
1525) and Niklaus Manuel (ca. 1484–1530). Bullinger's work was an
important innovation because he used a historical event, in this case
the founding of the Roman Republic, as a paradigm for contemporary
politics. Instead of creating the action for a political drama, he adapted
his historical source so that it had exemplary valence for Swiss politics.

Frischlin's *Hildegardis Magna* (1579) drew heavily on humanist interest in German history. In a letter defending the historicity of the
play, Frischlin cited the authority of the medieval historians Einhard
(ca. 770–840) and Lambert of Hersfeld (eleventh century), both of
whom enjoyed popularity in sixteenth-century printings, as well as
the more recent scholars Johannes Cuspinianus (1473–1529) and Johannes Stumpf (1500–ca. 1576).[27] The source for *Hildegardis Magna*
was Caspar Bruschius's *Monasteriorum Germaniae praecipuorum maxime
illustrium: centuria prima* (1551).[28] In that work, Bruschius briefly re-
counted a struggle between Charlemagne's wife, Hildegardis, and his
half-brother, Talandus. The events in the chronicle correspond nearly
exactly to the action in Frischlin's play. In order to undertake a campaign against the Saxons, Charlemagne entrusted his realm and wife
to the care of Talandus. During the king's absence, Talandus fell in
love with the queen and tried to seduce her. But through a rather
elaborate trick, Hildegardis managed to incarcerate him. Upon Charlemagne's return—here begins the action in *Hildegardis Magna*, act I,
scene 1—she decided to free Talandus. Unfortunately, Talandus went
directly to Charlemagne and charged that Hildegardis had imprisoned him so that she could commit adultery unimpeded. Enraged by
the story, the king ordered his wife removed to a forest to be blinded
and killed. By chance, a knight interceded in the sad execution of the
punishment and convinced the henchmen to bring the eyes of a hunting dog to Charlemagne. With her servant Rosina, Hildegardis fled
secretly to Rome, where, disguised as a man, she became a famous
doctor. Meanwhile, Talandus strangely suffered a malady which left
him blind. Because no one could help, he and Charlemagne traveled
to Rome to visit the renowned physician. Hildegardis, not recognized

in her male attire, required Talandus first to confess his sins, and afterward she cured him. Because Charlemagne wanted to express his thanks to the doctor personally, a meeting was arranged in St. Peters before the pope. After Hildegardis was recognized, the couple renewed their wedding vows with the pope's blessing. Naturally, the truth about Talandus came out. Charlemagne, always quick to mete out punishment, wanted him to be executed but commuted the sentence to perpetual banishment in deference to the queen's entreaties for mercy.

With its obvious similarities to *Susanna*, Frischlin easily fashioned the vignette into a five-act play: Hildegardis releases Talandus (act I); Talandus accuses her before Charlemagne (act II); Charlemagne condemns Hildegardis (act III); Hildegardis is miraculously rescued in the forest (act IV); Hildegardis is vindicated and Talandus punished (act V). Just as in his biblical dramas, Frischlin appropriated quotations, characterizations, and scenic structures from New Comedy.[29] For example, he created a parasite figure, Benzelo (not mentioned by Bruschius), to give depth to the exposition of Talandus as a wastrel. The scenes with Benzelo, however, do not develop into a discrete subplot, but they enhance the dramatic characterization of Talandus and provide the play with most of its Terentian coloration.

In order to focus on conciliar deliberations, Frischlin added two advisors not mentioned in Bruschius's account, Eberthalius, a prime minister (*magister aulicus*), and Ludobertus, the royal priest. Both confer with Charlemagne about his decision to punish Hildegardis. Instead of deferring to the royal will, they try, albeit unsuccessfully, to guide the king to responsible action. Knowing firsthand that Hildegardis is innocent (act II, scene 5), Ludobertus chastises the king about the latter's unjust condemnation (act III, scene 3). Likewise, Eberthalius is appalled by Charlemagne's inability to retain his composure so that the case can be investigated properly. He also recognizes the deceit, proclaiming that Talandus and Benzelo exemplify the rampant immorality of the times (act III, scene 7).

Although Bruschius reported this story in a matter-of-fact style without significant commentary, Frischlin purposefully cast Charlemagne as a derelict ruler and directed fierce criticism at Talandus. In the play, Talandus is fully aware of his own immorality and sycophancy; at one point he characterizes himself by evoking a perversion of the *genus demonstrativum*, one that is grounded on toadyism: "Neque culpanda culpo, neque laudanda laudo."[30] [I do not censure what should be censured, nor praise what should be praised.] In contrast to such unscrupulousness, Ludobertus steadfastly gives Charlemagne his opinion, even when it runs counter to the king's feelings:

> CA[rolus]. Eho, numnam dubitas, me absente corruptam esse
>   coniugem?
> LU[dobertus]. Dubito certe, et perquam vehementer. CA. at quam-
>   obrem? LU. quia tuam
> Uxorem istarum esse operarum, nemo unquam credidit: novum
>   hoc
> Et inauditum crimen si percrebescat: omnes aulici,
> Omnes cives, noti, ignoti, incolae advenae, fictum esse credent.[31]

> [Charlemagne: But you don't doubt that my wife committed adultery during my absence?
> Ludobertus: I doubt it very much, in fact, vehemently.
> Charlemagne: But why?
> Ludobertus: Because no one would ever believe your wife could do such a thing. When this new, unheard of charge becomes known, all the courtiers, all the citizens, nobleman and commoner, the residents, and the foreigners will think it has been trumped up.]

Ludobertus criticizes the king with striking frankness for the latter's lack of self-control: "sed velim tamen, ne quid in hac re tam grandi, temere agas: / Neu frustra te excrucies: neu falso suspectam habeas coniugem. / Sapientem omnia magis ratione, quam ira aut odio agere decet."[32] [I wish you wouldn't act so rashly in an affair of such importance; don't torment yourself over nothing; don't distrust your wife without reason. A wise man should act according to rationality, rather than anger and hatred.] Ludobertus's role, grounded in deliberative rhetoric, probes into the critical ethics important for a minister of state. Instead of glorifying the almost legendary figure of German history, Frischlin created a critical image of Charlemagne as an impulsive ruler and thereby demonstrated the advisor's duty to oppose inappropriate policy.

It was not without reason that Frischlin devoted considerable attention to the administrative structure of Charlemagne's court as well as the qualities which make for a just ruler. *Hildegardis Magna* was written for the festivities marking Ludwig's formal assumption of the duties of his hereditary office.[33] Ludwig had been exercising ducal powers since 1575, but in compliance with the details of Duke Christoph's will, he chose to assume his office formally in 1578–79. By adapting the historical material for a play about proper discharge of power as well as a ruler's relationship to his court, Frischlin could offer *Hildegardis Magna* as an appropriate contribution to the celebration of Ludwig's inauguration as duke.

The theme of marriage was popular among Lutheran dramatists; it provided an opportunity to propagate Lutheran doctrine on marriage and also helped evoke the marriage structure of New Comedy. Lutherans held that marriage helped maintain societal order,[34] and, at one point, Luther himself defended New Comedy because the theme of marriage was so prevalent in it: "Comödien gefallen mir sehr wol bey den Römern, welcher fürnehmste Meinung, Causa finalis, und endliche Ursache ist gewest, daß sie damit, als mit einem Gemälde und lebendigen Exempel, zum Ehestand locken und von Hurerey abziehen. Denn Policeyen und weltliche Regiment können nicht bestehen ohn den Ehestand. Eheloser Stand, der Cölibat und Hurerey, sind der Regiment und Welt Pestilenz und Gift."[35] In Luther's view, marriage was a basis of morality, economics, and political order. As a result of the controversy over the celibate priesthood, marriage emerged as a prominent issue in Lutheran anti-Catholic propaganda. There was a fortunate crossing of paths on the part of humanists interested in New Comedy and Lutheran dramatists writing about the institution of marriage. Marriage is a common theme in Frischlin's comedies (*Rebecca, Susanna, Frau Wendelgard, Hildegardis Magna, Ruth, Hochzeit zu Kana*, and, to a lesser extent, *Phasma*). But, with the exception of his minor works *Ruth* and *Hochzeit zu Kana*, Frischlin moved decisively beyond the Lutheran exaltation of marriage in order to treat other issues of sociopolitical order in the context of marriage.[36]

In *Hildegardis Magna* marriage is depicted not so much as the basis of societal order but rather as a symptom of a healthy political state of affairs. Charlemagne's weakness as a political leader led to a near tragedy for his wife, thus illustrating the need for reasoned administration based on a rational interaction between ruler and councillors. After Charlemagne's failure, it was only by chance that disaster was averted. The marriage motif at the end of the play suggests New Comedy, but, more importantly, the conclusion projects a harmonious court, purged of its divisive and immoral member.

In a limited sense, *Hildegardis Magna* has a critical perspective, one that was perhaps relevant to the court at Stuttgart: the ruler in the play is unidealized and must rectify his policy and conduct. The failings of Charlemagne stood as a dramatic warning to the young Duke Ludwig as he formally assumed the duties of his patrimony. In the prologue, Frischlin also appealed somewhat ironically to the interests of the court by describing the action of the play metaphorically as a hunt.[37]

This would have captured the attention of Ludwig and his courtiers, but it was surely well recognized that overindulgence in the hunt was one of Ludwig's failings. Since Frischlin consistently paid homage to Ludwig, it would be off the mark to imagine that he tried to goad the young ruler with overt criticism in *Hildegardis Magna*. Nonetheless, because he desired to maintain a critical stance vis-à-vis the political affairs of his day, Frischlin did not deliver an untarnished panegyric of the central political figure in the work. Given the ideological nature of much of Renaissance drama, such a willingness to question policy and those exercising temporal power is an important characteristic because it raises didactic literature beyond the pale of propaganda.

Frau Wendelgard was Frischlin's only experiment with historical drama in German.[38] It was performed in Stuttgart on 1 March 1579 on the occasion of Duchess Dorothea Ursula's birthday. The plot was taken from Johannes Stumpf's chronicle *Gemeiner Loblicher Eÿdgnosschaft Stetten-Landen und Völckern Chronicwürdiger Thaaten Beschreibung*.[39] In following the source closely—but adding an unhistorical subplot—Frischlin used the composition technique of his biblical comedies. The story is about Wendelgard, daughter of Heinrich I. After her husband, Ulrich of Buchhorn, was presumed to have died in battle against Hungarians in 915, she entered the cloister. Four years later, on the very day Wendelgard was celebrating a memorial for him, Ulrich returned; the couple was quickly reunited after Bishop Salomon of Constance released Wendelgard from her vows.

Though it has more polish than the German plays which Frischlin wrote in prison, *Frau Wendelgard* is nonetheless a minor work in his oeuvre, as Frischlin's decision not to publish it indicates. The comedy has no conflict, and it has more of an epic than dramatic character; long passages are narrations of political events with no bearing whatsoever on Wendelgard's story. Still, as Hieronymus Megiser's introductory letter to Dorothea Ursula shows, the play carries a heavy load of didacticism. Ulrich represented the brave lord who defended his land against infidels; Bishop Salomon was a churchman who served five emperors loyally and subordinately; and Wendelgard represented the faithful wife. As previously mentioned, many Lutheran plays glorified marriage, perhaps as a contrast to Catholic views of celibacy. Despite this and the fact that Wendelgard left the cloister to return to married life, there is no anti-Catholic invective in the play. Only in the epic vignettes narrated by Salomon did Frischlin address political issues. Possibly as a reflection of the Württemberg policy of maintaining close and good relations with the imperial court, Salomon emphasized his faithful service to five emperors, but he also narrated a lengthy account of his problems with two contumacious noblemen who were eventually executed. Though I cannot prove it, this may have been intended as a historical analogue for Ludwig's campaign, undertaken in 1579, against the rebellious Count Ludwig von Löwenstein.

Julius Redivivus, no doubt Frischlin's best-known work, should also be viewed from the perspective of rhetorical politicization of drama. *Julius Redivivus* has always caught the eye of scholars of German literature because Frischlin claimed to have composed the work "in laudem Germaniae." The sizable scholarship on the play shows a disproportionate interest in the laudatory qualities of the play and a general unwillingness to note its critical tendencies.[40] In spite of some shortcomings, Frischlin apparently felt that *Julius Redivivus* was his best play; it is in any event one of his most original and complex works. Although the official premiere took place in 1585 during the celebration of Ludwig's second marriage,[41] a performance of an earlier draft seems to have been produced in Tübingen in 1583 or 1584.[42]

Dialogues between ancients and moderns provide a framework for assessing the development of political institutions and humanist culture. Both aspects are bound up inextricably with the problem of Renaissance cultural imitation because Frischlin used the criteria of antiquity, embodied in the resurrected Cicero and Caesar, to evaluate the government and culture of his time. The comparison of ancient Rome and sixteenth-century Germany is slightly complicated by tendencies to contrast Germany of his day with ancient Germany as well as with sixteenth-century France and Italy. Caesar and Cicero say that they have come with a strong desire to see the *nova Germania* so different from the *vetus Germania* of their era. The idea for this type of cultural comparison was not original with Frischlin. Numerous descriptions of ancient and modern Germany had appeared after the rediscovery of Tacitus's *Germania* in the fifteenth century.[43] Particularly important in this tradition were tendencies both to exalt the German past and to laud the progress of contemporary Germany. Ulrich von Hutten (1488–1523) catalyzed the process of mythologizing the greatness of the German past in his extolment of the general Arminius, whom he ranked above Caesar and Alexander. Hutten's portrayal of Arminius as the embodiment of a heroic past probably figured in Frischlin's characterization of the military leader Hermannus in *Julius Redivivus*.[44] Hermannus says that he is a descendant of Arminius, and Caesar frequently addresses him as "Armini."

Frischlin drew heavily on the popular mythic conception of the German Empire as the heir to Roman *imperium*. Like other German humanists, Frischlin supplemented the concept of a *translatio imperii* with a transference of the entire literary culture of Rome, or a *translatio artium*. This type of glorification of sixteenth-century Germany by comparison to ancient Rome embodied a common ideal of humanist culture. According to Gustav Roethe, the idea for treating this topic through the prosopopoeic visit of Caesar and Cicero may have been suggested by Enea Sylvio Piccolomini's *Germania*, where Piccolomini asserted that ancient Germans, such as Ariovistus, would not be able to recognize their homeland, should they be resurrected to visit Germany.[45]

Nonetheless, reception of Tacitus in the Renaissance posed problems for the concept of cultural imitation. Most scholars thought that Roman culture should be imitated; yet Tacitus had extolled the simple virtues of the German people in order to contrast such basic values as bravery, loyalty, and familial cohesion with the growing corruptness of imperial Rome. Fortunately, literary imitation included the concept *aemulatio*, enabling imitation and progress to take place simultaneously. The paradigm of cultural imitation in *Julius Redivivus* is evaluated by Caesar and Cicero, both of whom are incessantly exposed to the German manifestation of *translatio imperii* and *translatio artium*. According to the ideal of cultural imitation expressed in the play, the greatness of Germany arises through imitation of the strengths of ancient tradition and avoidance of its weaknesses. Caesar aptly expressed this ideal of imitation extended to the realm of politics: "O Germanos beatos, si exterarum gentium mala / Pro disciplina et praeceptis habere possint, ut alios / Casus inde timeant."[46] [Blessed are the Germans if they, using the errors of others as lessons, fear the calamities others have suffered.]

Frischlin, however, was fully aware of inconsistencies inherent in a combination of Tacitean praise of old Germany and the Renaissance ideal of cultural imitation. Ideally, the Germans would have assumed the strengths of Roman culture while retaining the virtues of Tacitean Germany. In actuality, Frischlin drew parallels between the decline of Rome and the state of Germany. Hermannus, a figure with a Tacitean view of things, is outraged at the import of luxury goods from Savoy. He fears that these luxuries will weaken the moral fiber of the Germans, just as Asian finery had softened the rigor of the ancient Romans. In a scene very reminiscent of Aristophanes' *Acharnians*, Hermannus asks the French merchant Allobrox for item after item of military equipment, only to be mocked by the peddler with suggestions that the general purchase frivolous presents for his girlfriends.[47] Infuriated, Hermannus wants to have the merchant incarcerated immediately, but, in a dramatic deus ex machina, Mercury stops this rash action. The god of merchants encourages Hermannus to look for deeper reasons for Germany's troubles:

> Mercurius: An virtus bellica Germaniae solo pipere
> Saccaroque relanguescit? Hermannus: Etiam aliis rebus plurimis.
> Mercurius: Idem et ego reor; nam quae major est pestis Germaniae
> Quam gulae studium, quam crapulae, quam temulentiae![48]

> [Mercury: Is the military strength of the Germans softening be-
>   cause of pepper and sugar?
> Hermannus: Well, also because of many other things.
> Mercury: I agree. What greater pestilence is there in Germany than
>   the proclivity to indulgence, crapulence, and drunkenness?]

Hermannus readily accedes to the view that the *vetus disciplina*, as recorded in Tacitus, must be restored in Germany, but Mercury finds that the problem has even greater proportions, for he makes his criticism more specific, charging that moral turpitude among the ruling class is rampant:

> Equidem Germanos hodie reperias praeclaro loco
> Natos, qui cubitum prius nunquam abeunt quam sint ebrii
> Nec surgunt nisi crapulosi nec quicquam inceptant operum
> Nisi poti.[49]

> [Indeed, today you will find Germans of noble birth who never go
> to bed before they are drunk and never get up without a hang-
> over, nor do they begin any work unless they are drunk.]

In these fanciful discussions between ancient and modern the Tacitean critique of Rome enters into Frischlin's portrayal of the modern Germans; the paradigm of cultural imitation assumes a critical perspective because the modern Germans, so it seems, have acquired the vices of the ancient Romans.

Scholars have largely failed to see Frischlin's equivocation on the question of the progress of German culture. The incongruence between Renaissance imitation and Tacitus's *Germania* has not been adequately considered by those interpreting *Julius Redivivus* as an encomiastic tribute to sixteenth-century Germany. The inappropriateness of a one-sided approach to *Julius Redivivus* can also be seen in the numerous discussions of technology in the work. Both representatives of antiquity encounter the technological revolution in Germany with its staggering importance for cultural development. The great Latin poet Eobanus Hessus (1488–1540), whom Frischlin also resurrected, explains the process of printing to a dumbfounded Cicero. Cicero becomes so eager to learn more of this art that he begs Eobanus to take him to a printing shop. Hermannus, on the other hand, discharges a rifle in the first act to demonstrate the power of his weapon to an incredulous Caesar. At that point, the two Romans fall to the ground to worship Hermannus as the thundering Jupiter. Hermannus eventually convinces the awestruck pair that a German, not Vulcan or Daedalus, made the rifle. Intensely interested in the ensuing description of gunpowder and firearms, Caesar persuades Hermannus to take time out from his duties to conduct a tour through an armory.

Although the art of printing and the manufacture of paper are not encumbered with negative qualities, Frischlin strongly questions other technological advances. After the warmongering Caesar exits at the conclusion of act I, Cicero is left center stage to deliver an expression of the fright instilled in him by all the talk of modern weaponry:

Non expedit mihi hos sequi; nam sic timor
Praeoccupaverat animum meum, ut prope
Alienata constiterim mente. O saeculum
Illud felix, quod hisce caruit machinis.
Nam si Caesar, quo tempore bellum civicum
Nobis parabat, hisce armatus machinis
Fuisset, jam pridem nihil veteris Italiae
Restaret huic aevo reliquum.[50]

[There is no reason for me to follow them. Fear has gripped me so much that I have almost lost my mind. Fortunate was the age that did not have those devices! If Caesar had been armed with those things when he prepared for the civil war with us, nothing of ancient Italy would have remained for this age.]

According to Cicero, cowardice prompted the advancements in military technology because men became afraid to face each other eye-to-eye in combat. Cicero, however, ironizes his speech before the modern German audience by explaining that he did not mention his negative views of the advanced military technology to the Germans because he did not want them to think that he envied "their glory."[51]

The subject of military preparedness is replete with ambivalence. Morbid prognoses of catastrophic warfare dominate act V. Because he expects impending wars to flood his realm with damned souls, Pluto, the devil figure, wants Charon to construct two additional ferries for the heavy traffic. According to Pluto's prediction, the great war will stem from troubles in the Low Countries:

Deinde bellum instauratur quam maximum;
Nam Belgicos in armis esse milites,
Omnem juventutem, omnes aetatis gravis,
In quibus aliquid consilii et dignitatis est,
Ad arma prosilire tristissima, duces
Ac principes, qui eodem jure, legibus
Utuntur, dissentire inter se plurimum.[52]

[Furthermore, a great war is brewing again; the Belgic soldiers are in arms, the entire youth, all the old men who are wise and dignified are running to the sad arms, leaders and princes are in great disunion, though they live by the same laws.]

Pluto also mentions the constant Turkish threat and finally cites numerological predictions that the world will end within five years. In response to this forecast of imminent doom, Hermannus is trying to maintain the strength of Germany during a period of peace. He tells Cicero and Caesar, both somewhat taken aback by the presence of so much military might, that there is peace for the moment, but preparations for trouble must be made because foreign troops are planning to pass through his country en route to the Netherlands (act I, scene 2). At the heart of the vision of a future military disaster is the political confusion of the times. As Pluto said, political leaders, although they live by the same law, cannot establish political harmony.

In Frischlin's Renaissance idealization, the German political system is the legitimate heir to the Roman Empire. In act II, scene 3, Caesar introduces the topic of the empire by asking who holds power in Germany. Hermannus's answer confounds him: "Romanus imperator, quem vulgo omnes dicunt Caesarem."[53] The confusion and subsequent clarification emphasize the concept of cultural imitation, for Hermannus explains that the *imperium* passed from the Romans to the Germans. Frischlin elaborates the political comparisons to antiquity by equating the Prince Electors with the *Ephori* of Sparta.[54] Hermannus's exaltation of the Holy Roman Empire, however, is sharply undercut by the contrast of political reality. He waxes patriotic in his proud description of the ideal of the system and its mythic connection to the Roman *imperium*. Nonetheless, the reality of the empire constantly creeps into the play, particularly in the last two acts. The allusions to the turmoil in Germany as well as the condemnation of irresponsible princes render the portrayal of the German Empire in *Julius Redivivus* equivocal at best.

Humanism receives a more positive review. The greater part of act III, scene 1 comprises an encomium to German humanists, all of whom are compared to ancient men of letters. Some figures, however, are considered less than ideal. Cicero quibbles about Erasmus's style, citing *Ciceronianus* as an example of bad writing, and he also delivers a stinging condemnation of a work by Martin Crusius, Frischlin's arch-enemy.[55] It is also noteworthy that Eobanus Hessus, as the embodiment of German humanism in the play, enters the stage in a perturbed state because there has been a serious, but unspecified breach in his relationship with the Holy Roman Emperor (act II, scene 2).

One of the ideals of humanism was its internationalism. In this regard, humanism could provide a cohesiveness that was not to be found in the political configurations of the sixteenth century. Perhaps the Holy Roman Empire no longer embraced Europe, but Hermannus claimed that the Latin tongue still held dominion over the civilized world: "At haec lingua hodie totum orbem fere / Occupavit, hac doctissimi quique in Germania / Galliaque utuntur, hac loquuntur Dani atque Hungari."[56] [But this language has taken possession of most of the world; the most learned men in Germany and France use it, the Danes and Hungarians speak it.] Although his primary goal was to applaud German humanism, Frischlin did not omit a tribute to the Italian humanists—much to the delight of the two Romans:

> Habent Itali urbes magnificas, habent viros doctissimos,
> Habent Muretos, Sadoletos, Bembos, Sigonios, habent
> Manutios; quos si tu audires Latine verba proloqui,
> Nihil valerent Cornificii apud te, nihil Hortensii.[57]

> [The Italians have magnificent cities and very learned men. They have the Mureti, Sadoleti, Bembi, Sigonii, and Manutii. If you heard them speak Latin, your Cornificii and Hortensii would not seem a whit better.]

But, though this praise of Italian humanism emphasizes the internationalism of the movement, it indirectly suggests its limited success. Hessus's laudation is intended to console the Romans after they have been exposed to a crude chimney sweep who speaks Italian. To Hermannus and the two Romans, Italian is a barbarically decadent form of Latin. Frischlin thematizes vernacular languages here and in the action around the French merchant Allobrox, ostensibly to reveal the decay of Latin culture in neighboring countries and, by contrast, to highlight Germany's cultural refinement. Nonetheless, the use of vernacular languages puts pressure on Latin's claim to superiority, showing quite plainly that despite the flourish of humanism, Latin did not conquer the western world of letters.

The literary accomplishments of German humanism were embodied in the poet Eobanus Hessus.[58] Some scholars, such as Strauß and

Schade, have seen indications of a self-portrait by Frischlin in this figure.[59] Frischlin was able to suggest himself in the characterization of this poet because Hessus's temperament resembled his own. Both poets had enormous difficulty securing a steady livelihood. Hessus was apparently somewhat unconventional and, like Frischlin, seems to have been party to the humanist tradition of serious drinking. The instability he created for himself put Hessus perpetually in need of patrons to help him out of difficulties. In his first appearance in the play, Hessus alludes to unspecified problems, and hopes that he will be able to gain the favor of the emperor with a panegyric he has composed: "Quodsi vetor illi de acceptis coram queritari injuriis, / Num etiam librum, quem sacratissimo dicavi numini / Caesaris, eidem offerre non licet?"[60] [Though unable to complain to him in person about some injuries I have received, is it not permissible to offer him this book which I dedicated to the divine majesty of the emperor?] This panegyric could be the one Hessus delivered to Charles V in Augsburg in 1530. However, the situation of the poet estranged from his noble patron corresponds to a certain extent to that of Frischlin in 1584 and 1585. After the troubles surrounding his *Oratio de vita rustica* and his inability to gain the rank of *ordinarius* at Tübingen, Frischlin became a schoolmaster in Laibach (1582–84). However, he unexpectedly returned to Tübingen in 1584. Naturally, Frischlin worked to ingratiate himself to Ludwig in the hope, perhaps, that ducal support could eventually help him secure a full professorship at Tübingen. He produced *Julius Redivivus* in conjunction with the festivities marking the duke's second wedding in 1585 and also composed a long encomiastic description of the nuptials.[61] Thus Eobanus Hessus's attempt to curry the emperor's favor by presenting a *laudatio* could be a projection of Frischlin's intention of doing the same with his panegyric epithalamium.

One of the most important themes in *Julius Redivivus* concerns the political role of the humanist poet. Although ultimately the poet's role turns out to be rather intricate, Hessus's actions would seem to exemplify the adage "die Kunst geht nach Brot." Indeed, there is a strong sense of artistic dependence on patronage. At three points in the play, authors function as encomiasts for political leaders: Cicero delivers a laudatory introduction of Caesar to Hermannus (lines 327ff); Eobanus Hessus reads from his panegyric to the emperor (lines 645ff); and Hessus delivers an encomium to Julius Caesar (lines 1438ff). Frischlin clearly felt it was a poet's responsibility ex officio to commemorate the deeds and accomplishments of rulers. In return, however, the ruler would ideally be willing to support the arts. Caesar expresses the concept of political patronage for the arts rather optimistically: "nam poetarum ingenia / Semper grata fuere imperatoribus."[62] [Emperors always welcomed the talents of poets.] Nonetheless, several dialogues in *Julius Redivivus* suggest that the poet's function transcends the adulatory office one might associate with a poet laureate. Twice in the course of the play, Caesar claims that he does not prefer idle flattery to the hard truth. When Allobrox learns that he is speaking to a king, he chokes, complaining that he is afraid to speak because he does not know the art of flattery, "Je ne puis flatter."[63] Caesar, however, objects, asserting that one need only speak the truth.[64] Likewise, when Cicero asks whether Caesar would like to hear flattery, the latter responds, "Nihil prorsus, ac proinde vera te loqui / Velim."[65] [Not at all, I want you to say the truth.] As a corollary to the ideal poet, Caesar represents the ideal ruler who expects veracity, not cajolery.

Pluto puts forth the most lucid definition of the ideal poet, though he expresses it in negative terms. According to Pluto, it is the poet's responsibility to praise faults and censure virtues. Furthermore, Pluto is particularly ill-disposed toward those poets who dare to practice the Epicurean and Christian virtue of παρρησία, the commitment to voicing criticism openly. The devil promises the worst for these free-speaking poets who work against Satan's influence in the world:

Ego poetas volo adulari, assentari civibus nostris,
Volo laudare illos culpanda et rursus culpare laudanda.
Hoc si faxint poetae, praemium a nobis merebuntur
Et grati erunt deinceps Satanici consortibus regni.
Sin pergant veritatem effari et allatrare virtutes
Plutonis et increpare meorum flagitia servorum,
Faxo, ut vicissim vires experiantur nunc meas isti
Παρρησιάζοντες poetae.[66]

[I want poets to adulate and praise the citizens of hell, I want them to praise what should be criticized, and criticize what should be praised. If poets do this, they will earn a reward from me and will please the consorts of Satan's kingdom. But if they endeavor to tell the truth and to carp at the virtues of Satan and inveigh against the sins of my servants, then, in turn, I will make sure that those free-speaking poets feel my power.]

Although negatively stated, this outburst shows that Frischlin grounded his concept of poetics on rhetoric, especially demonstrative rhetoric. Frischlin knew παρρησία as a figure of thought in Roman rhetoric. In the pseudo-Ciceronian *Rhetorica ad Herennium*, a long passage is devoted to the figure of παρρησία, or *licentia*, as it was translated into

Latin.[67] The author of the *Rhetorica ad Herennium* emphasized the value of remonstrative *licentia* but also advised orators to palliate its sharpness by conjoining to it some words of praise. Frischlin took this rhetorical figure seriously; the very act of writing was for him rooted in the principle of the responsible, politically conscious poet exercising παρρησία.[68]

Rhetoric affected the dramatic structure of Frischlin's plays in different ways. With its traditional happy end, *Hildegardis Magna* optimistically projects a restoration of political morality. Following the practices used in his biblical comedies, Frischlin adapted his source to heighten its political didacticism. Several scenes are also examples of deliberative rhetoric, but, more importantly, the play itself is about conciliar rhetoric, from both a formal and an ethical standpoint. Despite its thought-provoking ambiguity, *Julius Redivivus* is another illustration of the impact of humanist ideology on dramatic form. Its structure, however, is unusual because it does not entail any plot development; the play's fantastic scenario merely sets the stage for discussions about politics and culture. In this regard it is clearly more similar to Aristophanes' political comedy than to New Comedy. The *Acharnians*, a play echoed in several scenes of *Julius Redivivus*, can provide a useful point of comparison. The subject of peace, in the absence of a coherent plot, gives the drama its center; the action and the satire of the play proceed from an impossible occurrence, in this case the private peace concluded between the Spartans and Dikaiopolis, an Athenian citizen. Frischlin used the concept of cultural imitation to give coherence to his play and shattered the convention of illusionistic drama with the resurrection of Cicero and Caesar in the sixteenth century. As is the case with Aristophanes, the phantasmagorical setting of the play enables humorous treatment of rather serious subjects. The irreality of the play lightens the critical tone in the assessment of culture and politics, just as the fractured reality of *Priscianus Vapulans*, as we will see, relieves the weightiness of its pedagogic and moral didacticism. With its comparative poles of antiquity and the Renaissance, imitation unifies the disparate segments of *Julius Redivivus*. The episodes revolve around discussions of humanist ideals of culture and politics, but sardonic humor, equivocal views, and absence of an illusion of reality contribute to make *Julius Redivivus* an ambivalent play. Despite the return of the Romans to Hades, the play does not convey a sense of dramatic resolution but rather produces an apocalyptic vision of the future which stands in stark contrast to the tenacious optimism of humanist ideology.

5. Humanism on the Stage

Humanists, as we have seen, composed dramas on a wide variety of subjects, but they also created a distinctively humanist genre, the play about humanism. In fact, several of the earliest humanist plays dramatized the value of the *studia humanitatis*: Wimpheling's *Stylpho*, Kerckmeister's *Codrus*, Bebel's *Comoedia vel potius dialogus de optimo studio iuvenum*, and, to a lesser extent, Reuchlin's *Henno* were conceived as propaganda for humanist education. Kerckmeister, Reuchlin, and Bebel promoted the quintessentially humanist ideal of attaining eloquence through the study of poetry. Wimpheling also dramatized the importance of poetry, though with less emphasis; his antihero Stylpho fails the qualification test for a benefice in part because he is unable to scan Virgil's first *Eclogue*.[1] Reuchlin limited his treatment of humanism to the lively choral interludes, in which he glorified poets in contrast to lawyers and civil servants.[2] Reading these songs, one senses the pleasure Reuchlin derived from devoting himself to his studies at Heidelberg, after a long, tumultuous career in Württemberg as a public servant. But in two particularly revealing plays, Bebel's *Comoedia* and Frischlin's *Priscianus Vapulans*, humanist drama, like humanism itself, extends significantly beyond the domain of the academy into areas of social and political concerns.

Bebel's play is not merely a dramatization of humanist ideals for education; it also demonstrates that humanist studies offered a measure of social mobility. The plot reveals how Vigilantius, its peasant hero, improves his social status through education. Rapardus, Vigilantius's father, acknowledges this goal in the opening lines: "Eamus, fili amantissime, quaerere dominum philologum Paraetianum nostrum consulturi, quo pacto tuam condicionem ampliorem et nobiliorem reddamus."[3] [My dear son, let's go find our learned master Paraetianus to consult with him on how we can make your status more distinguished and nobler.]

Comoedia also contains extensive defenses of poetry as well as an illustration of the importance of *eloquentia* for a political career. Act IV unfolds as a disputation on the values of Latin eloquence between the fledgling humanist Vigilantius and Lentulus, a dialectician and perhaps a student of the faculty of arts.[4] According to Lentulus, basic communicative ability, however crude and ungrammatical, constitutes sufficient command of Latin. He reveals himself as an opponent of humanism by professing exclusive concern for dialectics: "Nullum est studium praeter dialecticum."[5] In the midst of the dispute, a courtier appears on stage to support Vigilantius's advocacy of "casta et erudita Latinitas" with a short story similar to many of Bebel's *facetiae*. The *aulicus* recounts that a certain Cardinal Raimundo refused a request for an ecclesiastical preferment on the basis of the petitioner's barbarous Latin.[6] For Vigilantius and the courtier, *eloquentia* is the foundation of the liberal arts, the distinguishing quality of an educated person, and, consequently, the sine qua non for career advancement.

Bebel, the son of a peasant from the Swabian Alb, was the first important humanist at the University of Tübingen; he conducted humanist lectures there from 1496 until approximately 1518.[7] Melanchthon was also active at Tübingen for a short time (1512–18) and even delivered one of his best-known humanist speeches there, *De artibus liberalibus* (1517).[8] As part of the reforms of 1535–38, a *pedagogium* was established for young students, in which humanist subjects were well represented. Among the required subjects were grammar, rhetoric, epistolography, Virgil, Terence, and Erasmus's *Colloquia*.[9] In addition to letter writing, the students were also supposed to learn to write poetry. The university statutes of 1536, worked out in part by Joachim Camerarius (1500–1574) and Johannes Brenz (1499–1570), placed additional weight on rhetorical studies by requiring that students participate in "exercitia rhetorica."[10]

Frischlin's drama about humanism, *Priscianus Vapulans*, was commissioned for the celebration of Tübingen's first centennial. The play had its premiere on 20 February 1578 in the castle at Tübingen before the assembled dignitaries of the university and Ludwig's court.[11] The university celebrated its one-hundredth birthday a year late because an outbreak of plague had forced evacuation of the city in 1577.

Priscianus Vapulans marks the beginning of a phase of experimentation in Frischlin's dramatic career. With this play he departed from the well-traveled path of biblical drama and began to invent original plots for his comedies. Furthermore, *Priscianus Vapulans*, *Phasma*, and *Julius Redivivus* represent a radical departure from biblical drama insofar as there is no attempt in these plays to create an illusion that reality is represented on the stage.[12] There are ample indications that Frischlin eschewed the historical validity of his plots with purpose. While the biblical comedies were presented as historical truth, and *Hildegardis Magna* was published with a defense of its historicity, the three other comedies flaunt their fictionality. Historical fact and chronology are sometimes ignored to suit the framing of each play's message. The new sense of truth in Frischlin's dramas is not of a historical but rather of a moral nature. Nonetheless, to support the validity of his message, Frischlin included an extensive apparatus for both *Priscianus Vapulans* and *Phasma* to identify his sources. Many of the speeches in *Priscianus Vapulans* and *Phasma* are based on the writings of the characters who are speaking, though the contexts are fictional or even anachronistic. In *Julius Redivivus* Frischlin defended the imaginary construct of the plot; Cicero, at one point, falls out of his role to explain that comic poets enjoy freedom from the limits of history and plausibility and are therefore empowered, as in the present case, to bring the dead back to life, "Sicut comici solent resuscitare mortuos / In suis comoediis aut fabulis" [just as comic playwrights are accustomed to bringing the dead back to life in their comedies and plays].[13]

In the prologue of *Priscianus Vapulans,* Frischlin belabored the "newness" of the play, giving the audience a clear indication that it was different from his earlier biblical dramas:

Haec res agetur nobis, vobis fabula.
Non exquisite facta est, neque uti caeterae:
Non hic parasitus leno est, nec ferus Ismael,
Neque suspicax maritus, neque petulans senex.
Ridicula est res.[14]

[This plot we will act out, for you it is a play. It's not a polished work and it's not like the others. There's no parasitic panderer in it, no uncultured Ismael, no suspicious husband, no lascivious old man. The plot is absurd.]

The plot of *Priscianus Vapulans* revolves around the resurrection of the sixth-century grammarian Priscian and his suffering due to the terrible latinity of the later age. According to the ground rules of the play, every grammatical error does physical harm to him as the literal embodiment of grammar. The play has a figurative structure whereby Priscian, as a metonymy for Latin grammar, is made a theatrical reality; the metaphor of tormenting Priscian is expanded into the action of the play.

The plot is structured so as to project the validity of the humanist program for higher education. Viewed from this perspective, *Priscianus Vapulans* is a metaphor for the organization of the medieval university into faculties. In act I, Priscian encounters two scholastic philosophers, Franciscus de Mayronis (died 1327) and Chrysostomos Javellus (ca. 1470–after 1538),[15] engaged in mind-boggling *quaestiones* about subjects of metaphysics with bearing on theological orthodoxy.[16] With every solecism representing a blow to Priscian, the grammarian is left reeling at the end of the act, in dire need of medical care. In act II, the faculty of medicine is suggested by two doctors, Philonius and Lilius.[17] Because their ineptitude and bad latinity only worsen matters, Priscian seeks legal counsel in order to sue the physicians for malpractice (act III). Naturally, the lawyers' command of Latin leaves much to be desired.[18] Eventually the lawyers become rather angry about Priscian's enigmatic ramblings concerning grammar, but they are truly outraged when he cannot pay for their services. After deciding that Priscian is raving mad, the jurists have him tied up and sent to a church where the insane have allegedly been cured. There he falls into the hands of a monk and a priest, Breviarius and Quodlibetarius respectively. These two clerics, albeit fairly weakly, suggest the faculty of theology.[19] Further tortured by bad Latin, Priscian is deemed to be possessed by evil spirits. Efforts to exorcise the demons fail, and the whole encounter leaves Priscian on the threshold of death. At this point (act V), humanism comes on stage in the form of Melanchthon and Erasmus to save Priscian by introducing him to the accomplishments of humanist culture in Europe. Thus the main plot illustrates the humanist claim that the liberal arts, especially grammar and rhetoric, must provide a sound basis for study in the upper faculties of theology, philosophy, law, and medicine. The humanist salvation of Priscian at the end of the play is, by analogy, the revival of university education.

A subplot, which eventually devolves into a theological satire, complements the main plot's focus on the fate of latinity. The play is dramaturgically complex because Frischlin incorporated a detailed plot, around the peasant Corydon, on equal footing with Priscian's episodes. The scenes with Corydon carry the main action of the drama in acts II–IV. In act II, Corydon consults the doctors about an ailment his wife is feigning. In act III, he confers with the pettifoggers about how to get even with an adulterer because he has in the meantime discovered that his wife has had a liaison with a priest. In act IV, Corydon wreaks vengeance by beating the priest and exacting a large compensatory settlement.

Frischlin framed Corydon's three-act sequence with the anti-Catholic satire of acts I and V. Act I represents a satire not only of the poor latinity of the scholastic philosophers but also of scholastic defenses of Catholic orthodoxy. The appearance of Melanchthon and Erasmus in the final act also has theological meaning. Perhaps more than any others, they could be used to project a harmony of humanist learning and religion. Nonetheless, because both figures would have posed problems for the reception of *Priscianus Vapulans* in archorthodox Tübingen, Frischlin added a disclaimer that Erasmus and Melanchthon do not argue about articles of faith: "Neque Philippus aut Erasmus in hoc dramate de negotio religionis, aut de articulis fidei disputant: sed tantum de studiis agunt humanioribus, et de rebus, quae pertinent ad universos."[20] [Philipp and Erasmus do not dispute in this play about religious matters or articles of faith, but they are concerned with humanist studies and matters of general relevance.] In spite of this statement, it is obvious that Erasmus and Melanchthon represented ideals, though not in an orthodox Lutheran fashion, of Christian humanism. Melanchthon was a profound supporter of Luther and was the leading humanist of his day. In fact, Melanchthon was the first to record doctrines of Lutheranism systematically, a feat he accomplished in his *Loci Communes* (1521). In the play, however, Erasmus is the more resolute critic of the practices of the church. He openly encourages the hesitant Melanchthon to go to the rescue of Priscian in defiance of a papal bull permitting church officials to use bad Latin.[21] Erasmus provides an excellent counterpoint to the scholastic philosophers of act I because he had been at the forefront of humanist attack on scholastic methods of Bible exegesis.[22] In act I, Javellus and Franciscus de Mayronis profess the goal of harmonizing the teachings of both Aquinas and Scotus in their theological analyses. This, however, was precisely the kind of theology Erasmus vehemently opposed. He had aroused considerable controversy in orthodox circles with the methodology he espoused in the introduction to his Greek and Latin edition of the New Testament. In his essay "Methodus," he virulently assailed the *Vulgata* and scholastic philosophers Thomas Aquinas and Duns Scotus, as well as the theological practices of his own day. Erasmus's scorn for the old method was balanced by ardent appeals for a text-oriented, philological approach to theology:

> qui conveniat, ut theologus futurus sophisticas praeceptiunculas ediscat, ediscat qualiacunque in Aristotelem commentaria, ediscat Scoti conclusiones et argumenta, et idem operae gravetur dare libris divinis, ex quorum fontibus universa scatet theologia, quae modo vere sit theologia?[23]

> [How could it be suitable for a future theologian to learn by heart some sophistic maxims, some commentaries on Aristotle, the conclusions and arguments of Scotus, and yet he disdains to give the same effort to the Bible, from whose fountain all true theology springs forth?]

Erasmus's *ad fontes* theology was also closely related to the humanist approach to studying the arts and refining latinity. Humanist grammarians, for example, rejected medieval authorities such as Alexander de Villa Dei[24] and advocated instead the study of the classics themselves.

Because the work is in part a retrospective on humanism, the scanty scholarship on *Priscianus Vapulans* is dominated by a pejorative view of the play as being woefully epigonic. Gustav Roethe, whose essay on Frischlin otherwise contains some stimulating perspectives, claimed that *Priscianus Vapulans* was irrelevant, a contention Strauß had also made, and, furthermore, a dramatic flop: "daß man beim Jubelfest der Universität Tübingen durch so und so viel Stunden den gelehrten und langwierigen Priscianus sich gefallen ließ, beweist außerordentlich viel Bildung oder außerordentlich viel Geduld."[25] Roethe's severity is quite unfortunate, for the subsequent scholarly neglect of this play may be due to his condemnation. Criticism of the play on grounds of epigonism seems to be misdirected. It is essential to observe that, while Frischlin deliberately evoked the heyday of the humanists waging a *bellum grammaticale* as the basis for the commemorative function of the play,[26] he also embedded religious, social, and academic satire of considerable pertinence for his contemporaries in the reenactment of early German humanism.

No one would deny that the linguistic satire in the play explicitly recalls the early humanists' battles. The epistle and *facetia*, two important genres for Renaissance linguistic satire, figure prominently. The leitmotif of the play was probably taken from a *facetia* by Heinrich Bebel.[27] Using Priscian as a metonymy signifying Latin grammar, Bebel wrote that a priest gave Priscian a fatal blow with a solecistic attempt to say the weather was going to clear up:

> Est sacerdos non procul Ramasia flumine; qui cum superioribus diebus per fenestras caeli videndi gratia, an vel serenum vel pluviosum futurum esset, prospexisset, dixit ad suos convivas non sine summa iniuria grammaticarum sanctionum et cum letali vulnere Prisciani: "Caelus clarificat se." (Voluerat enim significare caelum serenum et ab aeris intemperie alienum fore.)[28]

> [There is a priest not far from the river Rems. When in previous days he looked out the window to see the sky whether it was going to be pleasant or rainy, he said to his guest (not without breaking grammatical rules and dealing a fatal blow to Priscian), "the sky is distinguishing itself." (He wanted to say that the sky would be clear and would be free of storms.)]

The linguistic satire in Bebel's *facetiae* exemplifies the humanist tradition Frischlin drew upon. Like *Priscianus Vapulans*, *facetiae* included a fair amount of anticlericalism, especially satiric exposures of immoral priests and monks. The humanists cultivated this form in order to exercise a sort of Roman *urbanitas*. The typical *facetia* was a witty, short narrative cast in elegant Latin prose.[29] The common mixture of *urbanitas* and crude satire in the collections of *facetiae* was responsible for the enormous appeal of the genre. Frischlin himself wrote *facetiae* and he knew the works of the Renaissance masters of *facetiae*, Poggio Bracciolini (died 1459) and Bebel.[30] He not only quoted from Poggio's and Bebel's *facetiae* in the text of *Priscianus Vapulans*[31] but also emulated the style of *facetiae* with his precarious combination of elegant Latin and drastic satire.

Priscianus Vapulans also contains an example of the satiric letter, a genre that was important, especially from a historical perspective, among the early German humanists. Act I, scene 1 is taken up with the discussion of a letter written by a former student of Franciscus de Mayronis. The remarkably bad Latin, the toadyism, and the high theological import of the student's philosophical inquiries suggest unmistakably the satire of the *Epistolae Obscurorum Virorum* (1515 and 1517).[32] This notorious collection of bogus letters, written probably by humanists in Erfurt and by Ulrich von Hutten, satirized the opponents of Johannes Reuchlin in his lengthy conflict with Johannes Pfefferkorn over the issue of destroying nonbiblical Hebrew writings.[33] Reuchlin's struggle to defend the integrity of most Jewish theological scriptures became a celebrated cause of the early humanists, especially because it allowed them to attack scholasticism. In the *Epistolae Obscurorum Virorum*, decadent Latin, adherence to medieval scholastic philosophy, and the moral hypocrisy of the obscurantists, a group of learned men in contact with the Cologne professor Ortwin Gratius, were persiflaged with impunity. In Frischlin's play a similarly pretentious and unfathomable letter is read in its entirety. Javellus then prescribes an obtuse, scholastic methodology for the student's investigations. The result is that the scholastics and the admiring student reveal their own shortcomings, much in the vein of the *Epistolae Obscurorum Virorum*. The obsequious salutation in the letter of the student, for example, was obviously inspired by the *Epistolae*:

Francisco de Maronis, septem liberalium artium
Candelabro aureo: radianti Theologorum apici: ordinis
Minorum lucifero: sacrae scripturae gazophylacio:
Haeresiarcharum malleo: virtutum Heroicarum omnium
Et non Heroicarum speculo dilucidissimo: meo
Domino dignissimo: domino praeceptori, humilimus suae
Dominationis discupulus et servitor vilissimus
Oscula pedum, loco salutis.[34]

[To Franciscus de Mayronis, the gold candelabrum of the seven liberal arts, the radiant crown of the theologians, the light-bearer of the Minorites, the treasury of the Holy Scriptures, the hammer of the heresiarchs, the most brilliant mirror of heroic and nonheroic virtues, my most worthy lord, lord preceptor, in the place of a salutation, the humble student and worthless servant of your lordship kisses your feet.]

The student concludes with the request that Franciscus send a copy of the *Vocabularius ex quo* to help him in his studies. This terrible Latin–German lexicon, first published in 1467, was another common object of scorn among humanists.[35]

Linguistic satire runs through *Priscianus Vapulans* from beginning to end. At some junctures, the linguistic satire embraces serious and prickly subjects. In act IV, Frischlin satirized the sacrament of confession from a linguistic perspective; Priscian is battered furthered by the unclassical Latin used by the clerics as they coax him to confess his sins:

> BR[eviarius]. Et si mihi confiteri vis, absoluam te. PR[iscianus]. ex his vinculis?
> BR. Non ex his tantum, sed te eripiam ex aliis etiam angustiis.
> PR. Oh gestio. sed quid vis confitear tibi? BR. primum hoc mihi
> Dices: an habeas seriam contritionem. PR. imo, mihi
> Attrita sunt omnia membra, attritae omnes ossium mihi
> Medullae: cor mihi contritum et iecur. BR. non male dicis.[36]

[Breviarius: But if you wish to confess to me, I'll absolve you.
Priscian: From these bonds?
Breviarius: No, not only from these, but from other bonds too.
Priscian: Yes, I want that. But what do you want me to confess?
Breviarius: First tell me if you have genuine contrition.
Priscian: Of course, all my arms and legs are attrited ("attritae sunt"), as is the marrow of my bones; my heart and liver are also bruised ("cor mihi contritum et iecur").
Breviarius: That sounds good.]

Priscian is confused, taking *contritio* in the classical sense of "misery" as derived from the verb *contero* ("to grind," or "to wear out"), while Breviarius and Quodlibetarius, who assume that *contritio* means "contrition," cannot understand Priscian's banter.

Bad latinity is one issue, perhaps one that did not seem all that momentous even to a Renaissance audience, but, as in his other plays, Frischlin expanded the scope of his criticism, here by viewing academics from religious and social perspectives. Because of the pervasive satire of Catholicism, *Priscianus Vapulans* can also be compared to the so-called *Kampfdramen* of the Reformation. This religious focus of the play, however, was not entirely an epigonic reenactment of the Lutheran dramatic practices of the 1530s and 1540s. The attack on Catholicism owes its origin to Frischlin's awareness of the growing ferocity of the Counter-Reformation in Hapsburg lands under Rudolf II.[37] The correlation of the academic and religious satire in *Priscianus Vapulans* suggests the struggle Frischlin had prepared to undertake in Graz in 1576/77; he had tried unsuccessfully to obtain leave from the University of Tübingen to assume the rectorship of a Protestant school in Graz that was trying to stem the growing influence of a nearby Jesuit institution.[38] The academic and religious revival of the Jesuits was probably on the mind of every Lutheran educator in the last quarter of the sixteenth century. Frischlin's correspondences with civic officials in Graz show conclusively that he was concerned about the momentum of the Catholic revival in that region.[39]

More than anything else, the attack on Catholicism serves as a foil for academic satire. Despite the humanist movement, the structure of the medieval university, with its emphasis on the faculties of theology, law, and medicine, remained intact throughout the sixteenth century. Melanchthon's assessment of the basic problem of humanism would have applied to the situation at Tübingen and other German universities: "Iurisperiti et Theologi hodie praevalent / Ludimagistris: et pluris fit unus hoc / Tempore rudis medicus, quam Grammatici decem."[40] [Today lawyers and theologians have much more status than school teachers, and nowadays one unskilled physician is esteemed more than ten grammar teachers.] In comparison to the three upper faculties, the faculty of the arts remained quite insignificant, even at universities where humanist reforms had taken place. Therefore, it was essential that Frischlin depict his academics as Catholics in order to avert allegations that he was trying to antagonize the Tübingen faculty.

It may have been risky for Frischlin, a man already alienated from the university hierarchy, to present such a critical view of academia. Although its premiere marked the one-hundredth anniversary of the University of Tübingen, there is not a single line of praise in *Priscianus Vapulans* for the institution. Furthermore, Frischlin had been seething with resentment over the university's treatment of him. When he was passed over for a vacant professorship of dialectics in favor of an undistinguished candidate, he protested by canceling all his lectures.[41] The duke and his court had to intervene to break the impasse between Frischlin and the faculty senate. Only in January 1578, one month before the premiere of *Priscianus Vapulans*, did the university and Frischlin come to terms about the latter's status. According to the settlement, Frischlin resumed his duties without a promotion but apparently with a significantly higher salary.

Yet, Frischlin ingeniously managed to formulate a critical statement about his own troubles and the situation at Tübingen. The figure of Priscian is strongly suggestive of Frischlin himself.[42] The portrayal of Priscian as a humanist who was out of sorts with, or abused by, the representatives of the upper faculties would correspond to Frischlin's view of his affairs in 1577/78. In his woodcuts for the Strasbourg editions of *Priscianus Vapulans*, Tobias Stimmer (1539–84) correlated Priscian with Frischlin by depicting the grammarian with a very long beard, Frischlin's hallmark.[43] From this perspective, it is not surprising that Priscian steps forward at the conclusion of the play to address the audience directly:

> Vos spectatores, non est, quod nos expectetis hic: apud
> Frobenium et Oporinum Priscianus roborabitur:
> Vos autem, quia et ipsi colaphos mihi impegistis plurimos:
> Nec dum veniam a me petiistis: tum demum eam impetrabitis:
> Si et post graves a me, atque iniurias abstinueritis manus:
> Et quod postremum est condimentum fabulae:
> Mihique gregique voletis huic applaudere.[44]

> [There is no reason, spectators, to wait for us here any longer. Priscian will recuperate at the print shops of Froben and Oporinus. But you, because you have beaten me so much, nor have you yet asked for my forgiveness; you will receive my pardon if and when you have stopped laying your grievous and injurious hands on me. And now, give us that which is the last condiment of a play: Applause for me and the troupe.]

In this finale Priscian removes his mask, as it were, to address the spectators in the persona of Frischlin, thus drawing a direct analogy between Priscian's opponents and those of the poet. The resuscitation of Priscian in the final act could stand as a representation of Frischlin's recent reconciliation with the university. A literal interpretation of this statement, one which is appropriate for the premiere of *Priscianus Vapulans*, reveals Frischlin admonishing his audience to stop attacking him as the obscurantists of the play tormented Priscian. In performances elsewhere, however, the conclusion would have been merely a plea to the audience to use better Latin.

Aside from Frischlin's personal complaints, *Priscianus Vapulans* contains a number of critical allusions to specific faculty members at the University of Tübingen.[45] The most direct barb in the play was shot at the Tübingen professor Martin Crusius. In act V, Melanchthon laments that a bad Greek and Latin grammar was replacing his own textbooks in the schools:

> nam quid ludimagistros dicam aliquos novitios?
> Qui praecepta cumulant Grammaticae Graecae atque Latinae, et libros
> Meos e puerorum excutiunt manibus, et substituunt
> Suos: ut melius scilicet videantur sapere, quam ego sapui.[46]

> [And what should I say about some of those new school teachers? They heap together precepts of Greek and Latin grammar and banish my books from the hands of students and substitute their own so that they might appear to know more than I did.]

The "praecepta Grammaticae Graecae atque Latinae" could refer only to Martin Crusius's *Grammatica graeca cum latina congruens*.[47] In the first edition of *Priscianus Vapulans*, there was also thinly veiled criticism of the Tübingen professor Georg Liebler, perhaps Frischlin's most important adversary in 1577. Erasmus praised the *Compendia* of Jakob Schegk, but lamented that an ungrateful student of Schegk, namely Liebler, had criticized use of the *Compendia*: "tum eiusdem (i.e., Scheccii) Compendia, / Ex manibus puerorum excussa ingrati discipuli / audacia."[48] [Then Schegk's *Compendia* were taken from the hands of students because of the audacity of an ungrateful student.]

In addition to Priscian's academic satire, Frischlin's critical voice can be heard in the peasant Corydon. The characterization of Corydon is indicative of Frischlin's concern for the problems of the peasant class. Corydon is often portrayed as a fool, but his status as a fool provides him with poetic license to speak frankly about the corruptness of the academics and churchmen in the play. I would suggest that Frischlin chose the name Corydon on the basis of Servius's well-known interpretation of the peasant's role in Virgil's second *Eclogue*: "Corydonis in persona Virgilius intelligitur."[49] Thus, turning Servius's interpretation around, the name Corydon suggests a peasant speaking in the persona of the author.

Social aspects of humanism do not play a significant role in Priscian's misadventures. Nonetheless, as is characteristic of Frischlin's subplots, social injustices come to the fore in Corydon's encounters with the academics. The full form of Corydon's name, "Menalcamynthathyrsidamoetacorydon," as an absurd combination of the names of noble peasants of Virgil's *Eclogues*, captures the twofold aspect of the rustic in Frischlin's play: though an uneducated farmer, Corydon has enough dignity to fight against the corruption around him. His importance as a dramatic pendant to Priscian is attested at the end of act IV; the amazing turnaround in Priscian's fortunes is prefigured in Corydon's triumph over the adulterous priest. Corydon's revenge corrects the inverted motif of the schoolmaster being beaten, for he flogs the corrupt priest who, according to the play, is the pupil in greatest need of instruction. This is not to say that Priscian does not have harsh words for Corydon's lapses into bad Latin, but Priscian and Corydon form a camaraderie of the rustic and enlightened academic, suffering in different ways from the same basic problems. With the peasant's experiences, Frischlin illustrated that corrupt Latin is not the only flaw of the debased doctors and lawyers, for Corydon exposes them as profiteering professionals preying upon the relatively defenseless lower classes.

Nonetheless, it is interesting to note the different sociological ramifications of the role of the peasants in the humanist plays of the Swabians Bebel and Frischlin. Written nearly a quarter-century before the worst outbreaks of the Peasants' War, Bebel's *Comoedia* depicts a flourishing peasant community. In the course of the play, Rapardus confers with other peasants about plans to send his son to a university. Hipponomos, who appears to be the equivalent of a village mayor, supports Rapardus's idea because Vigilantius will be able to help his peers and bring renown to the village: "Quodsi tecum esse volueris et institutum studium prosequi, evasurus es in eum hominem, qui omnibus tuis amicis adiumento et honori universisque companis tuis decus esse possis."[50] [But if you wish to use your mind and pursue the studies you have undertaken, you will become a famous man who can be a help and honor to all your friends and a glory to all the people of your village.] Relying on his *auctoritas* and *eloquentia*, Hipponomos manages to secure a place for Vigilantius with the best professor at the university. This would suggest not only that the peasantry is thriving but also that academic study offers the peasants social mobility.

In *Priscianus Vapulans*, despite the related interests of Corydon and Priscian, there is a sociological rift between peasant and academic. After having seen how easily the doctors and lawyers make their livelihoods, Corydon resolves to have his oldest son sent to a university. Like Strepsiades in Aristophanes' *Clouds*, Corydon plans to attain financial security by having his son trained to be a profiteering lawyer.

Corydon believes his son could learn the vapid sophistry of the academics and parlay that ability, with some deceitfulness, into a substantial income. While in search of a professor, Corydon meets Erasmus in act V. Erasmus quashes the scheme, contending that it is too late to educate the boy. Instead, the son should be content, according to Erasmus, to follow in the footsteps of his father: "Quia rusticam artem iam didicit, exerceat: / Et sorte sua, perinde ut tu pater, siet / Contentus."[51] [Since he has learned how to farm, let him do that. And he should be content with his lot, just as you, his father, are]. Although Frischlin was critical in the extreme, he did not have a revolutionary social consciousness. It also appears that the potential for social mobility of Bebel's time had contracted considerably. It is important to remember that Frischlin's own father, a Lutheran pastor, had been educated at the Tübingen *Stift*.[52] Through unusually distinguished academic and literary attainments, Frischlin rose from the respectable status of being the son of an educated pastor into the ranks of the lesser nobility. In *Priscianus Vapulans* the status of the peasant appears to be intrinsically good but subjected to the abuse of corrupt powers in society. The peasant, in Frischlin's view, deserves dignity, but, according to the implications of act V, he is excluded from the social mobility offered by the *respublica litteraria*.

The satirical techniques of *Priscianus Vapulans* are complex and variegated. Much of the satire resembles the antiacademic and anticlerical satire common in urban *Fastnachtspiele*. Act II, for example, begins with Dr. Lilius's examination of the urine of Corydon's wife. Frischlin's linguistic satire converges with popular satire of the medical profession in the outlandish prescription Lilius concocts for Corydon's wife. Popular satire also frequently reviled the corruptness and idiosyncratic jargon of lawyers. Johannes Reuchlin, for example, drew upon the motif of the avaricious pettifogger in *Henno*, as did Frischlin in *Priscianus Vapulans*. Frischlin's portrayal of the adulterous parish priest also rests on a broad tradition of anticlerical satire in late medieval and sixteenth-century literature.

Like so many Latin comedies of the Renaissance, the comic techniques of *Priscianus Vapulans* are indebted to the influence of many sources other than Roman New Comedy. In view of the absence of a plot built on trickery, or one leading to marriage, it would appear that New Comedy provided a model only for the act divisions and, to a limited extent, the colloquial Latin. Its satire and humorous scenario suggest more directly the comic techniques of Aristophanes. The occurrence of drastic comic devices, such as beatings, defecations, and urine examinations, constitutes a common denominator between

Aristophanic practices and those of sixteenth-century satire, especially as found in *Fastnachtspiele*. Frischlin knew of the motif of urine examinations and metaphorical defecations either directly from German *Fastnachtspiele* or indirectly through other humanists who had used these devices. Listing the components of Priscian's defecation suggests the cataloging technique in the *Narrenschneiden* of *Eccius Dedolatus* (1520), another humanist satirical drama influenced by both Aristophanes and German Carnival plays.[53] In general, it is important to note that humanists were always receptive to diverse, and often crude, satirical techniques. Even the *Epistolae Obscurorum Virorum* and the *facetiae* of earlier humanists combined linguistic with social and moral satire and did not shun sexual and scatological humor.

Priscianus Vapulans couples satire of professions that was common in vernacular literature with academic satire of poor latinity. Although Frischlin's stance is not wholly antiacademic, he was able to join the antiacademic satire of popular literature with a linguistically demanding satire of nonhumanist approaches to university study and research. The crudity and bawdiness of much of the humor balance the sophisticated linguistic satire. Priscian often provides an intellectual perspective, as in his mockery of confession and scholastic philosophy, whereas Corydon can provide a more emotive, sometimes physical attack on injustices.

As in most of his plays, Frischlin assumed laudatory and deprecatory postures in *Priscianus Vapulans*. The satiric voice, however, dominates here. Even the glorification of humanism, as played out in act V, reprises the criticism of the charlatans and obscurantists encountered in the first four acts. Frischlin created tension by using stereotypes of inane academics in a play commemorating the scholarly accomplishments of humanism. One can sense how this satire under different circumstances could have exploded into an attack on the *viri obscuri* of Tübingen. Frischlin, to be sure, followed traditions of humanist propaganda when he elected to satirize nonhumanist academics in his play. Nonetheless, the reenactment of that criticism, coupled with the complete absence of an encomiastic tribute to Tübingen, would have made *Priscianus Vapulans* an annoyingly ambiguous play for a Tübingen audience in 1578.

In one important respect, however, Frischlin's satire differs from that found in humanist works such as the *Epistolae Obscurorum Virorum* and *Eccius Dedolatus*. Because he did not enjoy the freedom of anonymity, Frischlin sometimes took an indirect approach to satire. If it is appropriate to extrapolate upon the basis of the identification of Priscian as Frischlin, then one can conjecture that Frischlin intended

to imply that humanism did not have a firm hold on the distinguished academics of the University of Tübingen. The play, thus read, combines direct satire of Catholicism with indirect criticism of the unimportance of humanism at Tübingen. The interpretation of the indirect in conjunction with the direct satire raises a basic artistic problem in *Priscianus Vapulans*. Indirect satire may sound like a contradiction in terms, but it was the only technique feasible for Frischlin. In his treatment of Catholic academics, Frischlin satirizes in an unmediated fashion because he assumes a stance that is ostensibly inapplicable to the Protestant professors at Tübingen. The criticism acquires indirect relevance to the Tübingen situation through the portrayal of Priscian as a destitute, abused, and unappreciated Nicodemus Frischlin. Only by linking his potentially controversial attack on academic obscurantism—something that would have raised suspicious eyebrows at Tübingen—to the more acceptable satire of Catholicism was Frischlin able to indulge himself in some indirect criticism of the University of Tübingen.

6. The Theology of Politics:
Phasma and Confessional Drama

Although the Middle Ages also experienced a succession of reform movements, the modern era dawned in Germany with the advent of the Reformation. For a considerable time thereafter, theology exerted a powerful influence over every aspect of culture and politics. As scholars have demonstrated convincingly, though to no one's astonishment, in the aftermath of the Reformation, drama became an important medium for propagating or opposing theological doctrine. In his essay on Reformation drama, Paul Böckmann explored the ways the doctrine of justification by faith alone informed Lutheran drama. Luther's disavowal of the determining significance of good works and his resulting concern for ethical motivation, in Böckmann's view, fostered the tendency to develop psychologically well rounded characters. As expressed in his introduction to Romans, Luther's concept that God judges man "nach des hertzen grundt" encouraged dramatists to look to the interior of their characters.[1] A significant extension of Böckmann's approach underlies Jean-Marie Valentin's essay on morality plays.[2] According to Valentin, the morality play underwent significant formal changes, as playwrights used it to different ends. In early morality plays, the political ramifications of theology are slight, but subsequently several playwrights, such as Manuel and Naogeorgus, composed religious drama that concerned the political in addition to the existential plight of man. The consequence I draw from Valentin's work is that theology and late Renaissance drama should not be construed without taking stock of political issues in sixteenth-century religious thought. In spite of the religious sincerity we might impute to some dramatists, the very act of writing a play with confessional propaganda had a highly political dimension. Without scanting the power of belief, we must recognize that advocacy of Protestant doctrine entailed a momentous decision to oppose the Catholic church. Unlike our own age, the sixteenth century, or the Middle Ages for that matter, could not have experienced a theological movement devoid of political ramifications. As the catch phrase of the Peace of Augsburg (1555), "Cuius regio eius religio," succinctly illustrates, we must study sixteenth-century ideologies from the perspective of the interdependence of theology and politics and not on the basis of theology alone.

Protestant drama, not to mention the frequently ignored efforts of Catholics, does not represent a radical departure from pre-Reformation practices. Virtually always composed and performed for a sharply circumscribed civic unit, drama veered toward both theological and political issues long before Luther had conceived of the ninety-five theses. Especially in satirical plays, dramatists treated religious questions in light of their social or political importance. Pre-Reformation dramas, such as Reuchlin's *Sergius* and Wimpheling's *Stylpho*, are often unconcerned with the quest for salvation but focus instead on social problems that arose from religious corruption or vent anticlerical sentiments. Conventions such as benefices and indulgences came under fire not because they were extrabiblical but because they tended to spawn corruption and, more importantly, imposed heavy fiscal burdens. Manuel's *Ablaßkrämer*, written after the beginning of the Reformation, illustrates the convergence of theological and political propaganda in drama.[3] Not at all a public enactment of deep-rooted religious convictions, the *Ablaßkrämer* represents an attempt to garner or solidify support among Bern's citizenry for a policy of banning indulgences. Consequently, the peasants of the play evince only secondary concern for their salvation; desire to recoup financial losses induces them to rough up a corrupt priest who had been peddling indulgences.

The political ramifications of theological innovation were quite evident to the reformers. Not only did established rulers break with the temporal power of the church, creating political fissures throughout the empire, but revolutionary ideas of political order also sprang up.[4] For example, in 1522 Luther left the Wartburg to quell rioting in Wittenberg. Andreas von Carlstadt (ca. 1480–1541) and the Zwickau prophets incited this as well as later outbursts of civil disorder, but soon there arose more severe cases of political revolutions. Thomas Münzer (ca. 1490–1525), among others, fueled the peasant uprisings with extremely effective theopolitical propaganda based on a political approach to biblical exegesis.[5]

Luther and Melanchthon responded in unison against the *Twelve Articles of the Peasantry*, and it would appear that the upheavals of the 1510s and the political nightmare of the 1520s engendered an increasingly emphatic insistence by Lutherans on a doctrine of strict political obedience. Melanchthon's *Loci Communes* (first edition, 1521) advanced a code of political behavior rooted in unconditional observance of the entrenched societal order. Like Luther, he considered the class system, with its inequalities, a God-given institution. Melanchthon politicized religious doctrine throughout the *Loci Communes*, but with

particular clarity in the chapter, "De magistratibus civilibus et dignitate rerum politicarum."[6] In the first sentence of this section in the
edition of 1535, he claimed that "plurimum prodest in Ecclesia exstare
veram et firmam doctrinam de Magistratibus et dignitate rerum civi-
lium" [it is very beneficial if there is in the church a true and strict
doctrine concerning rulers and the dignity of the state].[7] In no uncer-
tain terms, Melanchthon espoused a strictly antirevolutionary view of
political conduct by insisting that lower classes accept social inequity.
As is evident in Justus Jonas's authorized translation of *Loci Communes*, *gehorsam* became an ideal in Lutheran political thought: "Wis-
sentlicher ungehorsam gegen der weltlichen Oberkeit, und wider
rechte oder zimliche Gesetze, ist Todsünde, Das ist, solche sünde, die
Gott mit ewiger verdamnis straffet, . . . Gott hat die Welt den Regi-
menten unterworffen, und straffet ungehorsam ewiglich, derhalben,
das sein göttlich Gebot mutwilliglich ubertretten und veracht wird,
welches spricht, Du solt deiner Oberkeit gehorsam sein."[8]

There are similarities between this political code and the social criticism one meets in Protestant writings. In *Die Hochzeit zu Cana* (1538),
Paul Rebhun advocated abidance in the inflexible class system, es-
pousing, more or less, the kind of political conservativism encountered in Melanchthon's theology. For instance, Mary, who advises the
bride not to borrow a fine gown for her wedding, claims that it is God's
will that men have unequal clothing:

> Mein liebe muhm wilt folgen mir
> So darffst kein andern schmuck und zier
> Denn was dir Gott bescheret hat.
>
> ·
> Sieh wie er draussen auff der heid
> Die blümblein auch ungleich bekleid.
> Eins schmückt er schön, das ander nicht.[9]

This analogy, of course, translates into a theological defense of class-
society. In act III, where Mary sternly emphasizes that a wife should
be absolutely *gehorsam* to her husband, she cannot refrain from drawing a parallel between domestic and political order. A woman must not
disobey her husband because her subordination conforms to God's
plan; should she, however, eschew subservience, she would be the
equivalent of a political revolutionary:

> Dann gleich wie sonst auffrürer pflegn
> Den gmeinen pöbel zu erregn
> Zu widerstehn den öberherrn.

Also auch ander Weiber werdn
Durch solcher Weiber that verfürt
Das sie unghorsam auch berürt
Auch widerstrebns der öbern gwalt.[10]

Melanchthon espoused other concepts that pertain to theopolitical literature. In the course of his defense of society, Melanchthon had to address a common objection: how can it be that class-society is God's will, when it is patently clear that many rulers do not act in accord with God's will? Like others, he diffused this argument against class-society by differentiating between *Ambt* and *Person*. Whereas a person installed in the office of a judge or magistrate may be utterly possessed by Satan, the office itself remains a sanctified part of the God-given system and thereby commands complete respect and obedience. This distinction between *Ambt* and *Person* is frequently a crucial factor for understanding social satire by Protestants. Many plays of the sixteenth century include portrayals of different societal stations and offices. To a great extent, this marks a capitulation to accept the doctrine of the divinely granted, eternally fixed societal structure in lieu of exploring alternatives to it. Thus the most a socially conscious writer would undertake was an examination of the qualities incumbent upon the person holding a specific office. As critical as he was, even Frischlin never advocated changing societal order; his satire deals exclusively with individuals in various social stations and never questions the propriety of social order. The intensity of his criticism, with its emphasis on the corruptness of the upper classes, indicates, however, that Frischlin was on the threshold of superseding the Melanchthonian view of political order; but, despite his personal tragedies and incisive understanding of social injustice, Frischlin never ventured beyond the bounds of Lutheran political thought to put class-society itself into question.

Given the bitter strife of the first quarter of the sixteenth century as well as the virulent epidemic of new sectarian movements, it is hardly surprising that Lutheranism rapidly developed a rigid orthodoxy. Although in some ways a remarkable accomplishment, creation of a doctrinal code stirred further religious and political unrest. Political and religious propaganda merged into a single effort to create a conservative orthodoxy for the new faith with the goal of thwarting both religious deviation and political dissent. During the second half of the century, Württemberg became the driving force behind the development of Lutheran orthodoxy.[11] Earlier, Württemberg had not only been a stronghold for the doctrine of Schwenckfeld, but it had known

semiofficial support for the Swiss reformers. Duke Ulrich, who introduced the Reformation in Württemberg, had strong sympathies with
certain Swiss Protestants. However, in the aftermath of their own
political upheavals and the general crisis of the Schmalkaldic War, the
dukes of Württemberg embarked on a course of promoting Lutheran
orthodoxy in order to restore and solidify political order in their
duchy. Having inherited Duke Christoph's view of this issue, Ludwig
became keenly interested in promoting Lutheranism in all Protestant
regions. Despite his apparent lethargy in most affairs of state, Ludwig
was intensely concerned with theology; he even claimed to supervise
publication of theological tracts.[12] With Ludwig's support, Jakob Andreae (1528–90), the powerful Tübingen theologian, drafted and propagated the *Formula Concordiae* (1577) as part of the *Konkordienbuch*
(1580), works that to this day remain the basis of Lutheran doctrine.[13]

A great political dilemma of the sixteenth century was created by
the fragmentation of the reform movement. Protestant diplomacy was
monopolized by efforts to lessen the political weakness engendered by
the bitterness arising from confessional diversity. Beginning with the
Marburg Colloquy (1529), unification was to be the elusive goal of
Protestant theologians and politicians. As was the case with the Württemberg promotion of the *Formula Concordiae* in the 1580s, efforts to
reconcile the Protestants usually exacerbated interdenominational intolerance. In fact, the *Formula Concordiae* sharply curbed confessional
diversity on the local level and worsened the already problematic
relations between larger political units.

Frischlin also found himself engulfed in this quagmire of theology
and politics. As part of a propaganda campaign for the adoption of the
Formula Concordiae in Strasbourg, Lucas Osiander (1534–1604), the
court pastor at Stuttgart, commissioned Frischlin to translate several
invectives against Johannes Sturm into Latin. Although he translated
Osiander's views anonymously, the opposing side at Strasbourg easily
identified Frischlin as the composer. Through this, Frischlin became
enmeshed in a theological dispute of slight genuine interest to him.
Lambert Daneau (1530–95), the famous Calvinist leader, not only ha-
rangued Frischlin for his theological perspectives but also accused him
of having written anti-Calvinist propaganda to ingratiate himself to
Osiander—hardly an entirely specious charge. Frischlin responded
with *Spongia*,[14] and yet again with *Breve responsum*,[15] though he mainly answered the personal invective Daneau raised against him. A
curious aspect of this entire affair, one which suggests Frischlin participated in it only halfheartedly, was that Frischlin was a lifelong
admirer of Johannes Sturm. Even after this turbulent episode, Sturm

highly recommended Frischlin for a teaching position at Strasbourg in 1584/85.

In 1580 the industrious churchmen of Württemberg drew Frischlin into yet another propaganda project. To his dismay, the Stuttgart court commissioned him to translate a work by Jakob Schropp depicting an imaginary ecumenical council of Protestants. Schropp wanted to produce, at least in a fictional account, a Protestant alternative to the Tridentine Council. Frischlin worked unwillingly on this strange project until it was published in 1581 as *Acta oecumenici concilii supra controversia de coena Domini*.[16]

Frischlin's most important theological work, one unquestionably conceived as a contribution to the intensive Württemberg campaign for Lutheran orthodoxy, was *Phasma*. It was performed by students during Carnival of 1580 before the duke and members of the court and university, as well as the citizenry of Tübingen. Especially when viewed from the eschatological perspective of the final act, it constitutes a sustained and wholly intolerant invective against non-Lutheran confessions. Schwenckfeld, Zwingli, Carlstadt, Pius IV, and their followers, as well as those of Münzer and Calvin, are consigned in the final judgment to the eternal fires of hell. This weighty stuff, while it may have been patent reality in the eyes of his audience, would have made enemies for Frischlin in most of Europe. In all likelihood it was due to the sharpness of its invective against non-Lutherans that Frischlin withheld *Phasma* from publication.[17] In fact, in 1586 some of his enemies threatened to publish the play to embarrass Frischlin, who was then in exile wandering through various parts of Germany. Finally, however, the play was printed in 1592 under circumstances which have remained mysterious.[18]

The acrimony of *Phasma* is a little puzzling. Naturally, Frischlin did not need any more enemies. Furthermore, according to Strauß's reliable account, Frischlin was neither particularly biased in his religious outlook, nor did he have a propensity for quibbling over the fine points of theological doctrine. Although he too seems to have felt a genuine desire for the unification of the various forms of Christianity, most of his remarks to this effect lacked the rigidity of those of Württemberg theologians. In a poem addressed to Calvinist poets in Germany, he eloquently formulated a humane attitude toward this problem: "Non ego vos odi, quanquam diversa canentes: / Opto tamen nos ut copulet una fides."[19] [I do not hate you, though you sing differently; yet I do wish that one faith joined us.] Though he attacked Catholicism in some works, Frischlin had an open mind about individuals confessing that faith. He had Catholic acquaintances in Rottenburg am Neckar and even accepted a professorship at the University of Freiburg, a Catholic institution, only to rescind it at his wife's insistence. At the end of his German play *Frau Wendelgard*, he espoused an undoctrinaire view of the great religious schism; praising Bishop Salomon for his wisdom and political loyalty to five emperors, Frischlin concluded with the magnanimous thought:

> Wolt Gott es weren jhm geleich,
> All Bischoff in dem gantzen Reich.
> Es würd villeicht jetz besser stohn,
> Mit der zertrenntn Religion.[20]

In view of Frischlin's expressions of tolerance, it seems only natural that he did not risk earning the enmity of most of Germany by publishing the extremely aggressive and bigoted *Phasma*. By 1580, the date of his negotiations with the University of Freiburg, Frischlin knew all too well that he might eventually be compelled to make his career outside of archorthodox Württemberg. He probably wrote *Phasma* to ingratiate himself to the court and university; obviously, he would have enhanced his chances for eventually becoming *ordinarius* had he only been able to improve his image in the eyes of Andreae, his ardent opponent in the faculty senate. In line with this goal, Frischlin also composed an encomiastic tribute to Andreae as a *subscriptio* for a portrait of the latter. Nearly attributing divine inspiration to the theologian's words, Frischlin extolled the efforts to stem the Protestant factionalism but concluded, perhaps cautiously, by expressing the wish that Christianity might indeed profit from Andreae's work.[21]

The title of the play was taken from Donatus's description of the now fragmentary text of Menander's *Phasma*. As mentioned in the prologue, Menander entitled his work *Phasma* because in it a young man sees an apparition of a woman, albeit quite unsupernaturally, through a chink in a wall. Frischlin parodied Donatus's description of the play by construing the *phasma* ("apparition") as a dream induced by the devil to lead sectarians astray. Further inspiration for the title, again as stated in the prologue, was an account of a dream that Ulrich Zwingli (1484–1531) had had just before a decisive theological debate at Zürich. Frischlin mocked Zwingli's account of the divinely inspired dream by identifying the apparition—Zwingli called it a *phasma*—as the devil.[22]

Theological strife, the subject of the play, is dramatized as both the existential and political crisis of the century. The opening act addresses the difficulty for a lay person to find the path to salvation in the midst of the tendentious and volatile theological turmoil. The first scene transpires between the two peasants Corydon and Menalcas, wherein the latter is troubled by religious disunity and resulting uncertainty about salvation:

Nam hodie quid credam, aut cui credam, plane nescio.
. . . .
In religionis negotio et doctrina fidei vix reperies
Duos Doctores, qui idem per omnia sentiant:
Aut unam eandemque salutis viam commonstrent populo.[23]

[These days I just don't know whom or what I believe. In religious matters and doctrine of faith it's impossible to find two theologians who agree about everything or could show the people the same way to salvation.]

Doctrine without catholicity was the cross religious man of the sixteenth century had to bear. The inability of one confession to attain a consensus is painfully clear in act II, where Luther, the most persuasive proponent of Frischlin's faith, cannot convince Meliboeus to renounce Anabaptism.

Despite the open portrayal of the fiasco of Protestantism, Frischlin obviously supported the Lutheran side. Act III, for example, is carefully organized to impeach the teachings of Zwingli and Carlstadt. In a daring move, the act commences with an encounter between Catholic and Protestant opponents of Luther. The Catholics, represented by the monk Franciscus and the nun Brigitta, confront the Protestants on the sorest issue for the latter: the Protestant factionalism and the resulting epidemic of sectarianism. Though chastised for their abidance in various practices of the church, Franciscus and Brigitta do not falter before the viciousness of the two Protestant foes. Zwingli and Carlstadt can do little more than cite hackneyed criticisms of alleged immorality and greed in monastic communities. Frischlin, however, discredited these personal attacks by portraying the two Catholics as deeply religious and morally respectable. This relatively favorable depiction of the Catholics serves as an effective prelude to the Marburg Colloquy, because on the issue of the Eucharist, the major stumbling block of the colloquy, Luther probably stood closer to the Catholics than to other Protestants. As another prefiguration of the colloquy, Zwingli and Carlstadt debase their argumentation with the Catholics by resorting to irrational and vulgar invective. At the conclusion, Franciscus confounds his Protestant opponents by referring to the fierce infighting among the non-Catholics. When Zwingli insinuates that Satan fathered the Catholic church, the Catholics parry by quoting Luther's contention that the devil stands behind Zwingli's theology. At this point, Zwingli lashes out crudely at Lutheranism before the two Catholics:

> At nos istos (i.e., Lutheranos), qui hoc dicunt, ex ipso ortos Diabolo
> Affirmamus, et excrementum Satanae linguis et literis
> Nostris et ipsos esse, et doctrinam illorum dicimus.[24]

> [But we declare that the Lutherans who say this rose up from the devil, and in our writings and speeches we say that their doctrine is Satan's excrement.]

Naturally, the inveterate intolerance among the Protestants made a bad impression on those still within the Catholic fold. Franciscus and Brigitta prefer the confidence offered by the old traditions of the Catholic church to the newfangled theology of the reformers:

> FR[anciscus]. Si hoc ita est, ut tu dicis: abeas, valeas cum Luthe-
>   ranis tuis.
> Nam ego maiorum meorum vestigiis insistam,
> Et avitam religionem sectabor: id enim tutissimum erit.
> BR[igitta]. Idem et ego faciam, cur enim a fide antiqua recedam?
> Et illos sequar, qui sese mutuo tradunt Satanae?[25]

> [Franciscus: If that is the case, goodbye! Fare well with your Lu-
>   therans! I'm going to follow my ancestors' path, that is the old
>   religion, since it is the safest way.
> Brigitta: And I'll do likewise. Why should I leave the old faith and
>   follow those who deliver each other to Satan?]

Thus Frischlin discredited the Protestant splinter movements by showing the need to present a united front against Catholicism—the very issue at the heart of Andreae's *Formula Concordiae*.

The failure of Carlstadt and Zwingli in their disputation with the Catholics prefigures the outcome of their debate with Luther and Brenz. Before the encounter, the two opponents of Lutheranism pledge to remain stubbornly opposed to doctrinal compromise, no matter how compelling counterarguments may be.[26] True to their word, they are utterly unreceptive to the arguments Luther and Brenz adduce. The pathos and earnestness of Luther's rhetoric contrast starkly with the bombast of Zwingli's polemic. The issue of the Eucharist, the central problem in Frischlin's reenactment of the colloquy, forces suspension of the dialogue. But according to Frischlin's portrayal, Zwingli and Carlstadt bear responsibility for the collapse because their harsh rhetoric allows no room for further discussion or even mutual toleration:

> Car[olstadius]. At quinam vos estis Thyestae? qui carnes humanas comeditis?
> CI [i.e., Zvvinglius]. Et qui Anthropophagi, qui hominem dentibus discerpitis?
> Car. Quales Cyclopes? CI. Quales Canibales? Car. Quam immanes Deivori?
> CI. Quam horribiles Haematopotae? Car. Quinam Capernaitae? CI. Qui Sarcophagi?
> Car. Et quis Deus iste paniceus? CI. Et quis Iuppiter iste Elicius?
> Car. Christus impanatus? CI. Christus tostus et pistus? Car. ubique praesens in omnibus
> Cloacis, foricis, latrinis?[27]

> [Carlstadt: What kind of Thyesteans are you, who eat human flesh?
> Zwingli: What kind of man-eaters are you, who tear apart a man with your teeth?
> Carlstadt: What kind of Cyclops are you?
> Zwingli: What sort of cannibals are you?
> Carlstadt: What horrible God-eaters?
> Zwingli: What awesome blood drinkers?
> Carlstadt: Are you Capernaites?[28]
> Zwingli: Are you flesh-eaters?
> Carlstadt: Who is this God made of bread?
> Zwingli: Who is this Jupiter Elicius?[29]
> Carlstadt: Christ "in-grain-ate"?
> Zwingli: Christ is baked and milled.
> Carlstadt: Omnipresent in every sewer, privy, and pissoir?]

Neither reason nor cudgeling changes anyone's view of doctrinal issues. The debate on the Eucharist does not turn on logical analysis but rather on the Lutheran claim that some tenets must be accepted on faith, quite apart from rational considerations. Zwingli and Carlstadt vent the full force of their polemic by asserting that it is cannibalistic irrationality to believe that the faithful consume the body and blood of the Godhead. To this Brenz responds in calm cadence that many mysteries of Christianity are irrational:

> Noli tumultuari Carolstadi:
> Nam multa sunt, quae rationi adversantur, vera tamen sunt et verbo Dei

Nituntur: Itaque non ingenio humano, sed vera fide apprehen-
   denda sunt.
Quid enim tam absurdum dictu, quam aqua peccatum ablui?
Quid tam absonum, quam esu pomi totum genus humanum in ae-
   ternum exitium
Praecipitari?[30]

[Carlstadt, don't get so excited. There are many things that con-
tradict reason but are nonetheless true and proven by God's
word. They must be apprehended through genuine faith and not
through human intellect. What could be more absurd than to say
that sin is washed away by water? What is as incongruous as the
fact that the entire human race fell to eternal ruin because someone ate an apple?]

Frischlin repeatedly illustrates that the proliferation of confessions
placed an enormous strain on all theological doctrines. In act V, scene
2, the apostle Peter humorously reproaches Paul for having expressed
many concepts enigmatically: "Hic frater meus nonnulla scripsit intel-
lectu difficilia."[31] [This brother of mine wrote many things that are
difficult to understand.] Yet ultimately, Frischlin also abandons rational disputation and appeals to his audience emotionally; in act V he
resolves the debates with Christ's heavy-handed condemnation of all
non-Lutherans. The audience may not follow all the doctrinal hair-
splitting, but dramatic action undermines Luther's opponents; act II
reveals the alleged immorality of Anabaptists, act III the rashness of
Zwingli and Carlstadt, and act IV the putative role of the devil in the
Catholic church.

The combination of politics and religion forms the keystone in the
experimental structure of *Phasma*. The reenactment of the Marburg
Colloquy emphasizes the political aspect of confessional diversity.
Brenz, whose role Frischlin elevates well beyond its historical significance,[32] ends the theological discussion by stating his need to report
the outcome to his prince, the Duke of Württemberg. In the opening
scene, the wise peasant Corydon establishes a strong link between
politics and theology. Having expressed grave doubts about the sincerity of non-Lutheran Protestants, he concludes that the turmoil in
the church may soon lead to the destruction of political harmony:

ubi enim alius alio plus sapere vult, ibi
Oriuntur rixae et lites, turbatur Respublica,
Amittitur pax et tranquillitas Ecclesiae.[33]

[Whenever one person thinks he knows more than another, disputes and quarrels arise, the state is shaken, and the peace and tranquility of the church are lost.]

Act II concerns the sociopolitical issues which Anabaptism had raised. Influenced by Carlstadt and Münzer, as Luther emphatically points out, the peasant Meliboeus has dissolved his marriage and renounced ownership of property. Luther and Meliboeus debate the institution of marriage for an entire scene, though to no resolution. Meliboeus also argues for a radical view of society, contending that it is impossible for a Christian to be a member of the ruling class or hold an office elevating him above the common man:

> inter homines
> Christianos nulli debent esse Magistratus, nulli reges,
> Nulli principes: sed omnia communia omnibus, nihil cuiquam
> proprium.[34]

[Among Christians there shouldn't be any offices, any kings, any rulers; everything should be held in common by everyone, and no one should have property.]

Luther attempts to controvert this basic challenge to class-society with scriptural interpretation, but Meliboeus has also learned to defend his concept of a classless society with biblical citations. The confrontation is actually resolved only in a very oblique way; Meliboeus is discredited not on the basis of faulty argumentation but rather because of character deficiencies such as cavalier indifference to his family. Although the peasant cannot be persuaded to change his mind, Luther scores an ironic victory over him. Luther assures Meliboeus's wife, Thestylis, that the very laws and magistrates that Meliboeus abhors will help her recover her property and will grant her a legal divorce, freeing her to find a new spouse and rebuild her family. After all this, the second chorus reinforces the message of the act with its "Preces pro magistratu, contra Anabaptistas," a hymnlike song that not only vouches for the divine sanctity of the class-society but also advocates universal eradication of heresy:

> Ergo precamur supplices,
> Ut ordinem divinitus
> Hunc constitutum protegas,
> Omnesque reges asseras.
> . . . .
> Largire pacem regibus,

Ut mentibus concordibus
Novas repellant haereses,
Tibique soli serviant.[35]

[Thus as suppliants we pray that you protect this divinely established order, and that you watch over all rulers. . . . Bestow peace on rulers so that they in concord can repel new heresies and can serve you alone.]

More than any other work, *Phasma* reveals with striking clarity Frischlin's self-imposed limitation to social criticism. The conservative political ideology of the emergent Lutheran orthodoxy precluded sympathetic speculation about revolutionary political theories, as they indeed arose throughout the sixteenth century. Bound by the strictures of Lutheranism, Frischlin allowed his critical voice freedom only within the parameters of Lutheran political doctrine.

The historical perspectives of *Phasma* represent an amalgam of medieval and humanist outlooks as well as a tensive combination of religion and politics. The first four acts transpire as a historical survey of religiopolitical events of the sixteenth century. Though its date cannot be fixed exactly, act I represents a rural milieu of the 1520s in considerable turmoil because of the theology of Münzer and Carlstadt. In act II, Frischlin provides a reference to an approximate date: Luther mentions recent disturbances of Carlstadt at Orlamünde (1524/25). With act III, scenes 1–3, the action progresses to the Marburg Colloquy (1529). The subsequent dispute between Brenz and Schwenckfeld (act III, scene 4) may refer to theological developments of 1540, when the Schmalkaldic League, at Brenz's instigation, condemned Schwenckfeld's theology.[36] Act IV takes place at the conclusion of the Council of Trent (1563). In act IV, however, Frischlin took considerable liberties with historical accuracy by introducing characters anachronistically. Campeggio, the papal legate, could not have been present at the conclusion of the Council of Trent, for he had died in 1539. Frischlin also condensed history considerably by including a strong reference to Brenz's mission of 1551 to the Council of Trent at the beginning of act IV, scene 3. In all probability, Frischlin knew the history of the Reformation from his study of the writings of Johannes Sleidanus (ca. 1506–56), the first historian of the reform movements,[37] and consciously introduced these chronological leaps. To suit the needs of his drama, he radically compressed the sweep of history to create an illusion that less than a single day transpires.

Marked as it is by anachronism, act IV also introduces a different concept of history, namely the medieval view of history as the *Heilsge-*

schichte. To commence act IV the devil appears, revealing that the action of the play is leading to the final judgment of the principal players. Although the temporal survey of history continues, the timeless element of eternity is added by the devil's presence in act IV and then by the presence of Christ in act V. Revealing his plans for man's damnation in act IV, scenes 1 and 3, the devil delivers an *encomion paradoxon* of the development of sectarianism and Catholicism. The judgment scenes of the final act represent an extreme relativization of secular history from the perspective of the *Heilsgeschichte*, for all worldly events have significance only in terms of this last judgment. As in many Lutheran writings and plays, the Antichrist is the pope.[38] Frischlin's depiction of the final judgment does not limit damnation to the pope; it entails a sweeping condemnation of all who have not found their way into the Lutheran fold. Otherwise respectable individuals such as Franciscus, Brigitta, and Menalcas are consigned for eternity to hell.

The eschatological development of *Phasma* invites comparison with Naogeorgus's *Pammachius* (1538). Also focusing on political issues, in particular Paul III's announcement of a council to be convened at Mantua in 1536,[39] Naogeorgus portrays the rise of the temporal power of the church as proof of its theological corruption. He projects the imminent damnation of the pope as the Antichrist for an as yet unwritten and unrealized fifth act. In agreement with Christian doctrine, the final days will experience the reappearance of God's word on earth to counter the force of the Antichrist. At the end of the play, this event is prefigured by the announcement that a certain Theophilus has begun preaching the word of God in Wittenberg. Pope, devil, and sundry assistants conspire to impede the Lutherans with councils, theological disputations, sectarianism, and even wars. Apart from Luther, who is the Theophilus of the play, Naogeorgus's view of history is extremely abstracted and does not permit identification of dates or real personages. Although contemporary politics obviously played an important role in the genesis of the drama, the *Heilsgeschichte* is the moving force in Naogeorgus's interpretation of historical structure. Frischlin, however, arranged precise events of recent history to elucidate his interpretation of religion and politics. He focused sharply on historical detail of his own century but, like Naogeorgus, used the perspective of the *Heilsgeschichte* as a powerful satirical device. The combination of humanist interest in political theory and history with the theological perspective of Christian salvation indicates the tremendous political tension that grew out of authoritarian views of politics and salvation in sixteenth-century theology. Nonetheless, the apparent relativization of politics by the *Heilsgeschichte* is counterbalanced by the politicization of theology. If we take the interpretation of history in *Phasma* seriously, then it would appear that Frischlin, like many others, believed that the end of the world was imminent. Whatever his real sentiments were, the combination of sixteenth-century history with Christian eschatological thought enabled Frischlin to satirize non-Lutheran doctrine with greater specificity than did Naogeorgus in *Pammachius*.

Unlike his other plays, *Phasma* does not focus on political ethics for the apex of the social hierarchy but rather on the situation of the peasantry. Frischlin carefully framed the action of the entire play with two scenes (act I, scene 1 and act V, scene 5) in which Menalcas experiences the problems religious diversity posed for the peasant. At the beginning of the play, he complains bitterly to his friend Corydon about theological discord, for he, as a simple man, cannot hope to determine which confession will lead him to salvation. In act IV, Menalcas falls victim to the devil's argument that he should remain in the Catholic church and let priests and monks attend to his salvation. In the final scene of the play, Menalcas tries to explain his failing to Christ:

> O Domine, ego fui agricola,
> Homo illiteratus, et ruri deditus, quem pessimus hic Satan
> Monachi habitu misere circumvenit: sis propitius
> Mihi: et veniam concede ignorantiae.[40]

> [Oh Lord, I was a peasant, an illiterate man, devoted to farming.
> This horrible devil, dressed in a monk's habit, tricked me badly.
> Be kind to me, and forgive me for my ignorance.]

Despite Peter's plea for mercy, Menalcas receives eternal damnation. Whereas elsewhere he portrayed negative characters of the nobility, in *Phasma* Frischlin depicted the peasant breaking the strictures of his class. Meliboeus is damned only in part because of his second baptism and his rejection of marriage. More egregious was his political radicalism, which the triad of Christ, Peter, and Paul attacks vociferously. Meliboeus, who was hanged because of his political convictions, embodies the radical Christian peasant seeking to build an entirely new social order. In an impressive display of oratory, Peter condemns every aspect of Meliboeus's political ideology:

> ME[liboeus]. Ah mi Domine, ego propter te crucem et mortem
>   perpessus sum,
> Carnifici datus crudelissimo. . . .
> Pe[trus]. Ego dicam: haud enim ille mihi videtur passus crucem

Ut Christianus, sed ut homicida, qui bellum movit rusticum:
Sed ut fur, qui sua bona liberis suis e faucibus
Eripuit et aliis tradidit: sed ut facinorosus, qui multa commisit
Flagitia cum mulieribus obscoenis: sed ut curiosus alienarum
   rerum,
Qui ministerium verbi arripuit, ad quod nemo ipsum vocaverat.[41]

[Meliboeus: Ah, but my Lord, for your sake I was crucified and
   died, after having been turned over to the most cruel
   executioner. . . .
Peter: I will speak, for in my opinion he hardly seems to have been
   crucified as a Christian, but rather as a murderer and instigator
   of the Peasants' War. He died as a thief who took his property
   away from his children and gave it to others; he died as a crimi-
   nal who committed many sins with bad women; he died as a
   usurper of other people's duties since he took up the ministry of
   the word, to which no one had called him.]

As things turn out, Corydon is the ideal of the play. In the epilogue
Frischlin enjoins peasants to follow the example of Corydon, who left
the church but did not fall victim to the allurements of non-Lutheran
Protestantism:

Drumb welcher nit wils Teuffels sein/
   Der folge Christi Lehre fein/
Und laß den Pabst und all sein Lehr/
   Geb Gott dem Herrn allein die Ehr:
Er laß den Zwingel und Schwenckfeld/
   Die Seelenmörder/in der Welt/
Und folge dem frommen Bawren [i.e., Corydon] nach/
   Der spott des Teuffels mit seiner sprach.[42]

Corydon, the simple peasant who accepted his place in society but
revolted from Catholicism, found the narrow path, in Frischlin's opinion, to theological innovation without political radicalism. As such, he
embodies the peasant hero in Frischlin's depiction of a turbulent age.
   Given the fact that Frischlin not only encouraged but could also
count on substantial vernacular reception, it is not surprising that the
common man is so prominent in his oeuvre. *Phasma* holds the fore in
this regard, but subplots about peasants, as we have seen, are also
significant in *Rebecca*, *Susanna*, and *Priscianus Vapulans*. Frischlin's German plays also feature characters from the lowest walks of life. The
couple of modest means in Frischlin's *Hochzeit zu Kana* receives edify-
ing instruction about social responsibilities. Even *Frau Wendelgard* has
a satirical subplot about beggars that mainly provides comic relief,

though it is also critical of the indolent among the lower classes. But the peasants in *Rebecca, Susanna,* and *Priscianus Vapulans,* taken together, exhibit unusual integrity as they engage in difficult struggles to oppose the abusiveness of their social betters. In Frischlin's portrayal, these peasants strengthen social order by attacking corrupt men who exercise political power. Should we want to define Frischlin's peasant in Lutheran terms, we would conclude that he is entirely Melanchthonian in his allegiance to societal order but unusually strident in his opposition to corrupt nobility and stubborn in claiming his rights within the social order. Obviously, Frischlin conceived his plays with Duke Ludwig and the Stuttgart court in mind; consequently, the depiction of peasants is largely important as a means of showing the problems of corruption in the ruling classes. In spite of this, the focus on the common man and the positive portrayal of him may very well have increased Frischlin's popularity in vernacular translations.

Phasma provides some clues to how Frischlin produced his plays. Although he certainly wrote his comedies for educated audiences as one would have found at universities, schools, and most courts, the remarkable clarity of Frischlin's latinity would have placed his works within the reach of those who had absolved a Latin grammar school. Furthermore, Frischlin appears to have composed act summaries to enhance the intelligibility of his dramas.[43] Unlike the plays published under his direction, the imprint of *Phasma* includes German act summaries. At the beginning of the imprint, we are informed that "Cuiuslibet huius comoediae actus argumentum et summa germanice propter foeminas, et virgines, ut et alias Latini sermonis ignaras personas ab auctore ipso composita."[44] [An argument and a summary of each act of this comedy were written by the author in German for the sake of women, girls, and other persons without Latin.] Act V also includes a scene in German, in which Mary interrupts the judgment of Pius IV and his entourage to plea for nothing less than the damnation of all Catholics. She contends that monks and nuns have denigrated her with mendacious accounts of her involvement in bizarre and illicit escapades. Ironically, Frischlin cast Mary as the inversion of her common role in Catholicism. Instead of the loving mother who intercedes for the mercy of souls, Mary wants Christ to pay back her detractors:

> Ach lieber Sohn/ auch lieber Herr:
> Errette du mein Zucht und Ehr/
> Den Heilgen schender/ der mich zeucht/
> Ich sey ein Hur/ und sich nicht scheucht/
> Straff lieber Sohn geb im den Lohn.[45]

The shift to German effectively breaks up act V just as it had become much too serious, not to mention monotonous. The stern context even enhances the comic elements of the German scene; the coarse simplicity of Mary's German juxtaposes the juridical and theological pathos used in the series of condemnations.

The epilogue to *Phasma* is also unique in Frischlin's Latin comedies; in deference to Roman practices, Frischlin probably would have excluded it, had he published *Phasma*. As in German plays of the sixteenth century, the epilogue afforded Frischlin an opportunity to defend and interpret *Phasma*. An introduction to the epilogue excuses the use of German on the basis that it is necessary to address the illiterate critics in the audience: "Epilogus totius comoediae, nonnullorum illiteratorum illius calumniatorum haereticorum gratia, ab auctore ipso compositus, et post finem Comoediae recitatus."[46] [The epilogue to the entire comedy was written by the author himself for the sake of several illiterate, heretical detractors of it, and it was recited after the comedy.] The use of German is not entirely a satirical condescension to Frischlin's opponents but rather an attempt to make certain points in his defense clear to the audience. The German epilogue does not speak exclusively to the unlearned; a major part of the conclusion addresses those theologians who are likely to resent poetic treatment of serious theological dogma.

If the imprints of *Phasma* contain these German elements because they derive from a performance copy, we can conclude that Frischlin encouraged audience participation in the production of the drama. At the close of the Latin text, there are two German hymns preceding the epilogue. The first chorus, which the audience was probably meant to sing under the direction of Christ, is the famous Lutheran hymn "Erhalt uns Herr bey deinem Wort." In counterpoint to that, Satan and his followers sang a parody, "Erhalt die Römisch Kirch, O Gott/ / Und wehr deß Luthers hon und Spott/."[47]

Frischlin's practices in his other Latin plays suggest that he would not have included these or any of the other German materials in a publication of *Phasma*.[48] Nonetheless, the imprint of *Phasma* indicates that as a dramaturge Frischlin tried to reach various societal strata in his potential audience. The latinity would have limited the size and diversity of his audience, but the German act summaries would have compensated by making the plot much clearer to those with little Latin. There is also every reason to believe that Frischlin composed his Latin plays knowing that German translations would make them accessible to audiences with limited education. By Frischlin's time, translating neo-Latin plays into German had become a common practice, and Frischlin himself arranged to have several of his plays and panegyrics translated. Some of his plays even enjoyed multiple translations: *Rebecca* was translated into German five times, whereas *Phasma* has appeared four times in German[49] and once in Italian.[50]

A fascinating play from the perspective of the political forces of the age, *Phasma* became too problematic and ideological for Frischlin to handle. The age of confessionalism was fraught with theological squabbling over many basic aspects of Christianity, such as Christology, the Eucharist, and the nature of sin and salvation. From our perspective four centuries later, it might appear that the most reasonable approach to this dilemma was adiaphorism as espoused in part by Melanchthon; this could have cut through the Gordian knot of hopelessly conflicting theological dogma. Unfortunately, adiaphorism carried with it the distinct possibility of eroding the Protestant churches, a fate that was almost realized with the Augsburg *Interim* (1548). Although accommodation of Philippists and Calvinists was highly desirable, a Württemberg author in 1580 could not support adiaphorism because, under the political constellations of the time, such a policy would have been disadvantageous to the house of Württemberg. Despite certain inherent problems, the dukes of Württemberg committed themselves to a policy of abetting Lutheran concord, a program that resulted in the extremely important *Formula Concordiae* of Jakob Andreae and Martin Chemnitz. This effort proved successful in placating Gnesio-Lutherans and some Philippists, but, more importantly, it solidified doctrinal cohesiveness among Lutheran princes and clergy. As depicted indirectly in *Phasma*, such a policy became crucial in the aftermath of the Catholic reorganization accomplished at the Council of Trent. However, as Frischlin probably realized himself, the *Formula Concordiae* and the efforts to establish a Lutheran orthodoxy irrevocably ended the possibility of mutual accommodation of numerous Protestant groups. In any event, *Phasma* dramatizes how theology constricted, paradoxically, as a result of the confessional diversity of the late Renaissance. The powerful but arbitrary interpretation that the eschatological perspective foists onto history is biased and intolerant; yet it is consonant with the kind of political ideologies that were rife in sixteenth-century theology.

7. A Concluding Note

On the whole, humanists were not only prodigiously learned in literary matters but also intensely concerned about Renaissance politics. As Frischlin's works illustrate, the combination of philology and social criticism informed the development of humanist drama. The preponderance of didacticism in humanist literature obliges scholars to study works in terms of their underlying ideologies, and further to consider how ideologies may have shaped or influenced the development of literary forms.

A significant theoretical context for humanist literature was rhetorical imitation. On the one hand, Renaissance imitation took authors through the schoolroom of antiquity, frequently imposing a heavy burden of conventionality on them; it represented, in short, a comprehensive involution of philology, criticism, and composition. Nonetheless, imitation, either in the paraphrastic or parodistic varieties I have discussed, is inherently antithetical; it instills an approach to literature that impels its practioner both to copy and to supplant convention. As Renaissance theoreticians prescribed it, imitation entailed dissimilation. One of its cardinal precepts was that renascent forms and techniques, though derived from the ancients, must be made relevant to sixteenth-century culture. This aspect of imitative literature is self-evident in the question of composing Christian literature, but as far as comedy is concerned attempts to introduce political and social issues into imitations resulted in the development of comic forms which suggested New Comedy only on the surface.

Of the similarities between Renaissance and Terentian-Plautine comedy the predominance of the marriage plot is perhaps the most noticeable. As Renaissance dramatists recognized, biblical dramas, especially those dealing with marriage, could be modeled, with some alterations, on the structure of New Comedy. Moreover, restorative happy endings, as one finds in plays about the prodigal son and Susanna, do not differ in kind from those of New Comedy. The Rebecca story, for example, conformed to the marriage structure of New Comedy, though with the obvious exception that according to the Bible there was no complication or impediment to the union of the couple. Frischlin compensated for this absence by composing a contrastive subplot. But here, as in other plays, he used the subplot to heighten political didacticism. Though its political focus contravenes

Roman convention, *Hildegardis Magna* also leads to a kind of matrimonial conclusion that was consonant with New Comedy. Otherwise, Frischlin used the restorative conclusion in *Priscianus Vapulans*, where the appearance of Melanchthon and Erasmus, symbolizing the advent of humanism, reverses all the harm which Priscian endured.

The subplot, a key element of Frischlin's drama, has a specific function. Generally speaking, it too represents a departure from the basic single-stranded plot of New Comedy, but, more importantly, it serves in every instance to widen Frischlin's sociological purview by dramatizing the malaise of the peasantry. Of the subplots, that in *Priscianus Vapulans* is the most genuinely humorous since, after all, Corydon is not the victim of any grievous social injustice. *Rebecca* and *Susanna*, however, depict cruel exploitation of peasants with such intensity that considerable compassion is awakened for the afflicted.

Ancient rhetoric and its Renaissance descendants constitute another theoretical influence on humanist writings. Because imitation offered techniques for transposing literary genres, it fostered the confluence of poetics and rhetoric that, as scholars have noted, characterizes Renaissance literature. As the myriad of handbooks indicates, rhetorical theory was in full bloom, and Frischlin was avidly interested in it. He expounded on rhetoric in several works, and his concept of poetry drew heavily upon rhetorical analysis of literature. In the case of drama, we have seen that scholarship on the classics strongly affected humanist concepts of literature. Renaissance scholars, most notably Melanchthon, applied rhetorical methods to interpretations of drama. Melanchthon used the standard taxonomy of Roman rhetoric to classify elements of Terentian comedies. This has bearing on inquiry into political forms of humanist drama in part because rhetoric developed in antiquity as a branch of political science. Although Terence's plays lack political themes, Melanchthon's analysis laid the foundation for subsequent rhetorical interpretations of comedy that focused on political elements. By turning to the political comedy of Aristophanes, Frischlin formulated a concept of comedy that not only proceeded from the Roman system of rhetoric but also accommodated political subjects.

Imitation and rhetoric, though they perpetuated literary ornamentation in the Roman style, nonetheless drew authors into considerations of the Renaissance world from political, social, and cultural perspectives. Political rhetoric had a particularly strong impact on Frischlin; he not only politicized his biblical dramas with considerations of social injustice, but he also cast several scenes of *Rebecca* and *Susanna* in deliberative and juridical rhetoric, respectively. The rhetoric in *Hildegardis Magna* is predominantly conciliar, and the proper function of deliberative rhetoric in governance is the play's theme. While *Julius Redivivus, Priscianus Vapulans*, and *Phasma* are structurally quite different from the comedies just mentioned, Frischlin nonetheless created quasi-historical constructs in them to examine topics such as humanist culture, social inequity, sectarianism, and the politics of the German Empire. Because of its usefulness to the didactically minded poet, demonstrative rhetoric was pervasive in the Renaissance, and it obviously had a major impact on Frischlin's poetry. In *Julius Redivivus*, where the relationship of poetry to politics is a discrete theme, Frischlin defined the ideal poet in terms of demonstrative rhetoric, claiming that the poet must write critically, both in affirmative and satirical modes, about society, politics, and theology.[1]

As was so often the case for German humanists, the occasion for which a drama was written determined to some extent its theme and subject. An obvious example of this is *Priscianus Vapulans*, which was written to commemorate Tübingen's first centennial. The cultural-political significance of humanism is, appropriately, its theme, though, as we have seen, the perspective on Tübingen and the progress of higher education in Germany is tenaciously critical. Less obvious examples of occasional dramas are *Rebecca* and *Hildegardis Magna*. The marriage of Ludwig of Württemberg and Dorothea Ursula no doubt prompted Frischlin to choose the Rebecca story for his first drama, but issues with specific bearing on Württemberg politics, such as the education of a prince from the perspective of Duke Ludwig's minority, also figure prominently in the comedy. The political elements of *Hildegardis Magna* are largely self-evident, but here again the occasion for which it was written, namely the celebration of Ludwig's assumption of his office, influenced Frischlin's development of the plot. Charlemagne fails egregiously, both as husband and, more importantly, as ruler, because in his rage he turned a deaf ear to his trustworthy advisors. The most substantial additions to the source, the scenes of consultation between Charlemagne, Talandus, and the ministers of state, portray proper and improper council, a subject which was naturally pertinent to the duke as he formally accepted the reins of government. In each of these plays, however, general relevance for sixteenth-century culture transcends any special significance for the Stuttgart court.

Although Frischlin's dramas evince similarities, they can be divided fairly neatly into two groups. The first, which consists of the biblical comedies and *Hildegardis Magna*, uses the process of rhetorical mimesis. Here the influence of Terence was particularly deep, in part because Frischlin, like other humanists, imitated elements of Roman drama extensively in biblical comedy. But even in the case of biblical comedy the imitative process presupposed several basic departures from the conventions of Roman comedy. As sixteenth-century commentators on Terence reiterated, the plot of comedy should by definition be fictional; only the form of tragedy should be used to dramatize historical events or personages. In the mimetic process, the comic playwright strove for plausibility or verisimilitude to human nature in constructing a fictitious plot. Latin biblical comedy, on the other hand, was not constructed using the process of fictional mimesis that sixteenth-century humanists, following Aristotle and Donatus, ascribed to New Comedy; rather, it involved rhetorical imitation, whereby the historical or biblical narrative, perceived and portrayed as the truth, was rewritten in dramatic form. In a manner utterly foreign to Terentian comedy, biblical as well as historical comedy had an authenticated message.

The second group comprises those plays for which Frischlin created the plot. With varying degrees of success, *Priscianus Vapulans, Phasma,* and *Julius Redivivus* dramatize concepts of the Renaissance and Reformation. Because they derive from neither historical nor biblical sources, rhetorical mimesis is of lesser importance in them. In fact, by creating such imaginary and impossible plots, Frischlin eschewed the fictional mimesis of Terence altogether. Perhaps he was inspired by earlier humanist dialogues or satiric plays such as *Eccius Dedolatus,* though the influence of Aristophanes can by itself account for this development. The new kind of plot represents nothing short of a complete break with the illusionism of New Comedy. Likewise, these plays were not conceived as imitative parody or paraphrase, though the idiom of Roman comedy is used in them. In the process of departing from illusionistic drama, Frischlin intensified his satire and sharpened his focus on politics. In *Julius Redivivus* and *Priscianus Vapulans,* the resurrections remind one specifically of the fanciful setting of Aristophanes' *Frogs* and generally of his imaginative way of portraying the impossible. The fantastic and the absurd are, however, not capricious incidentals. *Priscianus Vapulans* and *Julius Redivivus* represent metaphorical enactments of humanist concepts and issues in German politics. The irreality of the plots lightens Frischlin's didacticism and to a certain extent relativizes any humanist ideology. By avoiding a tight development of plot, Frischlin focuses in the episodic vignettes of *Julius Redivivus,* as we have seen, on political and cultural questions. But humor, equivocation, juxtaposition of ideology, and its radical anti-illusionism render *Julius Redivivus* a richly ambivalent form of humanist drama.

Taking political rhetoric as a point of departure, I have defined Frischlin's approaches to satire and also described the political views espoused in the plays. Although Frischlin left unchallenged the validity of class-society, he did not always espouse the Lutheran view that it was a God-given institution. Much of Frischlin's satire criticizes courtiers and nobles. He never advocated eradication of the privileges of the nobility, but his inveterate attacks on what he perceived as rampant moral and political corruption in this class earned him the reputation of being a political radical of Thomas Münzer's stamp. The evidence provided by his plays and other writings does not support that charge, and it is somewhat ironic that in early 1580, just before the outbreak of his catastrophic feud with the nobility, he composed *Phasma*, the play that most clearly projects an unrevolutionary view of the peasant class and society in general. Nonetheless, although his political comedies found resonance at Ludwig's court and throughout Germany, Frischlin was too censorious in the eyes of the Württemberg nobility and the faculty at the University of Tübingen. As a student of his time, he critically examined politics, education, theology, and social responsibilities. Even when he reviewed the cultural accomplishments of humanism—a subject dear to his very existence as professor of poetry and history—he could not be complacent, but balanced approbation with incisive criticism. Yet, because of its intensity, his satiric literature ultimately exceeded the tolerance of his environment and resulted in the harsh realities of his short life.[2]

In closing, I would like to comment on the larger enterprise of German Renaissance scholarship. Like many scholars in my field, I have labored under the twofold liability of participating in a pioneering phase of research on both a forgotten author and a neglected period. Basic philological and literary-historical work for the sixteenth century has not been done. Not only are huge editorial projects required, but we also need to start, in some tentative way, to assemble a canon of significant works. The few texts and authors that are familiar seem to most non-Renaissance scholars to be asteroids suspended in vacuous space. The void in which scholarship presently resides obliges its practioners, I believe, to move beyond a specific text as much as possible in order to postulate larger trends, even at the risk of proving to have had a skewed perspective. In the foregoing essays I have tried to combine, as flexibly as I could, historical criticism with close readings of texts. Such a methodological syncretism works well for Renaissance German literature because it is supple enough to support the necessary task of unearthing the unknown, while providing room for interpretative readings. Historical criticism establishes the political and intellectual grounding, without knowledge of which German humanist literature often makes little sense. Close reading, however, enables us to test the results of contextual study; but more significantly, it is the only way, as far as I can see, to deepen our understanding of the formal elements of individual works.

Notes

Chapter 1

1. The following are comprehensive biographies of Frischlin: Bebermeyer, "Nicodemus Frischlin," and *Tübinger Dichterhumanisten*, pp. 47–79; Conz, *Nikodem Frischlin: der unglückliche wirtembergische Gelehrte und Dichter*; Lange, *Nicodemus Frischlin, vita, fama, scriptis ac vitae exitu memorabilis*; Scherer, "Nicodemus Frischlin"; and Zacher, "Nicodemus Frischlin." Among the more important essays on specific aspects of Frischlin's life are Schreiner, "Frischlins 'Oration vom Landleben' und die Folgen"; Stahlecker, "Martin Crusius und Nicodemus Frischlin"; and Wheelis, "Publish and Perish: On the Martyrdom of Nicodemus Frischlin."

2. As its title suggests, Strauß's *Leben und Schriften des Dichters und Philologen Nicodemus Frischlin* includes discussions of Frischlin's literary works. While Strauß exercises sound judgment in his appraisals, his analyses suffer from their excessively limited scope. Strauß's accomplishment lies not in the interpretation of individual works, but rather in the distillation of a coherent and reliable biography from the massive body of sources.

3. I might add that for a brief period Frischlin also lectured on astronomy; later he published a phenomenally learned astronomical treatise: *De astronomicae artis cum doctrina coelesti et naturali philosophia congruentia* (1586).

4. The first epithalamium was *De nuptiis . . . libri septem* (1577); the second *De secundis nuptiis . . . libri quatuor* (1585). The first epithalamium was also translated into German by Carl Christoph Beyer: *Sieben Bücher von der fürstlichen würtembergischen Hochzeit* (1578).

5. Toward the end of his life, Frischlin also published a lengthy panegyric to the dukes of Saxony: *Carmen panegyricum de quinque Saxoniae ducibus* (1588).

6. See Strauß, *Frischlin*, pp. 93–98, and Schulz-Behrend, "Nicodemus Frischlin and the Imperial Court."

7. Let me cite one example of this. After having had too much to drink one day in 1576, Frischlin broke some windows at Roseck, a castle in the vicinity of Tübingen. The aggrieved castellan, Jeremias Godelmann, brought the matter to the faculty senate at Tübingen, which was of course a great embarrassment to Frischlin. See Strauß, *Frischlin*, pp. 61–64.

8. This was the view of Marcus Wagner; see Schreiner, "Frischlins 'Oration vom Landleben' und die Folgen," pp. 128–29.

9. For the details of this long and complicated affair, see Strauß, *Frischlin*, pp. 386–94.

10. Quoted from Strauß, *Frischlin*, p. 459.

11. *Nomenclator trilinguis* (1586); *Grammatice Latina* (1586); *Rhetorica: seu institutionum oratoriarum libri duo* (1604). These are just prominent examples of the many scholarly works Frischlin published.

12. *Callimachi Cyrenaei Hymni (cum suis scholiis graecis) et Epigrammata* (1577); *Aristophanes* (1586); and *Tryphiodori Aegyptii, grammatici, et poetae, liber de Ilii excidio* (1588).

13. Though his paraphrases had been published earlier in separate editions, they were reissued in a collected edition after Frischlin's death: *Operum . . . pars paraphrastica* (1602).

14. All of which were published posthumously in *Operum poeticorum . . . pars elegiaca* (1601).

15. *Hebraeis*, edited by Martin Aichmann and Ulrich Bollinger, was first published in 1599.

16. See Roethe, "Frischlin als Dramatiker," p. lvii.

17. In 1584/85 Frischlin edited his plays for the *Operum poeticorum . . . pars scenica*, first printed by Bernhard Jobin in Strasbourg. The first edition of the *pars scenica* contained *Rebecca, Susanna, Hildegardis Magna, Julius Redivivus, Priscianus Vapulans, Venus*, and *Dido*. In the third collected edition (1589) Frischlin added *Helvetiogermani*. *Phasma*, though first printed posthumously in 1592, was added to the collected edition in 1595. Georg Pflüger, a schoolteacher in Ulm, produced an important edition of the collected dramas in 1608 with copious notes for students. See bibliography for a complete list of the *Operum poeticorum pars scenica*. For general remarks on Frischlin's relationship with Strasbourg printers, see Ritter, "Zu den Strassburger Drucken des Nicodemus Frischlin."

18. See Roloff, "Neulateinisches Drama," pp. 665–67.

19. Frischlin exerted especially strong influence on Jakob Gretser. See Dürrwächter, *Jakob Gretser und seine Dramen*, pp. 136ff., as well as Valentin, *Le théâtre des Jésuites*, 2:507–36.

20. In addition, while incarcerated at the end of his life (1590), he managed to compose two unpolished German dramas, *Ruth* and *Die Hochzeit zu Kana*, as well as summaries for three plays about Joseph. These works were first published by Strauß in 1857. For the sake of completeness, I should note that Frischlin wrote another play in German, *Weingärtner*, which was never published and is no longer extant. A poem by Frischlin concerning this play, "Apologia lepidissimae comoediae, cui titulum Vinitoris fecit," was printed in his *Operum poeticorum pars elegiaca*, fols. Yy 2r–4r. He also intended to compose a Christmas play entitled *Genethlia Christi*; the plan for it was published in Frischlin's *Methodus declamandi* (1606), pp. 162–65.

21. Some work, however, has been devoted to nondramatic works: Bebermeyer, *Tübinger Dichterhumanisten*, pp. 71–75, and Ludwig, "Nicodemus Frischlin," pp. 375–77, discuss the *facetiae*; Kohl, "Nikodemus Frischlin: Die Ständesatire in seinem Werke," pp. 119–56, describes the satires.

22. Janell's edition includes important essays on Frischlin by Walther Janell, Gustav Roethe, and Walther Hauff. I might add that, more recently, Richard Schade has edited Jakob Frischlin's German translation of *Julius Redivivus*.

23. Above all, Neumeyer's dissertation, "Nicodemus Frischlin als Dramatiker," provides an exhaustive compilation of Frischlin's borrowings from Ter-

ence and Plautus. Unfortunately, it lacks any description of Frischlin's theory or approach to imitation.

24. Kohl's dissertation, "Nikodemus Frischlin: Die Ständesatire in seinem Werke," also contains a useful biographical essay on Frischlin. For the sake of completeness, I should mention another, apparently handwritten dissertation on Frischlin, Fink's "Studien zu den Dramen des Nikodemus Frischlin." Unfortunately, I have been unable to locate a copy of it.

25. Tarot, "Ideologie und Drama," pp. 351–66, pursues a similar approach to early German drama in an analysis of Biedermann's *Cenodoxus* as an ideological form of tragedy.

Chapter 2

1. See Roloff, "Neulateinisches Drama," pp. 648–51. A thorough overview of the history of the humanist stage is available in Michael, *Frühformen der deutschen Bühne*, esp. pp. 67–86.

2. Melanchthon was an expert on ancient drama. For an edition of Terence's comedies, he wrote introductory essays, drawn largely from Donatus, that were reprinted throughout the century. In his *schola privata*, a sort of academic boardinghouse that was common during the sixteenth century, he frequently put on plays with his pupils. He also composed special prologues for ten dramas from the Roman canon. As a young man, he probably participated in a production of *Henno* to honor the author of that work, his great-uncle Johannes Reuchlin. See Ellinger, *Philipp Melanchthon*, p. 57.

3. See Vormbaum, *Evangelische Schulordnungen*, vol. 1, and the useful discussion in P. Expeditius Schmidt, *Die Bühnenverhältnisse*, pp. 5–20.

4. Skopnik, *Das Straßburger Schultheater: Sein Spielplan und seine Bühne*, p. 8. For more information on Johannes Sturm, see Sohm, *Die Schule Johann Sturms und die Kirche Straßburgs*, and Charles Schmidt, *Le vie et les travaux de Jean Sturm*.

5. See Roloff, "Neulateinisches Drama," p. 672.

6. See *Oratio in gymnasio in Ingolstadio publica recitata*, in Celtis, *Selections*, pp. 36–65.

7. In its context, "publica spectacula" almost certainly refers to plays, although the term itself could also mean public declamations.

8. The climactic statement comes near the end of the speech: "Quamobrem convertite vos, Germani, convertite vos ad mitiora studia, quae sola vos philosophia et eloquentia docere potest." Celtis goes on to ascribe political importance to the study of philosophy and eloquence. To illustrate the power of eloquence, Celtis quoted the famous simile in *Aeneid* I, 148–53 of the man who quells a riotous crowd with his words; see Celtis, *Selections*, p. 60.

9. Quoted from Roloff, "Neulateinisches Drama," p. 648.

10. Luther not only knew a great deal about classical drama but also was familiar with contemporary works. For general information on Luther's atti-

tudes toward drama, see Bacon, *Martin Luther and the Drama*, pp. 42–77. According to Kampschulte, *Die Universität Erfurt in ihrem Verhältnisse zu dem Humanismus und der Reformation*, 1:66, Luther probably attended Hieronymus Emser's lectures on Reuchlin's *Sergius*.

11. See Luther, *Werke* III, 1:431–32 (*Tischreden*, no. 867).

12. Ibid., p. 432. For the reception of Terence in the Renaissance, see Francke, *Terenz und die lateinische Schulcomoedie in Deutschland*, though a new study of this subject is badly needed.

13. See Strauß, *Frischlin*, p. 109.

14. See Frischlin, *Operum poeticorum pars scenica* (1589), p. 85: "Nam clamitant nonnulli homines nasutuli, / Leves personas in sacris Comoediis / Non introduci oportere, sed omnes graves: / Et quas imitari possit adolescentia: / Quae plaerunque ad malum siet proclivior. / Quasi vero nequam, flagitiosi, subdoli, / Periuri, blasphemi, salaces, ebrii, / Idcirco in scenam producantur, ut alii / Fiant similes malis, et non potius bonis: / Quorum virtutes et pie facta videant. / Habet Poeta bonorum exemplum, quo sibi / Licere id facere, quod alii fecerunt, putat. / Nam veteres Spartanos in more habuisse, ait: / Ut in conspectum liberorum servulos statuerent ebrios: ut turpitudine / Morum conspecta, ab isto vitio liberi / Terrerentur." Unless otherwise indicated, subsequent references to Frischlin's plays are taken from this edition of 1589.

15. Hrotsvitha, *Opera*, p. 113. Unless otherwise noted, all translations of Latin texts cited in this study are my own.

16. See Catholy, *Fastnachtspiel*, pp. 10–15. A good anthology of works is available in Wuttke, ed., *Fastnachtspiele des 15. und 16. Jahrhunderts*.

17. Some plays, such as Reuchlin's *Henno* and Frischlin's *Phasma*, premiered during Carnival but did not impugn the conventions of *Fastnachtspiele*.

18. See Waldis, *De Parabell vam vorlorn Szohn*, pp. 152–53, where Waldis criticizes Shrovetide plays produced in Rome.

19. See Gretser, *Udo von Magdeburg*, pp. 8–10, especially lines 81–83: "Nobis enim fuerit satis superque si / Quidam abstrahantur unam aut alteram / Horam a Licentia peccandi hoc tempore." Gretser wrote *Udo* to be performed in honor of Mary on Candlemas, which falls during Carnival.

20. See Birck's introductory epistles to his Latin versions of *Susanna* and *Judith* in Birck, *Sämtliche Dramen*, 2:170–76, 276–78.

21. Melanchthon discussed the political value of humanism frequently, though a succinct statement can be found in his speech "In laudem novae scholae," printed in Melanchthon, *Werke in Auswahl*, 3:63–69. At the end of the speech, Melanchthon summarized the civic importance of education: "Quare in primis in bene constituta civitate, scholis opus est, ubi pueritia, quae seminarium est civitatis, erudiatur, valde enim fallitur, si quis sine doctrina solidam virtutem parari posse existimat, nec ad respublicas gubernandas quisquam satis idoneus est sine scientia earum litterarum, quibus ratio omnis regendarum civitatum continetur." Erasmus's interest in political edu-

cation was enormous; I would single out his important work on the education of the prince as an illustration of his belief in the political benefits of humanist studies. See *Institutio Principis Christiani* (1515), in Erasmus, *Ausgewählte Schriften*, 5:112–357.

22. Under pressure, he eventually published an apology for the oration: *Entschuldigung/ und endtliche bestendige Erklärung Doctoris Nicodemi Frischlini, gestelt an den löblichen Adel/ teutscher Nation* (1585). For excerpts from the speech, see Strauß, *Frischlin*, pp. 173–84.

23. *Oratio de vita rustica*, in *Orationes insigniores aliquot* (1605), p. 307. The *Orationes* were first printed in 1598.

24. Some information on this subject can be found in Kiesel, *Bei Hof, bei Höll*, pp. 21–128.

25. Luther, *Werke* II, 12:108. Many dramatists were inspired by this concept. Paul Rebhun, for example, wrote two biblical dramas in German and even appended Luther's prefaces to Tobit and Judith to his edition of *Susanna* (1536).

26. Luther's prefaces to these two apocryphal books have frequently been cited by scholars of sixteenth-century drama. Unfortunately, the ramifications of Luther's argumentation have not been analyzed. See, for example, Holstein, *Die Reformation im Spiegelbilde der dramatischen Litteratur*, pp. 20–21; Creizenach, *Geschichte des neueren Dramas*, 3:354.

27. For a slightly longer discussion of the patristic background to this type of apology, see my dissertation, "Nicodemus Frischlin and Sixteenth-Century Drama," pp. 10–17. More recently, Parente, *Religious Drama*, pp. 26–27, follows the argument I laid down in my dissertation. A general study of the reception of patristic literature in sixteenth-century Germany is a pressing *desideratum*. Dyck, *Athen und Jerusalem*, pp. 35–41, has a brief discussion of this topic.

28. See Augustine, *De Doctrina Christiana* III, 94: "Et quis talia non dicit indoctus nec omnino sciens qui sint vel quid vocentur hi tropi? Quorum cognitio propterea scripturarum ambiguitatibus dissolvendis est necessaria quia, cum sensus, ad proprietatem verborum si accipiatur, absurdus est, quaerendum est utique, ne forte illo vel illo tropo dictum sit quod non intellegimus, et sic pleraque inventa sunt quae latebant."

29. Others, especially Gregory the Great and Cassiodorus, made significant contributions to this tradition. In his influential *Origines*, Isidore of Seville used the Bible to illustrate many aspects of rhetoric and poetics. Nonetheless, Isidore's orientation to literature was predominately classical; the number of his Bible citations is modest in comparison to the number of quotations from Roman literature.

30. See Bede, *De Arte Metrica et De Schematibus et Tropis*, esp. I, 25.

31. Melanchthon, *Elementorum Rhetorices libri duo* (1532), fols. F 1v–2r.

32. Boltz, *Publii Terentii Aphri sechs verteütschte Comedien* (1544), fol. A 3v. The first edition of this work was printed by Morhart in 1539.

33. Kerckmeister, *Codrus*, p. 64.

34. Frischlin, *Oratio de exercitationibus oratoriis et poeticis ad imitationem veterum* (1587), in *Orationes insigniores aliquot*, pp. 112–68. Hereafter this speech is cited as *Oratio de imitatione*.

35. *Oratio de imitatione*, p. 157. See also Curtius, *Europäische Literatur und lateinisches Mittelalter*, pp. 96–97.

36. See *Oratio de dignitate et multiplici utilitate poeseos habita Tubingae*, in *Operum poeticorum . . . paralipomena* (1610), p. 162: "Comica non pauci sacris immista libellis / Esse putant: sacroque pedes incedere socco. / Qualia Susannae memorantur gesta, pudicae / Virginis et castum ardenter retinentis amorem. / Huic fere consimilem sacri fecere Tobiae / Historiam, ludus tanquam si scenicus esset." Strauß, *Frischlin*, p. 28, also quoted this passage but observed neither the Lutheran nor the patristic background of the concept.

37. See Friedrich Dedekind's introduction to his revised edition of *Der Christliche Ritter* (1590), fols. A 7r–7v, for another citation of Luther's idea of the biblical origin of drama:

> Es ist freylich eine alte löbliche weise und gewonheit/ das Geistliche Gedicht und Comoedien, die liebe jugend damit als einem Spiegel/ bild und Exempel der furcht Gottes und aller tugend zu berichten/ zu reitzen/ und darinne zu uben gemacht und gespielet werden/ Als bey den Jüden/ Judith/ Tobias/ Susanna/ und andere mehr sein/ und wol zu vermuten ist/ das dergleichen viel mehr sey gewesen/ darinne sie sich auff ire Sabbath und Feste geübet/ und der jugend und gemeinem Mann also mit lust Gottes wort und werck eingebildet haben/ Wie D. Lutherus in den Vorreden auff die Bücher Judith und Tobia urteilet und zeuget.

38. See Atkinson's discussion in his edition of Gnapheus's *Acolastus*, pp. 47–72.

39. See Könneker, *Hans Sachs*, p. 8.

40. Naogeorgus, *Iudas Iscariotes Tragoedia nova et sacra* (1552), fol. A 3r.

41. *Phasma* (1592), fol. H 3r: "Soll man dann / Geistliche sachen auff die bahn / Fürbringen/ in eim Spiegelfecht/ / Durch ein Comedi also schlecht? / Als wenn die Gottesdiener gut / Verloren hetten all iren mut/."

42. See Franz, "Bücherzensur und Irenik," pp. 123–94.

43. See Strauß, *Frischlin*, p. 229.

44. *Phasma*, fol. H 3v.

45. Frischlin's works were subject to censorship and criticism by theologians at the University of Tübingen and by members of the court of Duke Ludwig.

46. Frischlin, *Epistolae et Praefationes*, appended to his *Methodus declamandi*, pp. 149–50.

Chapter 3

1. Herrick, *Comic Theory in the Sixteenth Century*, p. 1.

2. Wimpheling's *Stylpho* and Reuchlin's *Henno* are available in modern edi-

tions by Schnur. For Bebel, see his *Comoedia* (Barner, ed.). Both of Celtis's plays, *Ludus Dianae* and *Rhapsodia*, were reprinted in Celtis, *Ludi Scaenici* (Pindter, ed.). Locher's *Ludicrum Drama de sene amatore* was reprinted in Reinhardstoettner, *Plautus: Spätere Bearbeitungen*, pp. 240–46.

3. *Sergius* is available in Reuchlin, *Johann Reuchlins Komödien* (Holstein, ed.), pp. 107–26. Unfortunately, with the exception of *Ludicrum Drama*, Locher's plays have never been reprinted. See bibliography for the imprints mentioned here. For a discussion of Locher's early plays, see Coppel, "Jakob Locher und seine in Freiburg aufgeführten Dramen;" concerning his *Tragedia, Spectaculum, Iudicium Paridis*, and *Ludicrum Drama*, see my essay, "Politics, Poetry, and Whimsy: On the Humanist Dramaturgy of Jakob Locher."

4. I do not mean to suggest that biblical drama was unimportant in the Middle Ages. For general information on this and other aspects of medieval drama, see Brett-Evans, *Von Hrotsvit bis Folz und Gengenbach: Eine Geschichte des mittelalterlichen deutschen Dramas*. The best historical survey of sixteenth-century biblical drama is in Holstein, *Die Reformation im Spiegelbilde der dramatischen Litteratur*, pp. 75–159, though a new comprehensive study is very much needed. Otherwise, two recent articles on the subject are useful: Valentin, "Aux origines du théâtre néo-latin de la réforme catholique," and Lebeau, "De la comédie des humanistes a la 'divine comédie.'"

5. A measure of the play's success can be gleaned from its publication history: by 1585 it had gone through at least forty-six printings (see Gnapheus, *Acolastus* [Bolte, ed.], pp. xxiv–xxvii). By singling out Gnapheus's accomplishment, I do not mean to slight the very important dramas by Georg Macropedius; for a thorough introduction to his works, see Best, *Macropedius*.

6. See Michael, *Das deutsche Drama der Reformationszeit*, pp. 202–4.

7. This is by no means a new observation, though I should note that in his edition of *Acolastus*, pp. 26–43, Atkinson argued that the principal model was *Andria*. For a list of Gnapheus's borrowings from classical sources, see Bolte's edition of *Acolastus*, pp. xvi–xxiv.

8. Gnapheus, *Acolastus* (Atkinson, ed.), p. 84.

9. See Böckmann's description of Gnapheus's "parabolische Struktur," in Böckmann, *Formgeschichte*, pp. 305–11.

10. See Birck, *Sämtliche Dramen*, 1:8 (the dedicatory epistle for *Exechias*): "Nec te pigeat id suscipere; quod me ne nunc quidem aedere pudet. Germanica sunt, Germanici poetae nomen apud vestrates audio. Terentius apud suos magis celebrabatur, quam si Atticas (quod poterat) Romae dedisset, Nec tum deerant, qui Menandri fabulas intelligerent. Populi tum nobis, non doctorum tantum applausus demerendus erat."

11. See Lebeau, "Sixt Bircks *Judith* (1539)." A comprehensive study of Birck's dramas is still needed; Levinger's *Das Augsburger Schultheater* is largely limited to consideration of the type of stage Birck used for his productions.

12. On the humanist reception of Hrotsvitha, see Zeydel, "The Reception of Hrotsvitha by the German Humanists after 1493."

13. This is the view expressed by Abbé, *Drama in Renaissance Germany and Switzerland*, p. 47.

14. Petrarch voiced this opinion in *Epistulae ad Familiares,* XXII, 2:133–39: "Sum quem priorum semitam, sed non semper aliena vestigia sequi iuvet; . . . sum quem similitudo delectat, non identitas, et similitudo ipsa quoque non nimia, in qua sequacis lux ingenii emineat, non cecitas, non paupertas; sum qui satius rear duce caruisse quam cogi per omnia ducem sequi." Quoted from Petrarca, *Le Familiari,* 4:108. For more information on Petrarch, see Gmelin, "Das Prinzip der Imitatio in den romanischen Literaturen der Renaissance," pp. 98–173. Pigman, "Versions of Imitation," is a stimulating essay on the various types of imitation, especially eristic imitation.

15. See Zielinski, *Cicero im Wandel der Jahrhunderte,* pp. 182–86, for a brief survey of the battles of the Ciceronians.

16. *Dialogus cui titulus Ciceronianus sive de optimo dicendi genere,* in Erasmus, *Ausgewählte Schriften,* 7:1–355. Some scholars, for example, Joachim Camerarius and J. C. Scaliger, objected to Erasmus's views. For Camerarius's approach, see Gerl, "*De imitatione* von Camerarius."

17. See Erasmus's letter to Francis Vergara, a passage which has since become a *locus classicus* on the subject of Renaissance imitation: "Apud hos prope turpius est non esse Ciceronianum quam non esse Christianum: quasi vero si Cicero nunc revivisceret, de rebus Christianis non aliter loqueretur quam aetate sua loquebatur, quum praecipua pars eloquentiae sit apposite dicere. Nemo negat Ciceronem dicendi virtutibus excelluisse, quamquam non omne dicendi genus convenit personis vel argumentis quibuslibet. . . . Nihil enim moror inanem oratoris bracteam, et decem verba hinc atque illinc ex Cicerone emendicata. Totum Ciceronis pectus requiro. . . . Ut formae pictor, ita dictionis rhetor absolutum exemplum a multis petat oportet." Quoted from *Opus Epistolarum Erasmi Roterodami,* 7:194 (no. 1885).

18. See Auerbach, *Literatursprache und Publikum,* pp. 25–53.

19. Erasmus, *Ciceronianus,* pp. 134–36.

20. Ibid., p. 168.

21. Melanchthon, *Elementorum Rhetorices libri duo,* fol. H 7r.

22. Ibid., fol. H 8r–8v.

23. Ibid., fol. E 6r.

24. It is interesting, for example, to see the diversity of models Melanchthon recommended for epideictic composition: "Sed quoniam extant exempla, in quibus ratio huius generis tractandi cerni potest, nihil opus est longioribus praeceptis. Isocrates relinquit laudationem Evagorae, Plinius Traiani. Extant et recentes Panegyrici dignissimi qui legantur, Erasmi in Philippum Regem Hispaniae, Huteni Poema de principe Alberto Moguntino Archiepiscopo. Sunt psalmi quidam generis demonstrativi, qui describunt Christum." Melanchthon, *Elementorum Rhetorices libri duo,* fol. D 3r. This analysis of Erasmus and Melanchthon is derived from my dissertation, "Nicodemus Frischlin and Sixteenth-Century Drama," pp. 29–34. More recently, Parente, *Religious Drama,* pp. 39–41, espouses a similar view.

25. Hess, *Deutsch-Lateinische Narrenzunft,* p. 163, stated his intention to write a study of this work, though, to my knowledge, it has not yet appeared.

26. *Oratio de imitatione,* p. 157.

27. See ibid., p. 146: "Quid veteribus licuit: cur non et nobis liceat?" For a useful discussion of *imitatio* in Roman literature, see Reiff, *Interpretatio, Imitatio, Aemulatio.*

28. *Oratio de imitatione*, p. 157.

29. *Oratio de praestantia et dignitate Virgilii Aeneidos* was printed in *Orationes insigniores aliquot*, pp. 1–111.

30. All of Frischlin's paraphrases were collected in *Operum pars paraphrastica.*

31. *Venus* and *Dido* were included in Frischlin's *Operum poeticorum pars scenica* (1585, etc.). Frischlin also published *Dido* separately in 1581.

32. See *Methodus declamandi*, p. 2: "Is enim imitatur, qui similia scribit antiquis, non qui eadem."

33. Ibid., pp. 1–2.

34. See *Oratio de imitatione*, p. 125, where Erasmus is criticized for using poetic diction in prose works; Frischlin also chastized Erasmus in *Julius Redivivus*: "Eobanus: Quid Erasmus Roterodamus? Cicero: . . . tum faciendae orationis ac / Exornandae auctor locupletissimus, nisi / Quod verborum delectum non apte adhibuit" (act III, scene 1). For this pedantic criticism, he drew upon the research of J. C. Scaliger, who had been embroiled in a knotty dispute with Erasmus over aspects of *Ciceronianus* until the latter's death in 1536; see Strauß, *Frischlin*, p. 262. For details of the controversy, see Hall, *The Life of Julius Caesar Scaliger*, pp. 94–114, as well as Telle, *L'Erasmianus sive Ciceronianus d'Etienne Dolet*, and Magnien, "Erasme et Scaliger."

35. See *Oratio de imitatione*, p. 148: "Est enim parodia sententia inversa, mutatis vocibus, ad ridicula, sensum retrahens, ut Scaliger finit. Habet tamen etiam in seriis locum, neque tantum carmine, sed etiam in prosa, sed proprie tamen in carmine, unde etiam parodiae nomen habet." For comparison, see Scaliger, *Poetices Libri Septem* (1561), p. 46: "Est igitur Parodia Rhapsodia inversa mutatis vocibus ad ridicula sensum retrahens."

36. *Oratio de imitatione*, p. 157. Frischlin also quoted a parody of Ovid by Eobanus Hessus which is less sympathetic to the model. Hessus rendered the original, "Est Deus in nobis, agitante calescimus illo / Sedibus aethereis spiritus iste venit," as "Est Pluto in vobis, agitante calescitis illo / Sedibus infernis spiritus iste venit" (p. 158).

37. This was an important issue in Frischlin's edition of Callimachus's *Hymni et Epigrammata*. See the preface to the Callimachus edition, reprinted in *Epistolae et Praefationes*, appended to Frischlin's *Methodus declamandi*, p. 118: "Etsi enim deploranda est priscorum vatum caecitas, quod tam praepostero animorum studio, profanos ac commentitios Ioves, Apollines, Dianas, Ceres, et Minervas colere ac celebrare maluerunt, quam verum Israelis Deum: tamen propterea e Scholis Christianis (ut multi censent) non erunt exterminandi ac profligandi."

38. See Hofmann, *Die Artistenfakultät an der Universität Tübingen*, esp. p. 143.

39. *Oratio de imitatione*, p. 163. Frischlin had also planned to compose paraphrases of Juvenal and the entire *Aeneid.*

40. See *Julius Redivivus* (Janell, ed.), p. lxxvii:

Delineavi iam olim pro Terentio isto profano, in quo pueri discunt artes meretricias, delineavi, inquam, Eunuchum, Adelphos et Heautontimorumenon, tres comoedias novas et sacras, in quibus omnis historia Josephi continetur. Nam in Eunucho exponitur historia Josephi venditi a fratribus, amati et proditi a Putipharis uxore, conjecti in carcerem, liberati a Pharaone et constituti in principem locum in regno Aegypti. In Adelphis negotiantur fratres Josephi in Aegypto: Simeon luditur a Serapione, servo Josephi et ejusdem Graece loquentis interprete; idem conicitur in vincula, adducitur Benjamin, ad extremum Josephus summa cum gratulatione a fratribus agnoscitur. In Heautontimorumeno Jacobus propter Josephum jam olim amissum et propter Simeonem captivum et propter abductum Benjaminem se ipsum excruciat; filii reversi ex Aegypto patrem laetissimo nuntio exhilarant, dubius pater de profectione confirmatur a Jehova et tandem a Josepho et a Pharaone senex pater summo cum applausu omnium Aegyptiorum excipitur. Consignavi etiam Hecyram, in qua historia Ruth explicatur et in scaenam producitur. Verum ut has comoedias non absolverem hactenus, fecit tum infortunium quoddam meum et mea illa in locis peregrinis negotii plena vita.

41. Roethe, "Frischlin als Dramatiker," p. xxvii, aptly observed that the four planned plays and the two completed Latin comedies would equal the number of extant plays in Terence's oeuvre.

42. *Operum poeticorum pars scenica*, fol.):(3v.

43. When Georg Pflüger edited Frischlin's plays for schoolboys in 1608 (reprinted in 1612), he meticulously identified most of the borrowings from Terence and Plautus in his annotations.

44. It should be mentioned that Frischlin, like many other dramatists, made a sharp distinction between *comoediae sacrae* and *comoediae profanae*. A *comoedia sacra* was an adaptation of a scriptural story, whereas a *comoedia profana* was a play about any other subject matter. Frischlin used *comoedia profana* to refer to ancient comedy as well as his own nonbiblical plays.

45. *Operum poeticorum pars scenica*, p. 1. Terence's play begins with the following exchange between Simo and Sosias: "SI. Vos istaec intro auferte: abite.—Sosia, / ades dum: paucis te volo. SO. dictum puta: / nempe ut curentur recte haec? SI. immo aliud. SO. Quid est / quod tibi mea ars efficere hoc possit amplius? / SI. nil istac opus est arte ad hanc rem quam paro, / sed eis quas semper in te intellexi sitas, / fide et taciturnitate. SO. exspecto quid velis." Terence is quoted according to Terence, *Comoediae* (Kauer and Lindsay, eds.).

46. *Zwo schöne Geistliche Comoedien/ Rebecca unnd Susanna* (1589), fol. A 3r.

47. *Pseudolus*, line 133; Plautus is quoted according to Plautus, *Comoediae* (Lindsay, ed.).

48. Frischlin, *Operum poeticorum pars scenica*, p. 15.

49. In his defense after the uproar over his *De vita rustica*, Frischlin claimed that all his statements about the nobility were taken from earlier writers. Among the voluminous materials on Frischlin in the Hauptlandesarchiv in

Stuttgart is a 131-page autograph, "Grundtlicher unnd Nottwendiger Bericht Nicodemi Frischlini Poetae L.," which lists all the sources he used for *Oratio de vita rustica*; it would be an essential pendant to a critical edition of the speech.

50. Frischlin made this plea by adducing examples from classical antiquity for cooperation between emperors and poets. See the first edition of *Rebecca* (1576), p. 4.

51. See Strauß, *Frischlin*, pp. 93–98. Frischlin was also eventually raised into the ranks of the lower nobility; see Schulz-Behrend, "Nicodemus Frischlin and the Imperial Court," pp. 172–80.

52. *Rebecca*, p. 6.

53. Previously, the date of the premiere had been problematic because Frischlin did not mention the play in his epic glorification of the wedding. In a manuscript of Salomon Schweigger entitled "Beschreibung der Raisz von Wirtenberg nach Constantinopell und Jerusalem bis in Teütschlandt," Joachim Boeckh uncovered solid evidence that the play was first performed at the wedding. The manuscript is a preliminary version of Schweigger's *Ein newe Reyßbeschreibung* (1608). Unlike the book, the manuscript version contains a clear account of Schweigger's participation in a production of *Rebecca* for the duke's wedding; he played the role of Gastrodes and felt that it was a portent of his future *Wanderlust*. See Boeckh, "Gastrodes: Ein Beitrag zu Salomon Schweiggers *Ein newe Reyßbeschreibung* und zu Nicodemus Frischlins *Rebecca*." Furthermore, Frischlin indicated in its full title that *Rebecca* was composed specifically with the wedding of Ludwig and Dorothea in mind: *Rebecca. Comoedia nova et sacra, ex XXIIII. capite Geneseos, ad Plauti et Terentii imitationem scripta: et ad nuptias illustriss. Principis ac Domini, D. Ludovici Ducis Wirtembergici ac Teccii: Comitis Montis Peligardi, etc. adornata.*

54. In *Operum poeticorum pars elegiaca*, fols. N 1r–Q 8r.

55. *De nuptiis . . . libri septem.*

56. *Rebecca*, p. 5.

57. *Operum poeticorum pars scenica*, pp. 8–9.

58. See Trometer, "Die polemischen Züge in den Isaak-und-Rebekka-Dramen des sechzehnten Jahrhunderts," for a brief discussion of these plays. The following are the authors of the versions, with the date of each play in parentheses: Hans Tirolf (1539), Leonhard Culmann (1547), Peter Praetorius (1559), Thomas Brunner (1569), and Christian Zyrl (1572). Culmann's *Von der Hochzeyt Isaacs und Rebecce* is available in Senger, ed., *Leonard Culmann*, pp. 463–519. Brunner's *Die schöne und kurtzweilige Historia / von der Heirat Isaacs und seiner lieben Rebecca* has been edited by Michael and Heinen.

59. *Operum poeticorum pars scenica*, p. 22.

60. The letter is described by Sattler, *Geschichte des Herzogthums Würtenberg*, 5:66.

61. Frischlin's letter is quoted by Sattler, ibid.:

Quot putas, O mi ocelle patriae nostrae dulcissime, Dux Ludovice, quot putas fuisse inter Tuttlingenses illos nobiles, qui florentibus Huldrici rebus similes se gesserint tui Degenfeldii, Anwilani, Herteri et similium progenitores, de quibus Lutherus graviter concionatur? Cum obsideretur Reutlingum, Wilhelmus Herter, ut publicae habent literae, proclamavit ad cives, nisi deditionem facerent, fore, ut experiantur extrema mala et primum emisit telum in hostes. Ubi autem fuit exulante optimo Principe? Tutlingae fuit et bellum illi indixit. Cum urbs foederata caperetur, nihil obstabat Nobilitati fides data foederi. Cum Princeps esset restituendus, omnes fidem datam foederi Suevico praetendebant. . . . Nunquam credidisset Ulricus Dux tantam perfidiam cadere in homines, quibus ipse benefecerat, quantum postea experta est. . . . Nunquam credidisset Elector Joh. Fridericus patrem Electorem verum locutum esse, quando illum his verbis monuit: Er soll dem Adel nicht zu viel trauen, nisi hoc eo tempore post expertus fuisset, quo apud Mulhusium a suis proditus atque in hostium manus traditus fuit.

62. *Operum poeticorum pars scenica*, p. 8: "Nam hodie, qui in aulis Principum / Versantur, et consilia rei dant publicae, / Multi non domini, sed sua commoda promovent."

63. Ibid., p. 73.

64. See Pilger, "Die Dramatisierungen der Susanna," pp. 176–85, and Casey, *The Susanna Theme*, pp. 99–115, for summaries of Frischlin's *Susanna*.

65. In the sixteenth century, a *Susanna* was attributed to Macropedius. Best, *Macropedius*, p. 15, however, doubts Macropedius's authorship for this play. I should add that in 1532 Johannes Placentius published a *Susanna* in Antwerp. Though I have not been able to consult the text, it appears from Brown's summary that it exerted no influence on Frischlin. See Brown, "The *Susanna* of Johannes Placentius."

66. Heinrich Julius wrote two versions of *Susanna*; both are reprinted in Heinrich Julius, *Die Schauspiele des Herzogs Heinrich Julius von Braunschweig*. *Susanna* was included in Schonaeus's *Terentii Christiani Pars Secunda*. Israel's version is summarized in detail by Casey, *The Susanna Theme*, pp. 133–42.

67. *Phormio* is the one remaining play not covered by Frischlin's plans for dramas or *Rebecca*. It is, however, impossible to argue for a specific relationship between *Susanna* and *Phormio*, as could be done with *Rebecca* and *Andria*.

68. See Roethe, "Frischlin als Dramatiker," p. xxxiii.

69. *Operum poeticorum pars scenica* (Pflüger, ed.), fol. (:) 4v.

70. *Operum poeticorum pars scenica*, p. 96.

71. See Rebhun, *Susanna*, p. 80: "Die widwen uns auch das bewehrn / Das/ wer die rach bevilch dem herrn / Das der auffs best gerochen werd / Mehr/ denn er selbst hett begehrt/." For a discussion of Rebhun's play, see Könneker, *Die deutsche Literatur der Reformationszeit*, pp. 165–73.

72. *Operum poeticorum pars scenica*, pp. 157–58.

73. Ibid., p. 145.

74. Ibid., p. 145.

75. Ibid., p. 140.

76. See Pilger, "Die Dramatisierungen der Susanna," pp. 135–41.

77. Jakob Frischlin translated both works in *Zwo schöne Geistlich Comoedien*. Andreas Calagius also translated both works: *Rebecca, ein sehr lustige, und gar newe Comoedia, vom seligen Ehestande* (1599); and *Susanna, eine zumal lustige und gar newe Comoedia* (1604). *Rebecca* was again translated by Christian Schön, *Eine schöne liebliche und nützliche Comoedia, von des Patriarchen Isaacs Freyschafft* (1599), and by Johannes Konrad Merck, *Rebecca* (1616). According to Goedeke, *Grundriß*, 2:140, another translation was done by four Strasbourg students in 1608; it, however, does not seem to be extant.

78. *Operum poeticorum pars elegiaca*, fol. I 4r.

79. *Oratio de imitatione*, p. 168.

Chapter 4

1. Trunz, "Der deutsche Späthumanismus um 1600 als Standeskultur," p. 153.

2. All of Frischlin's major plays were translated in the sixteenth century, though the German translation of *Priscianus Vapulans*, mentioned by Jakob Frischlin in *Zwo schöne Geistlich Comoedien*, fol. A 6v, does not seem to be extant.

3. Although there was not universal agreement in antiquity and the Renaissance, Aristotle, Quintilian, and the vast majority of theoreticians distinguished three canonical genres of rhetoric. Cicero, however, claimed that since every speech is specific and unique each one should be considered, in formal terms, sui generis. Melanchthon added the *genus didascalicon*, but otherwise concentrated his attention on the three canonical genres. See Melanchthon, *Elementorum Rhetorices libri duo*, fol. A 7r. For a general description of the ancient definitions of these genres, see Lausberg, *Handbuch der literarischen Rhetorik*. Many of Frischlin's ideas and definitions can be found in his *Rhetorica*, a purposefully eclectic work which derives elements from Quintilian, Cicero, Aristotle, Scaliger, Melanchthon, Ramus, and Erasmus.

4. *Methodus declamandi*, p. 2.

5. See ibid., p. 4.

6. Melanchthon, *Opera omnia*, 19:695: "In Andria genus orationis deliberativum est. Tota enim fere fabula in eo consistit, polliceaturne patri Pamphilus accepturum se uxorem; Davus suadet et fallitur, ipse sibi dissuadet. Itaque et dicendi exemplum habes hanc consultationem, ut alias multas narrationes et figuras praetereamus."

7. See Herrick, *Comic Theory in the Sixteenth Century*, pp. 26–30, 106–29.

8. See ibid., pp. 77–79.

9. The influence of Aristophanes on German humanism deserves a thorough study. Three useful but limited treatments can be found in Süß, *Aristophanes und die Nachwelt*; Hille, *Die deutsche Komödie unter der Einwirkung des Aristophanes*; and Friedländer, "Aristophanes in Deutschland."

10. In 1586, Frischlin published an edition and translation of Aristoph-

anes' *Plutus, Knights, Clouds, Frogs,* and *Acharnians.* He had intended to edit and translate the entire corpus of Aristophanes, but the difficulties he met after 1580 prevented him from completing the project.

11. Weinberg, in *A History of Literary Criticism in the Italian Renaissance,* 2:743–50, calls Scaliger's work the first non-Aristotelean poetics of the Renaissance. For a partial translation of Scaliger's *Poetica,* see Scaliger, *Select Translations from Scaliger's Poetics.* Padelford, however, does not include *Poetica* I, 9, the crucial chapter on drama, in his translations.

12. The *partes attinentes* included *titulus, modi, cantus, thymele sive sultatio,* and *apparatus.* The *accessoriae partes* were the *prologus, argumentum, chorus,* and *mimus.*

13. See Aristotle, *De Arte Poetica* XVII, 2. For a description of the tripartite division of drama, see Herrick, *Comic Theory in the Sixteenth Century,* pp. 106–29.

14. *Aristophanes,* p. 17r: "Ibi plerunque mirabiles incidunt controversiae et disputationes de suscepto negocio."

15. Ibid., p. 17r: "Catastrophe inopinatum consiliorum, et rerum gestarum eventum continet: sive is laetus sit, sive tristis, sive utrunque. Haec pars apud Aristophanem aut simplex est, aut multiplex. Simplicem voco Catastrophen, ubi non admiscentur novae personae, quae prius in theatrum non venerint: . . . Multiplicem vero, quando idem eventus aliquibus bono, aliquibus malo cedit, et varii utriusque generis homines introducuntur, quorum aliqui eodem exitu rerum praeteritarum laetantur, aliqui contristantur." Elschenbroich is probably wrong when he cites the unfortunate endings for characters in *Phasma* as something Frischlin would have considered problematic. See Elschenbroich, "Imitatio und Disputatio in Nikodemus Frischlins Religionskomödie *Phasma,*" pp. 345–46.

16. The attempt to divide Aristophanic comedy into five acts posed many problems, as Frischlin admitted: "at vetus plures videtur Actus habuisse. Ideoque difficile mihi fuit Aristophanicas Comoedias, Latinorum more, in actus distinguere, et actus ipsos in scenas subdistinguere. Qua in re, si quibus non satisfacio, ab illis admoneri et doceri cupio" (*Aristophanes,* p. 16v.). Nonetheless, Frischlin's act divisions were used in all subsequent editions until Brunck abandoned them in his edition of 1781–83.

17. *Aristophanes,* pp. 16r–16v.

18. See Melanchthon's edition of Terence in Melanchthon, *Opera omnia,* 19:693: "Vetus comoedia erat carmen quoddam non dissimile tragoediae, quo liberius taxabantur vitia hominum, et habuit non tantum ficta argumenta, sed interdum etiam res gestas, quae cum eorum, qui gesserant, nomine decantabantur."

19. Aristotle's brief definition of comedy, in *De Arte Poetica* IX, 5, influenced a trend to define comedy in terms of the structure of New Comedy: "This now becomes clear in the case of comedy: they [i.e., comic poets] make their own plots and then they assign names to the things that occur" (my translation). J. C. Scaliger, of course, follows Aristotle in his definition of comedy: "at Comoedia fingit omnia, atque personis, maxima ex parte, pro re

imponit nomina." But Scaliger's discussion in his *Poetica* III, 97 fully appreciates the importance of political satire in Aristophanes.

20. *Aristophanes*, fol.)(2v.

21. See Plutarch, *Moralia*, section 853 ("Comparatio Aristophanis et Menandri"). Plutarch's critique peaks in a general dismissal of Aristophanes: "For he [i.e., Aristophanes] seemed to have written poetry not for a decent man; rather, he wrote his disgraceful and licentious words for the . . . [textual problem], and the blasphemous and bitter words for the slanderous and malicious" (my translation).

22. See, for example, Erasmus's *De Ratione Studii* in his *Opera Omnia* I, 2:115, where he recommends that Aristophanes be read in the schools to foster eloquence but claims that Menander would be preferable, had his plays survived: "Quo quidem in genere primas tribuerim Luciano, alteras Demostheni, tertias Herodoto. Rursum ex poetis primas Aristophani, alteras Homero, tertias Euripidi. Nam Menandrum, cui vel primas daturus eram, desideramus."

23. *Aristophanes*, p. 9r.

24. Ibid., p. 15v.

25. Heinrich Bullinger and Hans Sachs composed Lucretia dramas in 1526 (printed 1533) and 1527 (printed 1560) respectively. Sachs (1530) and Hans Rudolf Manuel (ca. 1565) wrote plays about Virginia.

26. Hartmann, in Bullinger, *Lucretia-Dramen*, pp. 9–26, describes the political elements of *Lucretia*.

27. Frischlin cited these sources to corroborate the meeting of Hildegardis and Charlemagne in Rome as depicted in the play. See *Operum poeticorum pars scenica*, pp. 256–57.

28. The brief story of Hildegardis is in Bruschius, *Monasteria*, pp. 25v–27v. For information on Bruschius, see Horawitz, *Caspar Bruschius*; for more recent bibliography, see Wiegand, *Hodoeporica*, pp. 452–56.

29. The use of the *palliata* in *Hildegardis Magna* is well documented by Georg Pflüger in *Operum poeticorum pars scenica*, fols. L 1v–7r. See also Neumeyer, "Nicodemus Frischlin als Dramatiker," pp. 21ff.

30. *Operum poeticorum pars scenica*, p. 214.

31. Ibid., p. 203.

32. Ibid., pp. 202–3.

33. The ceremonies marking this occasion involved the entire nobility of Württemberg. See Sattler, *Geschichte des Herzogthums Würtenberg*, 5:50–53.

34. See Holstein, *Die Reformation im Spiegelbilde der dramatischen Litteratur*, pp. 19–20, and Trometer, "Isaak-und-Rebekka-Dramen," pp. 699–705.

35. Luther, *Werke* III, 1:432 (*Tischreden*, no. 867).

36. I should emphasize that there is no overt anti-Catholicism in *Hildegardis Magna*. The first edition of the play was even dedicated to Abbot Eberhard of Kempten; see *Hildegardis Magna* (1579), fols. A 2r–A 8v. Hildegard also enjoyed some popularity among Jesuit playwrights. See Szarota, *Das Jesuitendrama im deutschen Sprachgebiet*, 2:1229–43, 2356–59.

37. See *Operum poeticorum pars scenica*, pp. 166–67: "Poeta vos ad venan-

dum invitat hodie / In hoc theatro scenico. Nam bestias / Producturum se ait, ferasque plurimas: / Eas ut observetis, orat maxime. / Nam hoc studio scit vos oblectari impendio: / Cum sit solenne fortibus viris opus: / Et belli quasi praeludium, venatio. / Haec sylva est Arduenna vetustissima Belgii: / In qua lupus Talandus Hildegardim ovem / Persequitur: eam Leo, maritus Carolus / Hodie canibus vorandam dat Lorariis."

38. *Frau Wendelgard* was reprinted in Strauß, ed., *Deutsche Dichtungen von Nicodemus Frischlin*, pp. 3–63. It was also edited by Kuhn and Wiedmann in 1908, and by Rothweiler in 1912.

39. I have consulted the second edition (1586); the first edition appeared in 1548.

40. Wheelis noticed some of the critical perspectives in his article, "Nicodemus Frischlin's *Julius Redivivus* and Its Reflections on the Past." His essay summarizes the views of his dissertation, "Nicodemus Frischlin: Comedian and Humanist," a work solely devoted to discussing *Julius Redivivus* and some aspects of David Friedrich Strauß's career. The most extreme example of a one-sided approach to *Julius Redivivus* is Ridé, "Der Nationalgedanke im *Julius Redivivus* von Nicodemus Frischlin." Ridé's article is based on his *L'image du Germain*, 2: 956–970.

41. See Schade, "*Julius Redivivus*: Entstehung und Stuttgarter Aufführung," for a discussion of the play in the context of this performance. Essentially the same discussion appeared as "Nicodemus Frischlin und der Stuttgarter Hof: Zur Aufführung von *Julius Redivivus*." A further elaboration of the discussion has now appeared as "Frischlin's *Julius Redivivus* (1585): Comedy, Court and Personal Politics" in Schade, *Studies in Early German Comedy 1500–1650*, pp. 97–122.

42. *Julius Redivivus* was first printed in 1585 as part of Frischlin's *Operum poeticorum pars scenica*, though with a separate title page; see *Julius Redivivus* (Janell, ed.), p. lxxiii.

43. Ridé, *L'image du Germain*, and Borchardt, *German Antiquity and Renaissance Myth*, offer a wealth of information on this subject.

44. See Roethe, "Frischlin als Dramatiker," p. xlv; Hutten, *Opera omnia*, 4:407–18.

45. Roethe, "Frischlin als Dramatiker," p. xlvi.

46. *Julius Redivivus*, lines 940–42. References to *Julius Redivivus* are made to the edition of Janell.

47. See *Acharnians*, lines 1097–1142, in Aristophanes, *Comoediae* (Hall and Geldart, eds.).

48. *Julius Redivivus*, lines 1743–46.

49. Ibid., lines 1755–58.

50. Ibid., lines 586–93.

51. Ibid., lines 605–7: "Sed non ausim tamen hoc Germanis dicere, / Ne me suam sibi invidere gloriam / Existiment."

52. Ibid., lines 1943–49.

53. Ibid., line 897.

54. Ibid., lines 944–47.

55. Ibid., lines 1273–79.

56. Ibid., lines 368–70.

57. Ibid., lines 1582–85.

58. For information on Hessus, see Krause, *Helius Eobanus Hessus.*

59. See Strauß, *Frischlin*, pp. 130–42, and Schade, *"Julius Redivivus*: Entstehung und Stuttgarter Aufführung," p. 168.

60. *Julius Redivivus*, lines 614–16.

61. *De secundis nuptiis . . . libri quatuor.*

62. *Julius Redivivus*, lines 1454–55.

63. Ibid., line 1073.

64. Ibid., line 1074: "si modo possit verum dicere."

65. Ibid., lines 1496–97.

66. Ibid., lines 1841–48.

67. See *Rhetorica ad Herennium*, IV, 36, 48–IV, 37, 49.

68. See my discussion of παρρησία in Price, "Nicodemus Frischlin's Rhetoric," pp. 537–38.

Chapter 5

1. See Wimpheling, *Stylpho*, p. 30.

2. See Reuchlin, *Henno*, pp. 22, 26, 32. In the fourth song Reuchlin even appeals to professionals to leave their careers in order to become poets.

3. Bebel, *Comoedia*, p. 16.

4. Ibid., p. 46, Lentulus speaking: "Ego sum optimus artista."

5. Ibid., p. 50.

6. Ibid., p. 54.

7. See Haller, *Die Anfänge der Universität Tübingen*, pp. 212–35. Before Bebel, the humanists Samuel Karoch and Jakob Locher had been active at Tübingen, though unfortunately it is no longer possible to determine what they did there. See also Oberman, *Werden und Wertung der Reformation*, pp. 17–28.

8. The speech has been reprinted in Melanchthon, *Declamationes*, pp. 1–13. For a discussion of Melanchthon's dissatisfaction at Tübingen, see Oberman, *Werden und Wertung der Reformation*, pp. 22–27.

9. This information is taken in large part from Barner, *Barockrhetorik*, pp. 418–25. See also R. Roth, *Urkunden zur Geschichte der Universität Tübingen aus den Jahren 1476 bis 1550*, pp. 176–85. According to "Herzog Ulrichs Ordnung vom 30. Januar 1535," three schools were to be established at Tübingen: a grammar school, a *pedagogium*, and an *academia*. Humanist studies were to be well represented in the *pedagogium*, and Ulrich mandated that the curriculum be controlled: "Doch wellen wir hierinn der Lerer Thiranny und herttigkait, die yetzuzyten sie üben möchten nit zulassen, Sondern ußgeschaiden haben. Und sollen gemelte Magistrj in pedagogio leren Grammaticam, Terencium, Virgilij Biecher, Ciceronis Epistolas oder Plinij, Schemata Rethorices und Grammatices, Erasmi Colloquia, Copiam Verborum et Rerum und Parabolas etc. Darzu sollen dise Knaben mit sonderm vleis angehalten

werden, damit sie wol lernen ain Carmen und ain Epistolam zumachen." As part of the *academia*, there were also to be *lectiones communes* in which humanist studies were emphasized.

10. Frischlin conducted the rhetorical exercises at Tübingen from 1571 to 1579.

11. See Strauß, *Frischlin*, p. 122, and Sattler, *Geschichte des Herzogthums Würtenberg*, 5:49.

12. Strauß, *Frischlin*, p. 122, associated this development with Frischlin's growing knowledge of Aristophanes; he felt that in some ways *Priscianus Vapulans* and *Julius Redivivus* showed similarities to Aristophanic comedy. Roethe, "Frischlin als Dramatiker," pp. xxxviii–xxxix, attacked this correlation with Aristophanes rather clumsily.

13. *Julius Redivivus*, lines 343–44.

14. *Operum poeticorum pars scenica*, p. 353. This is an imitation of Plautus, *Captivi*, lines 55–58: "Non pertractate facta est neque item ut ceterae: / neque spurcidici insunt versus inmemorabiles; / hic neque peiiurus leno est nec meretrix mala / neque miles gloriosus."

15. For information about Franciscus de Mayronis, see P. Bartholomäus Roth, *Franz von Mayronis*. Chrysostomos Javelli is chiefly known for his commentary on the first part of *Summa Theologica*; he also argued the concept of predestination against Luther.

16. The debate with Priscian about the issue of *ubiquitas* is probably an allusion to the squabbles between Lutherans and Calvinists over this aspect of Christology. See Roustan, "De N. Frischlini comoediis latine scriptis," p. 31.

17. Philonius is the pseudonym of Balescon de Tarento, a doctor who was active 1380–1418. Lilius is Aloisi Giglio (1510–70), a doctor and astronomer who made some important contributions to the calendric reforms of Gregory XIII.

18. The jurists are called Nevisanus and Barberius. Giovanni Nevizzano died in 1540. Frischlin refers in the margins of the play to Nevizzano's *Sylvae nuptialis libri sex* (1516). Barberius is Jean Berbier d'Yssingeaux (died after 1480). Frischlin also cites Berbier's handbook for law students, *Viatorium iuris utriusque*.

19. The prologue to *Priscianus Vapulans* supports my contention that Frischlin wished to suggest theology with the two clerics of act IV: "Quare animam agens [i.e., Priscianus] duos accedit Theologos, / Ut ab illis capiat paululum solatii."

20. *Operum poeticorum pars scenica*, p. 450–51.

21. See *Operum poeticorum pars scenica*, p. 434, where Erasmus dismisses a papal privilege that minimized the importance of the use of correct Latin by priests: "Nihil hoc te privilegium perterreat. / Nam commune id habent cum asinis indoctissimis / Indocti antistites."

22. From a Lutheran perspective, Frischlin portrayed Erasmus quite sympathetically. After all, although he at one time had sympathies with Luther, Erasmus remained loyal to the church. Luther and Erasmus had furthermore become embroiled in a famous dispute over the doctrine of free will. See

Erasmus, *De libero arbitrio*, in *Ausgewählte Schriften*, 4:1–195

23. Erasmus, *In Novum Testamentum Praefationes*, in *Ausgewählte Schriften*, 3:68.

24. Alexander's *Doctrinale* was a tenacious authority since its composition in the twelfth century. According to Reichling, *Das Doctrinale des Alexander de Villa-Dei*, p. xlv, it was printed over 250 times between 1470 and 1588.

25. Roethe, "Frischlin als Dramatiker," p. xxxviii.

26. To a very limited extent, Frischlin may have been indebted to Andrea Guarna's *Bellum Grammaticale* (1514).

27. Roethe, "Frischlin als Dramatiker," p. xxxix, first observed this; the monk's mistake was the masculine use of the ordinarily neuter "caelus" in "caelus clarificat se."

28. Bebel, *Facetien*, p. 169.

29. For information about *facetiae*, see Vollert, *Zur Geschichte der lateinischen Facetiensammlungen des 15. und 16. Jahrhunderts*, and, more recently, Bowen, "Renaissance Collections of *Facetiae*."

30. Frischlin's efforts in this genre, first published ten years after his death, were frequently printed with those of his two precursors. See Frischlin, *Facetiae selectiores* (1600). Bebermeyer reprinted some of Frischlin's *facetiae* in *Tübinger Dichterhumanisten*.

31. See *Operum poeticorum pars scenica*, pp. 428, 447.

32. Book I of the *Epistolae Obscurorum Virorum* appeared either at the end of 1515 or at the beginning of 1516; the second volume, written largely by Ulrich von Hutten, was first published in 1517.

33. For a thorough account of the feud, see Brod, *Johannes Reuchlin und sein Kampf*.

34. *Operum poeticorum pars scenica*, p. 355.

35. See *Epistolae Obscurorum Virorum* I, 8 and *Priscianus Vapulans*, act V. I might add that the apotheosis of humanism in act V is reminiscent of another favorite pastime of the humanists: the listing of books "qui legendi sint." Many humanists made reading lists, Bebel, Erasmus, and Melanchthon among them. Frischlin incorporates the bibliographic tribute to humanism rather primitively. Priscian must be given humanist antidotes for all the nonhumanist literature he has ingested. Erasmus suggests purging Priscian with antidotes, "alterius agemus." The antidotes, listed in *Operum poeticorum pars scenica*, pp. 438–42, comprise works by humanists, classical authors, and church fathers. The purgation also gives Frischlin the opportunity to list books that should not be read. In addition to the purgative, there is another list of scholarly monuments, for Priscian must also begin his convalescence.

36. *Operum poeticorum pars scenica*, p. 422.

37. For Rudolf's important role in the Catholic revival, see Evans, *Rudolf II and His World*, pp. 84–115.

38. See Strauß, *Frischlin*, pp. 64–65.

39. See Seuffert, "Frischlins Beziehung zu Graz und Laibach." The following undated correspondence, taken from Seuffert, p. 260, is almost certainly from 1577; it illustrates Frischlin's concern about the Jesuits:

Nachdem Ich bin von E. G. und St. Stiefft praedicanten M. Johanne
Plenniger schrieftlich erinnert worden, wie das die Jesuwitische sect zu-
verkleinerung unserer Religion ein famos schrieftt unnd Echo publicirt,
wellichen dann er neben seinem schreiben mier ubersendet, hab Ich nit
können underlassen, nach dem Ich vermerckht, das gemelte Jebusiten,
als die In euerer Haubtstadt ihr geschmeiß wieder die erkhandte warheit
auszubietten sich understehn, fürnemlich E. G. und St. aufgerichtenn
newen Christlichen schuelen zu wieder drueß sollich ihr grob fliekh und
stickwerckh spargiren. Ihren (ungerumbt) mit einem artlichern Echo zu
antwortten, unnd Sie mit Reichs muntz gegen ihren kupfernen Vierern
zu zalen. Welchen ich dann hiemit E. G. und St. zu einem gegenstreich
deticirt, unnd verehrt haben wiel, mit biett solchen also uff und anzu-
nehmen, damitt E. G. und St. nicht gedenckhen woll, das ich zu der
gleichen Stückhwerkhen geartet und geneigt, Sonndern das viel mehr
darumb geschehen sein, das die, in Ihrem sün, allein wizigen leut, nicht
denckhen möchten, das wo es mit dergleichen Calumniis aus gerichtet
wer, wier hierin gar erlegen wehren.

I would add to Seuffert's discussion that the "Echo" Frischlin mentions is
an anti-Jesuit poem which was printed in *Operum poeticorum pars elegiaca*,
fols. Kkk 3r–5r.

40. *Operum poeticorum pars scenica*, p. 433.

41. See Strauß, *Frischlin*, pp. 69–74. Initially, it appeared that one of Frischlin's enemies, Professor Georg Liebler, was going to be able to place his son-
in-law in this position. Although that attempt was stopped because Liebler
could get his son-in-law an even better position at Tübingen, the faculty senate passed over Frischlin in favor of Georg Burckard.

42. The grammarian was known not only for his *ad fontes* methodology for
grammar, but also for his highly imitative panegyric to the Emperor Anasta-
sius. See Helm, "Priscianus."

43. Compare especially the woodcut for act V (p. 432) with the portrait of
Frischlin at the beginning of the *Operum poeticorum pars elegiaca*, fol.):(1v.
Strauß, *Frischlin*, p. 187, retells a story that Frischlin once put his beard in his
mouth in order not to be recognized by his enemies.

44. *Operum poeticorum pars scenica*, pp. 449–50.

45. For some of the details in this paragraph, I am indebted to the percep-
tive remarks of Roustan, "De N. Frischlini comoediis latine scriptis,"
pp. 24ff. Roustan believed that there might also be an intended allusion to
Jakob Schegk in the persiflage of the philosophers enamored of Aquinas and
Scotus, for Schegk respected their thought very much.

46. *Operum poeticorum pars scenica*, p. 436.

47. Crusius, *Grammaticae graecae cum latina congruentis pars prima [et altera
pars]* (1562–63).

48. *Priscianus Vapulans* (1580), fol. E 7r.

49. In view of his lifelong study of Virgil, it is extremely likely that Frischlin knew Servius's commentary. The quote is taken from Servius, *In Vergilii
Carmina Commentarii*, 3, part 1: 18.

50. Bebel, *Comoedia*, p. 32.

51. *Operum poeticorum pars scenica*, p. 445.

52. See Strauß, *Frischlin*, pp. 12–13. Frischlin's father, Jakob, studied at the university, most notably with the famous botanist Leonard Fuchs. Jakob was one of the first students of the Tübingen *Stift* after Duke Ulrich established it.

53. See *Eccius Dedolatus* (Best, trans.), pp. 20–21. The Latin text is available in *Eckius Dedolatus* (Szamatólski, ed.).

Chapter 6

1. See Böckmann's chapter "Das lutherische Glaubensprinzip als Voraussetzung," in Böckmann, *Formgeschichte*, pp. 289–300.

2. Valentin, "Die Moralität im 16. Jahrhundert: Konfessionelle Wandlungen einer dramatischen Struktur."

3. Although a new edition of his works is needed, all of them are available in Manuel, *Niklaus Manuel. Der Ablaßkrämer* is also available in a diplomatic edition by Zinsli.

4. See, for example, "Martin Luther oder die Fürstenreformation," in Meusel, *Thomas Müntzer und seine Zeit*, pp. 41–118.

5. See, for example, Bloch, *Thomas Münzer als Theologe der Revolution*.

6. Because of its numerous revisions, the *Loci Communes* is a difficult book to work with. In Melanchthon, *Opera omnia*, vol. 21, editions are organized into three groups: that of 1521, those of 1535–42, and those of 1543–59; these are called *prima*, *secunda*, and *tertia aetas*, respectively. As far as I can determine, the chapter "De magistratibus civilibus et dignitate rerum politicarum" first appeared in the edition of 1535.

7. Melanchthon, *Opera Omnia*, 21:542.

8. Ibid., 22:613.

9. Rebhun, *Dramen*, pp. 103–4.

10. Ibid., pp. 123–24. Such a combination of religious and political indoctrination can also be seen in the epilogue of *Susanna*, where Rebhun reviewed the roster of characters to define what constitutes, to his mind, proper conduct for those from various classes.

11. See Hermelink, *Geschichte der evangelischen Kirche in Württemberg*, esp. pp. 104–26.

12. See ibid., p. 107, where Ludwig is quoted: "ich habe eines und anderer Theologen Schriften gelesen, wie meine Räte und Diener wissen; wie auch meiner Theologen Streitschriften, ehe und dann sie von mir gelesen, nicht publiziert werden."

13. See ibid., pp. 119–26. I should also mention that Martin Chemnitz actively participated in the drafting of the *Formula Concordiae*.

14. *Spongia Laonici Antisturmii, a Sturmeneck, Equitis Germani, adversus Lamberti Danaei, Calvinistae Gallicani Antiosiandrum. Pro Luca Osiandro* (1580).

15. *Breve responsum . . . adversus iniuriosas contumelias, quas Lambertus Danaeus . . . scripsit* (1581).

16. See Strauß, *Frischlin,* p. 165.

17. Elschenbroich, "Imitatio und Disputatio in Nikodemus Frischlins Religionskomödie *Phasma,*" p. 362, argues that Frischlin's secret purpose in *Phasma* was to compose a "dogmatische Travestie." His assertion is based on the view that Zwingli is portrayed positively (with which I disagree) and on the fact that Frischlin's brief evocation in act III of Plautus's *Amphitruo* creates a "mythologische Travestie" of the arguments concerning the Eucharist. While the latter suggestion is interesting, I find the entire argument unconvincing, especially when one considers the heavy-handed support of Lutheranism throughout the play.

18. According to *Verzeichnis der im deutschen Sprachbereich erschienenen Drucke des XVI. Jahrhunderts,* 7:269–70, there are four slightly different printings of *Phasma* from 1592. I quote from the Tübingen copy of *Phasma: hoc est; comoedia posthuma, nova et sacra: de variis haeresibus et haeresiarchis; qui cum luce renascentis per Dei gratiam Evangelii hisce novissimis temporibus extiterunt* (Impressum in Jazygibus Metanastis, Anno Christi-Nati 1592. Antichristi vero revelati 75). The *Verzeichnis* claims that Jazyges Metanastae is a fictitious designation and that the work was actually printed by Jobin in Strasbourg.

19. *Operum poeticorum pars elegiaca,* fol. D 2v. Roustan, "De N. Frischlini comoediis latine scriptis," pp. 33–35, also discusses this topic.

20. *Deutsche Dichtungen von Nicodemus Frischlin,* (Strauß, ed.), p. 62.

21. See Frischlin, *Operum poeticorum pars elegiaca,* fol. Ddd 7v; at the end of the poem, Frischlin opined: "Atque tua multum templa iuventur ope."

22. See Elschenbroich, "Imitatio und Disputatio in Nikodemus Frischlins Religionskomödie *Phasma,*" p. 351.

23. *Phasma,* fols. A 3v–A 4r.

24. Ibid., fol. C 4v.

25. Ibid.

26. Ibid., fol. C 1v: "CI. sententiam / Nostram de Sacramento Coenae esse veram, et mordicus / Retinendam: neque ab ea latum unguem recedendum. CA. scilicet. / Neque enim me Lutheri movet autoritas. CI. Neque me Brentii / Crassa subtilitas."

27. Ibid., fol. D 2r.

28. Capernaites is a reference, primarily, to John 6:26–58. "Capernaite" was a pejorative term in sixteenth-century theological polemics. It designates someone who believes in transubstantiation.

29. "Jupiter Elicius" means "Jupiter drawn from heaven." It is an allusion to Ovid, *Fasti* III, 327–28.

30. *Phasma,* fol. D 2r.

31. Ibid., fol. F 4v.

32. I should also mention that Frischlin's wife was the grandniece of Johannes Brenz.

33. *Phasma,* fol. A 4v.

34. Ibid., fol. B 3v.

35. Ibid., fol. B 7v.

36. See Elschenbroich, "Imitatio und Disputatio in Nikodemus Frischlins Religionskomödie *Phasma*," p. 363. Schwenckfeld was also an important opponent of Andreae; see, for example, Kolb, "Jakob Andreae," pp. 53–68.

37. Frischlin lectured on Sleidanus at Tübingen; he also provided some references to Sleidanus in marginal notes to *Phasma*.

38. See, for example, Manuel's *Von Papsts und Christi Gegensatz*, in *Niklaus Manuel*, pp. 103–11, and Naogeorgus's *Pammachius*, in Naogeorgus, *Sämtliche Werke*, vol. 1.

39. See Roloff, "Heilsgeschichte, Weltgeschichte und aktuelle Polemik: Thomas Naogeorgs *Tragoedia Nova Pammachius*." In 1536, Paul III proclaimed that a council would take place the next year in Mantua, but it was never convened.

40. *Phasma*, fol. G 5v.

41. Ibid., fol. G 4r.

42. Ibid., fol. H 2v.

43. See P. Expeditius Schmidt, *Die Bühnenverhältnisse*, pp. 111–14, for German act summaries for other Latin texts; German act summaries were apparently used in Magdeburg Terence performances in 1592.

44. *Phasma*, fol. A 3v.

45. Ibid., fol. F 7r.

46. Ibid., fol. G 8v.

47. Ibid., fol. G 7v.

48. There are also indications in the text that the play would have been printed without the German segments. The scene with Mary, for example, does not affect the numeration of scenes. And the Latin text comes to a conventional conclusion with Paul's words: "denique huic Comoediae plausum dare Comicum" (ibid., fol. G 6v.).

49. *Phasma* was translated by Arnold Glaser in 1593 and by Johannes Bertesius in 1606. The play also appeared anonymously as *Eine anmuthige Comoedie, von der wahren/ alten Catholischen/ und Apostolischen Kirchen* (1671) and was also partially translated in 1839 by Immanuel Hoch as *Die Religionsschwärmer oder Mucker*.

50. *Comedia piacevole: della vera, antica, Romana, catolica & apostolica chiesa* (1611).

Chapter 7

1. Frischlin was consequently a staunch advocate of poetic freedom, and he even claimed *licentia academica* in some of his apologetic writings. See, for example, a passage from Frischlin's lecture on Sallust that Strauß quotes on page 203: "Daher hat ein Academia ihre Freiheit, die Professores haben Macht, den Hippocentauris ihre Bubenstuck und Schelmstuck zu sagen, und sind nicht schuldig, einem jeden Scharrhansen darum Red und Antwort zu

geben. Das seyn Freiheiten Academiae; wo das nicht ist, so hat man keine Freiheiten."

2. As a final word on Frischlin, I note with pleasure that, although as yet no volumes have appeared, Adalbert Elschenbroich has undertaken the enormous task of producing a critical edition of Frischlin's works. A description of the project can be found in Elschenbroich, "Eine textkritische Nikodemus Frischlin-Ausgabe."

Bibliography

Works by Frischlin

With the exception of the dramas, for which I have tried to compile a complete list of sixteenth- and seventeenth-century imprints, I have listed only those works by Frischlin that have been cited in the text or notes. In general, I have tried to abbreviate titles as much as possible; however, owing to my desire to indicate the contents of each book as fully as possible, some of the abbreviated titles remain rather lengthy. Locations of the Frischlin-imprints I have used are given in brackets. Perhaps the best bibliography of Frischlin-imprints, though one limited to works printed in the sixteenth century, is in *Verzeichnis der im deutschen Sprachbereich erschienenen Drucke des XVI. Jahrhunderts*, 7:261–74. Although there are a few manuscripts scattered in libraries throughout Europe, the most important archival materials on Frischlin are housed in the Hauptstaatsarchiv Stuttgart.

Collected Dramas

Operum poeticorum Nicodemi Frischlini Poetae . . . pars scenica: in qua sunt, comoediae quinque, Rebecca, Susanna, Hildegardis, Iulius redivivus, Priscianus vapulans, Tragoediae duae, Venus, Dido. [Argentorati:] Apud Bernhardum Iobinum, 1585. [Stuttgart, Wolfenbüttel; this edition has separate title pages for each play.]

Operum poeticorum . . . pars scenica: in qua sunt, comoediae quinque, Rebecca, Susanna, Hildegardis, Iulius Redivivus, Priscianus Vapulans. Tragoediae Duae, Venus, Dido. [Argentorati:] Excudebat Bernhardus Iobin, 1587. [Yale, Stuttgart, Tübingen, Wolfenbüttel]

Operum poeticorum . . . pars scenica: in qua sunt, comoediae sex, Rebecca, Susanna, Hildegardis Magna, Iulius Redivivus, Priscianus Vapulans, Helvetiogermani. Tragoediae duae, Venus, Dido. [Argentorati:] Excudebat Bernhardus Iobin, 1589. [Yale, Tübingen, Wolfenbüttel]

Operum poeticorum . . . pars scenica: in qua sunt, comoediae sex, Rebecca, Susanna, Hildegardis Magna, Iulius Redivivus, Priscianus Vapulans, Helvetiogermani. Tragoediae duae, Venus, Dido. [Argentorati:] Excudebat Bernhardus Iobin, 1592. [Stuttgart, Wolfenbüttel]

Operum poeticorum . . . pars scenica: in qua sunt comoediae septem: Rebecca, Susanna, Hildegardis, Iulius Redivivus, Priscianus Vapulans, Helvetiogermani, Phasma. Tragoediae duae: Venus, Dido. Argentorati: Excudebant Haeredes Bernhardi Iobini, 1595. [Tübingen]

Operum poeticorum . . . pars scenica, in qua sunt comoediae septem: Rebecca, Susanna, Hildegardis, Iulius redivivus, Priscianus vapulans, Helvetiogermani, Phasma. Tragoediae duae: Venus, Dido. Witebergae: Impensis Clementis Ber-

133

geri, Bibliop. Witeb. [Typis Simonis Gronenbergii], 1596. [Stuttgart, Tübingen, Wolfenbüttel]

Operum poeticorum . . . pars scenica: in qua sunt: comoediae sex, Rebecca, Susanna, Hildegardis Magna, Iulius Redivivus, Priscianus Vapulans, Helvetiogermani. Tragoediae duae, Venus, Dido. Argentorati: Excudebant haeredes Bernh. Iobini, 1596. [Wolfenbüttel]

Operum poeticorum . . . pars scenica: in qua sunt; comoediae sex: Rebecca, Susanna, Hildegar. Iulius Redivi. Priscian. Vapul. Helvetiogerm. Tragoediae duae: Venus, Dido. His novissime accesserunt eiusdem autoris elegia in ebrietatem: epistolae duae, carmine elegiaco scriptae: et omnium pene scriptorum elenchus. Argentorati: Excudebant haeredes Bernh. Iobini, 1598. [Stuttgart, Wolfenbüttel]

Operum poeticorum . . . pars scenica, in qua sunt comoediae septem: Rebecca, Susanna, Hildegardis Magna, Iulius Redivivus,Priscianus Vapulans, Helvetiogermani, Phasma. Tragoediae duae, Venus, Dido. Witebergae: C. Berger, 1601. [Wolfenbüttel]

Operum poeticorum . . . pars scenica: in qua sunt; comoediae sex, Rebecca, Susanna, Hildegardis Magna, Iulius Redivivus, Priscianus Vapulans, Helvetiogermani. Tragoediae duae, Venus, Dido. His novissime accesserunt eiusdem autoris elegia in ebrietatem: epistolae duae, carmine elegiaco scriptae: et omnium pene scriptorum elenchus. Argentorati: Apud Tobiam Iobinum, 1604. [Yale, Stuttgart, Wolfenbüttel]

Operum poeticorum . . . pars scenica, in qua sunt comoediae septem: Rebecca, Susanna, Hildegardis Magna, Iulius Redivivus, Priscianus Vapulans, Helvetiogermani, Phasma. Tragoediae duae, Venus, Dido. Witebergae: C. Berger, 1607. [Wolfenbüttel]

Operum poeticorum . . . pars scenica: in qua sunt, comoediae sex, Rebecca, Susanna, Hildegardis Magna, Iulius Redivivus, Priscianus Vapulans, Helvetiogermani. Tragoediae duae, Venus, Dido. Edited by Georg Pflüger. Argentorati: Apud Johannem Carolum, 1608. [Wolfenbüttel]

Operum poeticorum . . . pars scenica: in qua sunt comoediae sex, Rebecca, Susanna, Hildegardis Magna, Iulius Redivivus, Priscianus Vapulans, Helvetiogermani. Tragoediae duae, Venus, Dido. Edited by Georg Pflüger. Argentorati: Apud Johannem Carolum, 1612. [Yale, Stuttgart, Wolfenbüttel]

Operum poeticorum . . . pars scenica, in qua sunt comoediae septem: Rebecca, Susanna, Hildegardis, Iulius Redivivus, Priscianus Vapulans, Helvetio-Germani, Phasma. Tragoediae duae: Venus, Dido. Witebergae: Typis Iohannis Gormanni, impensis Clementis Bergeri, Bibliop., 1621. [Stuttgart]

Operum poeticorum . . . pars scenica, in qua sunt; comoediae sex Rebecca. Susanna. Hildegar. Iulius Redivivus. Priscian. Vapul. Helvetio Germ. Tragoediae Duae, Venus, Dido. Edited by Georg Pflüger. Argentorati: Apud Johannem Carolum, 1621. [Stuttgart]

Operum poeticorum pars scenica: in qua sunt, comoediae sex: Rebecca. Susanna. Hildegar. Iulius Redivi. Priscian. Vapul. Helvetiogerm. Tragoediae duae: Venus. Dido. . . . Elegia in ebrietatem: epistolae duae carmine elegiaco scriptae et omnium pene scriptorum elenchus. Argentorati: Prostat in officina haered. Laz. Zetzneri, 1626. [Stuttgart]

Operum poeticorum . . . pars scenica, in qua sunt comoediae septem: Rebecca, Su-

sanna, Hildegardis, Iulius Redivivus, Priscianus Vapulans, Helvetio Germani, Phasma. Tragoediae duae: Venus, Dido. Witebergae: Apud Haered. Clementis Bergeri, Typis Johannis Röhneri, 1636. [Yale, Stuttgart]

Deutsche Dichtungen von Nicodemus Frischlin, theils zum erstenmal aus den Handschriften, theils nach alten Drucken. Edited by David Friedrich Strauß. Bibliothek des litterarischen Vereins in Stuttgart, 41. Stuttgart: Litterarischer Verein, 1857.

Individual Plays

DIDO

Dido. Tragoedia nova, ex quarto libro Virgilianae Aeneidos: in quo ardentissimus amor Didonis in Aeneam, et tragicus eiusdem exitus, describitur. Accessit ludorum circensium, qui proximo Maio celebrati sunt Stuccardiae, descriptio. Tubingae: Apud Alexandrum Hockium, 1581. [Stuttgart]

FRAU WENDELGARD

Fraw Wendelgardt/ Ein New Comedi oder Spil/ auß glaubwürdigen Historien gezogen/ von Fraw Wendelgardt/ Kayser Hainrichs/ des Ersten/ auß Sachsen/ Tochter/ und ihrem Ehegemahel/ Graff Ulrich von Buchhorn/ Herrn im Litzgew/ am Bodensee: was sich Anno 915. und Ann. 919. mit inen zugetragen. Nützlich und kurtzweilig zulesen. Gehalten zu Stutgardt/ den 1. Tag Martii/ Anno M. D. LXXIX. Tübingen: Bey Alexander Hock, 1580. [Wolfenbüttel]

Fraw Wendelgard/ Ein New Comedi oder Spil. Franckfort am Mayn: Wendel Hummen, 1589. [Tübingen]

Comoedia Teutsch Fraw Wendelgarth. . . . Jetzund aber widerumb auß Reimen in prosam vertirt, und zu Marpurg vor Bartholomaei anno 1642 gehalten worden. Marpurg: Bey Caspar Chemlin, 1642. [Stuttgart]

Fraw Wendelgard. Edited by Alfred Kuhn and Eugen Wiedmann. Stuttgart: Grüninger, 1908.

Frau Wendelgard: Eine deutsche Komödie von Nikodemus Frischlin, 1580. Edited by Paul Rothweiler. Ellwangen: Ipf- und Jagst-Zeitung, 1912.

HELVETIOGERMANI

Helvetio-Germani, comoedia nova, neque illepida et lectu, actuque iucunda, atque utilis. Helmstadii: Excudebat Iacobus Lucius, 1589. [Stuttgart, Tübingen, Wolfenbüttel]

HILDEGARDIS MAGNA

Hildegardis Magna, comoedia nova: de admiranda fortuna Hildegardis, quae Hiltebrandi Suevorum et Alemannorum Ducis filia et Caroli Magni Regis Francorum uxor fuit: scripta in laudem totius Alemanniae. Inseruntur multa passim, quae ad illorum temporum historiam pertinent. Tubingae: Apud Georgium Gruppenbachium, 1579. [Stuttgart, Tübingen, Wolfenbüttel]

Hildegardis Magna. Tubingae: Apud Alexandrum Hockium, 1583. [Stuttgart]

Hildegardis Magna. Altdorphii: Excudebat Balthasar Scherffius Universitatis Typographus, 1625. [Tübingen]

JULIUS REDIVIVUS

Julius Redivivus. Mit Einleitungen von Walther Hauff, Gustav Roethe, Walther Janell. Edited by Walther Janell. Lateinische Litteraturdenkmäler des 15. und 16. Jahrhunderts, 19. Berlin: Weidmannsche Buchhandlung, 1912.

PHASMA

Verzeichnis der im deutschen Sprachbereich erschienenen Drucke des XVI. Jahrhunderts, p. 270, lists three slightly different printings from the same year with the following title: *Phasma: hoc est; comoedia posthuma, nova et sacra: de variis haeresibus et haeresiarchis; qui cum luce renascentis per Dei gratiam Evangelii hisce novissimis temporibus extiterunt.* Impressum in Iazygibus-Metanastis, 1592. [Yale, Stuttgart, Tübingen, Wolfenbüttel]
Phasma. Excusum anno Christi nati 1592. [Stuttgart, Wolfenbüttel; this is yet a fourth printing from 1592.]
Phasma. Impressum in Iazygibus-Metanastis, 1598. [Stuttgart, Wolfenbüttel; Wolfenbüttel also has a second printing of the same year.]
Phasma. Impressum in Jacygibus-Metanastis, 1612. [Yale, Stuttgart]
Phasma. Impressum in Jazygibus-Metanastis, 1619. [Stuttgart, Tübingen]

PRISCIANUS VAPULANS

Priscianus Vapulans, . . . comoedia lepida, faceta, et utilis, in qua demonstrantur soloecismi et barbarismi, qui superioribus seculis omnia artium et doctrinarum studia, quasi quodam diluvio inundarunt: scripta in laudem huius seculi. Argentorati: Apud Bernhardum Iobinum, 1580. [Yale; this is the 1580 printing without the woodcuts by Tobias Stimmer.]
Priscianus Vapulans. Argentorati: Apud Berhardum Iobinum, 1580. [Harvard, Wolfenbüttel; this includes woodcuts by Stimmer.]
Priscianus Vapulans. Erphordiae: Apud Esaiam Mechlerum, 1581. [Wolfenbüttel]

REBECCA

Rebecca, comoedia nova et sacra, ex XXIIII capite Geneseos, ad Plauti et Terentii imitationem scripta: et ad nuptias illustriss. Principis ac Domini, D. Ludovici Ducis Wirtembergici ac Teccii: comitis Montis Peligardi, etc. adornata. Francofurti: Ex typographia Andreae Wecheli, 1576. [Stuttgart, Wolfenbüttel]

SUSANNA

Susanna, comoedia nova, sacra et lectu iucunda atque utilis: in qua foeminei pudoris exemplum proponitur. Tubingae: Apud Alexandrum Hockium, 1578. [Stuttgart]
Susanna. [Tubingae:] Apud Alexandrum Hockium, 1583. [Wolfenbüttel]

Translations of Frischlin's Plays

HILDEGARDIS MAGNA

Ein schöne Comedien von Fraw Hildegardin Hertzog Hildebrandts in Schwaben Tochter, Keysers Caroli Magni Gemahlin. Strasbourg: Antoine Betram, 1599. [Strasbourg; I have not seen this imprint.]

JULIUS REDIVIVUS

Iulius Caesar et M. T. C. Redivivi. Translated by Jakob Frischlin. Speyr: Bei Bernard Dalbin, 1585. [Yale, Stuttgart, Tübingen]
Iulius Caesar cum M. T. C. Redivivus. Translated by Jakob Frischlin. Speyr: Bernard Dalbin, 1592. [Wolfenbüttel]
Commedia Julius Redivivus. Translated by Jakob Ayrer. Nürnberg: Balthasar Scherff, 1618. Reprint in *Ayrers Dramen.* Edited by Adalbert von Keller. Stuttgart: Litterarischer Verein, 1865.
Julius Redivivus. Translated by Jakob Frischlin. Edited by Richard E. Schade. Stuttgart: Reclam, 1983. [Reprint of 1585 edition]

PHASMA

Phasma. Translated by Arnold Glaser. Gryphißwalt: Augustin Ferber, 1593. [Stuttgart, Wolfenbüttel]
Phasma. Translated by Johannes Bertesius. Leipzig: Nic. Nerlich, 1606. [British Museum; I have not seen this printing.]
Eine anmuthige Comoedie, von der wahren/ alten Catholischen/ und Apostolischen Kirchen/ in welcher von denen eingeführten Personen alle Controversien und Streitigkeiten erörtert werden. Romanopoli [Augsburg?], 1671. [Wolfenbüttel; this is an anonymous translation of *Phasma.*]
Die Religionsschwärmer oder Mucker; als da sind: Wiedertäufer, Nachtmahlsschwärmer und Schwenkfelder. Ein Fastnachtspiel. Translated by Immanuel Hoch. Stuttgart: G. L. Friz, 1839. [This is a partial translation of *Phasma.*]
Comedia piacevole: della vera, antica, Romana, catolica & apostolica chiesa. Romanopoli [Augsburg?], 1611. [Wolfenbüttel; this is an Italian translation of *Phasma.*]

REBECCA

Zwo schöne Geistliche Comoedien/ Rebecca unnd Susanna. Translated by Jakob Frischlin. Franckfort am Mayn: Bey Johann Spiessen, in Verlegung Wendel Hommen, 1589. [Stuttgart]
Rebecca, ein sehr lustige, und gar newe Comoedia vom seligen Ehestande. Translated by Andreas Calagius. Liegnitz: Nicolaus Schneider, 1599. [Wroclaw; I have not seen this printing.]
Eine schöne liebliche und nützliche Comoedia, von des Patriarchen Isaacs Freyschafft. Translated by Christian Schön. Wittenberg: Bey Zacharias Lehman, 1599. [Wolfenbüttel]
Rebecca. Translated by Johannes Konrad Merck. Ulm, 1616. [Ulm]

SUSANNA

Zwo schöne Geistliche Comoedien/ Rebecca unnd Susanna. Translated by Jakob Frischlin. [See listing above under *Rebecca.*]

Susanna, eine zumal lustige und gar newe Comoedia. Translated by Andreas Calagius. Görlitz: Johann Rhambaw, 1604. [Wolfenbüttel]

Other Works by Frischlin

Aristophanes, veteris comoediae princeps, poeta longe facetissimus et eloquentissimus, repurgatus a mendis, et imitatione Plauti atque Terentii interpretus, ita ut fere carmen carmini, numerus numero, pes pedi, modus modo, latinismus graecismo respondeat. Francoforti ad Moenum: Excudebat Iohannes Spies, 1586. [Yale, Stuttgart]

Breve responsum . . . adversus iniuriosas contumelias quas Lambertus Danaeus ex aliorum relatu acceptas, circa initium et finem suae fulginosae Encausticae scripsit. Tubingae: Excudebat Georgius Gruppenbachius, 1581. [Stuttgart, Tübingen]

Callimachi Cyrenaei Hymni (cum suis scholiis graecis) et Epigrammata. Edited and translated by Nicodemus Frischlin. [Genevae:] Excudebat Henricus Stephanus, 1577. [Yale, Stuttgart]

Carmen panegyricum de quinque Saxoniae ducibus. Witebergae: Typis Clementis Schleichii, 1588. [Wolfenbüttel]

De astronomicae artis cum doctrina coelesti et naturali philosophia congruentia, ex optimis quibusque Graecis Latinisque scriptoribus, theologis, medicis, mathematicis, philosophis et poetis collecta, libri quinque. Francoforti ad Moenum: Excudebat Ioannes Spies, 1586. [Yale, Stuttgart, Tübingen]

De nuptiis illustrissimi Principis, ac Domini, D. Ludovici, Ducis Wirtembergici et Teccii, Comitis Mompelgardii, etc. cum illustrissima Principe ac Domina, D. Dorothea Ursula, Marchionissa Badensi, etc. Stuccardiae, anno 1575. Mense Novembri celebratis. Libri septem, versu heroico conscripti a Nicodemo Frischlino. Tubingae: Georgius Gruppenbachius, 1577. [Yale, Stuttgart, Tübingen, Wolfenbüttel]

De secundis nuptiis illustrissimi Principis ac Domini, D. Ludovici, Ducis Wirtembergici ac Teccensis etc. cum illustrissima Duce ac Domina, D. Ursula, Duce Bavariae, Comite Palatina Rheni, etc. praeterito Maio, huius 1585. Anni celebratis Stuccardiae, libri quatuor: versu conscripti heroico. Tubingae: Apud Georgium Gruppenbachium, 1585. [Stuttgart, Tübingen, Wolfenbüttel],

Entschuldigung/ und endtliche bestendige Erklärung Doctoris Nicodemi Frischlini, gestelt an den löblichen Adel/ teutscher Nation. In wölcher lautter dargethon würdt/ daß er in seiner Oratione de vita rustica (wie auch in andern seinen Schrifften) den löblichen Adel anzutasten/ zuverkleinern/ oder zuschmähen niemalen bedacht gewesen. Tübingen: Bey Georgen Gruppenbach, 1585. [Tübingen]

Facetiae selectiores: quibus ob argumenti similitudinem accesserunt, Heinrici Bebelii, P. L. facetiarum libri tres. Sales item, seu, facetiae ex Poggii Florentini oratoris libro selectae. Nec non Alphonsi Regis Arragonum, et Adelphi facetiae. Argentorati: Typis haeredum Bernhardi Iobini, 1600. [Yale, Stuttgart]

Grammatice Latina, compendiose scripta, ac in octo libros distributa. Francoforti ad Moenum: Excudebat Ioannes Spies, 1586. [Stuttgart, Wolfenbüttel]

"Grundtlicher unnd Nottwendiger Bericht Nicodemi Frischlini Poetae L." 18 December 1580. MS. A 274, Büschel 42, #18. Hauptstaatsarchiv, Stuttgart.

Hebraeis. Continens duodecim libros: quibus tota regum Iudaicorum, et Israeliticorum historia, ex sacris literis ad verbum desumpta, carmine heroico Virgiliano describitur. Edited by Martin Aichmann and Ulrich Bollinger. Argentorati: Ex officina typographica Iobiniana, 1599. [Yale, Stuttgart, Tübingen, Wolfenbüttel]

Methodus declamandi (posthuma) in laudatione, thesi de laudibus mulierum demonstrata: Cui praeterea annexae sunt eiusdem epistolae et praefationes. Argentinae: Typis Iohannis Caroli, 1606. [Stuttgart, Tübingen]

Nomenclator trilinguis, Graeco-Latinogermanicus, continens omnium rerum, quae in probatis omnium doctrinarum auctoribus inveniuntur, appellationes continens, quarum aliquot millia nusquam sunt obvia. Francoforti ad Moenum: Excudebat Ioannes Spies, 1586. [Munich]

Operum . . . pars paraphrastica: qua continentur, P. Virgilii Maronis: Bucolica, ex Plauto et Terentio: Georgica, ex Catone, Varrone, Columella, et Plinio: Aeneidos libri duo priores, ex Livio, Caesare et Cicerone. Q. item Horatii Flacci Venusini, Epistolarum libri duo: tum A. Persii Flacci Volaterrani, Satyrae sex: . . . paraphrasi . . . exposita et enucleata. Francofurti ad Moenum: Typis et sumptibus Iohannis Spiessii et haeredum Romani Beati, 1602. [Stuttgart, Tübingen, Wolfenbüttel]

Operum poeticorum . . . paralipomena: ex recensione Valentini Clessii P. L. Continentur hoc opere, poemata, maiori ex parte typis ante non excusa, videlicet, V. libri carminum heroicorum et octo satyrae adversus Iac. Rabum Apostatam. Darmbstadii: Excudebat Balthasar Hofmann, impensis Ioannis Iacobi Porsii, 1610. [Stuttgart]

Operum poeticorum . . . pars elegiaca: continens viginti duos elegiacorum carminum libros, ad imitationem Ovidii, et optimorum hoc in genere authorum scriptos, qui nunc demum post obitum auctoris congesti et pro materiae diversitate digesti . . . eduntur. Quibus adhaerescunt eiusdem auctoris odarum libri tres: anagram. unus. Cum praefatione M. Georgii Pfluegeri, in qua etiam inter caetera, paucis vita auctoris contra malevolorum quorundam morsus defenditur. Argentorati: Excudebant haeredes Bernh. Iobini, 1601. [Yale, Stuttgart, Tübingen, Wolfenbüttel]

Orationes insigniores aliquot. Edited by Georg Pflüger. Argentorati: Excudebat Iohann Carolus, 1605. [Harvard, Stuttgart, Tübingen, Wolfenbüttel]

Panegyrici tres de laudibus D D. Maxaemyliani II. et Rodolphi II. Tubingae: Apud Alexandrum Hockium, 1577. [Stuttgart, Wolfenbüttel]

Rhetorica: seu institutionum oratoriarum libri duo: nunc primum, in gratiam studiosae iuventutis, typis excusi: opera et impensis Hieronymi Megiseri. Lipsiae: Imprimebat Michael Lantzenberger, 1604. [Stuttgart, Wolfenbüttel]

Sieben Bücher von der fürstlichen würtembergischen Hochzeit. Translated by Carl Christoph Beyer. Tübingen: Bey Georgen Gruppenbach, 1578. [Yale, Stuttgart, Wolfenbüttel]

Spongia Laonici Antisturmii, a Sturmeneck, Equitis Germani, adversus Lamberti Danaei, Calvinistae Gallicani Antiosiandrum. Pro Luca Osiandro. Tubingae: Excudebat Georgius Gruppenbachius, 1580. [Stuttgart, Wolfenbüttel]

Tryphiodori Aegyptii, grammatici, et poetae, liber de Ilii excidio. Edited and translated by Nicodemus Frischlin. Francofurti ad Moenum: Apud Ioannem Wechelum, impensis Wendelini Hom., 1588. [Stuttgart, Wolfenbüttel]

Other Primary Sources Cited

Alexander de Villa Dei. *Das Doctrinale des Alexander de Villa-Dei.* Edited by Dietrich Reichling. Berlin: Hofmann, 1893.

Aristophanes. *Comoediae.* Edited by F. W. Hall and W. M. Geldart. 2 vols. Oxford: Clarendon Press, 1906.

Aristotle. *De Arte Poetica.* Edited by Rudolf Kassel. Oxford: Clarendon Press, 1965.

Augustine. *De Doctrina Christiana.* Edited by Guilelmus M. Green. Corpus Scriptorum Ecclesiasticorum Latinorum, 80. Vienna: Hoelder-Pichler-Tempsky, 1963.

Bebel, Heinrich. *Comoedia vel potius dialogus de optimo studio iuvenum.* Edited and translated by Wilfried Barner. Stuttgart: Reclam, 1982.

————. *Facetien.* Edited by Gustav Bebermeyer. Bibliothek des litterarischen Vereins in Stuttgart, 276. Leipzig: Hiersemann, 1931.

Bede. *De Arte Metrica et De Schematibus et Tropis.* Edited by C. B. Kendall. Corpus Christianorum Scriptorum Latinorum, 123A. Turnhout: Brepols, 1975.

Birck, Sixt. *Sämtliche Dramen.* Edited by Manfred Brauneck. 3 vols. Berlin: de Gruyter, 1969–80.

Boltz, Valentin. *Publii Terentii Aphri sechs verteütschte Comedien auß eygen angeborner Lateinischer Sprach auffs trewlichst transferiert.* Tübingen: Morhart, 1544.

Brunner, Thomas. *Die schöne und kurtzweilige Historia/ von der Heirat Isaacs und seiner lieben Rebecca.* Edited by Wolfgang F. Michael and Hubert Heinen. Bern: Peter Lang, 1983.

Bruschius, Caspar. *Monasteriorum Germaniae praecipuorum maxime illustrium: centuria prima.* Ingolstadii: Apud Alexandrum et Samuelem Weyssenhornios fratres, 1551.

Bullinger, Heinrich, and Hans Sachs. *Lucretia-Dramen.* Edited by Horst Hartmann. Leipzig: VEB Bibliographisches Institut, 1973.

Celtis, Conrad. *Ludi Scaenici.* Edited by Felicitas Pindter. Budapest: Egyetemi Nyomda, 1945.

————. *Selections from Conrad Celtis, 1459–1508.* Edited and translated by Leonard Forster. Cambridge: Cambridge University Press, 1948.

Crusius, Martin. *Grammaticae graecae cum latina congruentis pars prima [et altera pars].* Basileae: Oporinus, 1562–63.

Culmann, Leonhard. *Von der Hochzeyt Isaacs und Rebecce.* In *Leonhard Culmann,* edited by Matthias W. Senger, pp. 464–519. Nieuwkoop: de Graaf, 1982.

Dedekind, Friedrich. *Der Christliche Ritter.* Ulssen: Michel Kröner, 1590.

Eccius Dedolatus. Translated by Thomas W. Best. Lexington: University of Kentucky Press, 1971.

Eckius Dedolatus. Edited by Siegfried Szamotólski. Lateinische Litteraturdenkmäler des 15. und 16. Jahrhunderts, 2. Berlin: Speyer and Peters, 1891.

Epistolae Obscurorum Virorum. Edited and translated by Griffin Stokes. London: Chatto and Windus, 1909.

Erasmus von Rotterdam. *Ausgewählte Schriften.* Edited by Werner Welzig. 8 vols. Darmstadt: Wissenschaftliche Buchgesellschaft, 1967–75.

———. *Opera Omnia.* Amsterdam: North-Holland Publishing Company, 1969– .

———. *Opus Epistolarum Erasmi Roterodami.* Edited by P. S. Allen and H. M. Allen. 12 vols. Oxford: Clarendon Press, 1906–58.

Gnapheus, Gulielmus. *Acolastus.* Edited and translated by W. E. D. Atkinson. London, Ontario: University of Western Ontario, 1964.

———. *Acolastus.* Edited by Johannes Bolte. Lateinische Litteraturdenkmäler des 15. und 16. Jahrhunderts, 1. Berlin: Speyer and Peters, 1891.

Gretser, Jakob. *Jakob Gretsers "Udo von Magdeburg."* Edited by Urs Herzog. Berlin: de Gruyter, 1970.

Heinrich Julius. *Die Schauspiele des Herzogs Heinrich Julius von Braunschweig.* Edited by Wilhelm Ludwig Holland. Bibliothek des litterarischen Vereins, 36. Stuttgart: Litterarischer Verein, 1855.

Hrotsvitha von Gandersheim. *Opera.* Edited by Karl Strecker. Leipzig: Teubner, 1906.

Hutten, Ulrich von. *Opera quae reperiri potuerunt omnia.* Edited by E. Böcking. 7 vols. Leipzig: Teubner, 1859–69.

Kerckmeister, Johannes. *Codrus.* Edited by Lothar Mundt. Berlin: de Gruyter, 1969.

Locher, Jakob. *Libri Philomusi. Panegyrici ad Regem. Tragedia de Thurcis et Suldano. Dyalogus de heresiarchis.* Strasbourg: Grüninger, 1497.

———. *Ludicrum Drama de sene amatore.* In Karl von Reinhardstoettner, *Plautus: Spätere Bearbeitungen plautinischer Lustspiele,* pp. 240–46. Leipzig: Wilhelm Friedrich, 1888.

———. *Spectaculum a Jacobo Locher more tragico effigiatum. In quo christianissimi Reges adversum truculentissimos Thurcos consilium ineunt expeditionemque bellicam instituunt inibi salubris pro fide tuenda exhortatio.* Printed with *Iudicium Paridis de pomo aureo de triplici hominum vita de tribus deabus que nobis vitam contemplativam activam ac voluptariam represent et que illarum sit melior tutiorque.* N.p., n.d. [Ingolstadt, 1502].

Luther, Martin. *D. Martin Luthers Werke.* 61 vols. Weimar: Hermann Böhlau, 1883–1983.

Manuel, Niklaus. *Der Ablaßkrämer.* Edited by Paul Zinsli. Bern: Francke, 1960.

————. *Niklaus Manuel.* Edited by Jakob Baechtold. Frauenfeld: Huber, 1878.

Melanchthon, Philipp. *Declamationes.* Edited by Karl Hartfelder. Lateinische Litteraturdenkmäler des 15. und 16. Jahrhunderts, 4. Berlin: Speyer and Peters, 1891.

————. *Elementorum Rhetorices libri duo.* [Antwerp:] Ioan. Grapheus typis excudebat, 1532.

————. *Opera quae supersunt omnia.* Edited by C. G. Bretschneider and H. E. Bindseil. 28 vols. Corpus Reformatorum, 1–28. Braunschweig: Apud C. A. Schwetschke et Filium, 1834–60.

————. *Werke in Auswahl.* Edited by Robert Stupperich. 7 vols. Gütersloh: Gerd Mohn, 1951–75.

Naogeorgus, Thomas. *Iudas Iscariotes Tragoedia nova et sacra, . . . Quoquo duae Sophoclis Tragoediae, Aiax Flagellifer et Philoctetes, ab eodem auctore carmina versae.* N.p., n.d.; introductory letter signed Stuttgart, 12 September 1552.

————. *Sämtliche Werke.* Edited by Hans-Gert Roloff. Berlin: de Gruyter, 1975– .

Ovid. *Fastorum Libri Sex.* Edited by E. H. Alton, D. E. W. Wormell, and E. Courtney. Leipzig: Teubner, 1978.

Petrarca, Francesco. *Le Familiari.* Edited by Vittorio Rossi and Umberto Bosco. 4 vols. Florence: G. C. Sansoni, 1933–42.

Plautus. *T. Macci Plauti Comoediae.* Edited by Wallace Lindsay. 2 vols. Oxford: Clarendon Press, 1904–5.

Plutarch. *Moralia.* Edited by Berthold Häsler. Leipzig: Teubner, 1978.

Rebhun, Paul. *Dramen.* Edited by Hermann Palm. Bibliothek des litterarischen Vereins, 49. Stuttgart: Litterarischer Verein, 1859.

————. *Susanna.* Edited by Hans-Gert Roloff. Stuttgart: Reclam, 1967.

Reuchlin, Johannes. *Henno.* Edited and translated by Harry C. Schnur. Stuttgart: Philipp Reclam, 1970.

————. *Johann Reuchlins Komödien.* Edited by Hugo Holstein. Halle: Buchhandlung des Waisenhauses, 1888.

Rhetorica ad Herennium. Edited by Gualtiero Calboli. Bologna: Pàtron, 1969.

Scaliger, Julius Caesar. *Poetices Libri Septem.* Lugduni: Apud Antonium Vincentium, 1561.

————. *Select Translations from Scaliger's Poetics.* Translated by Frederick Morgan Padelford. Yale Studies in English, 26. New York: Henry Holt, 1905.

Schonaeus, Cornelius. *Terentii Christiani Pars Secunda.* 1599. Reprint. Coloniae Agrippinae: Iodocus Kalcovius, 1652.

Schropp, Jakob. *Acta oecumenici concilii supra controversia de coena Domini.* [Translated by Nicodemus Frischlin.] Tubingae: Georg Gruppenbach, 1581.

Servius. *In Vergilii Carmina Commentarii.* Edited by Georg Thilo and Hermann Hagen. 4 vols. Leipzig: Teubner, 1881–1902.

Stumpf, Johannes. *Gemeiner Loblicher Eÿdgnosschaft Stetten-Landen und Völkkern Chronicwürdiger Thaaten Beschreibung.* Zürich: in der Froschow, 1586.

Terence. *P. Terenti Afri Comoediae.* Edited by Robert Kauer and Wallace Lindsay. Oxford: Clarendon Press, 1926.

Waldis, Burkard. *De Parabell vam vorlorn Szohn*. In *Die Schaubühne im Dienste der Reformation*, edited by Arnold Berger, 1:141–206. Leipzig: Reclam, 1935–36.

Wimpheling, Jacob. *Stylpho*. Edited and translated by Harry C. Schnur. Stuttgart: Reclam, 1971.

Wuttke, Dieter, ed. *Fastnachtspiele des 15. und 16. Jahrhunderts*. Stuttgart: Reclam, 1978.

Secondary Sources Cited

Abbé, Derek van. *Drama in Renaissance Germany and Switzerland*. New York and London: Cambridge University Press, 1961.

Auerbach, Erich. *Literatursprache und Publikum in der lateinischen Spätantike und im Mittelalter*. Bern: Francke, 1958.

Bacon, Thomas I. *Martin Luther and the Drama*. Amsterdam: Rodopi, 1976.

Barner, Wilfried. *Barockrhetorik: Untersuchungen zu ihren geschichtlichen Grundlagen*. Tübingen: Niemeyer, 1970.

Bebermeyer, Gustav. "Nicodemus Frischlin." *Neue deutsche Biographie* 5:620–21. Berlin: Duncker and Humblot, 1953– .

_____. *Tübinger Dichterhumanisten: Bebel, Frischlin, Flayder*. 1927. Reprint. Hildesheim: Georg Olms Verlagsbuchhandlung, 1967.

Best, Thomas. *Macropedius*. New York: Twayne, 1972.

Bloch, Ernst. *Thomas Münzer als Theologe der Revolution*. Berlin: Aufbau Verlag, 1960.

Böckmann, Paul. *Formgeschichte der deutschen Dichtung*. Hamburg: Hoffmann and Campe, 1949.

Boeckh, Joachim G. "Gastrodes: Ein Beitrag zu Salomon Schweiggers *Ein newe Reyßbeschreibung* und zu Nicodemus Frischlins *Rebecca*." *Wissenschaftliche Zeitschrift der Martin Luther Universität Halle-Wittenberg, Gesellschafts- und Sprachwissenschaftliche Reihe* 10, part 4 (1961): 951–57.

Borchardt, Frank. *German Antiquity and Renaissance Myth*. Baltimore and London: Johns Hopkins Press, 1971.

Bowen, Barbara C. "Renaissance Collections of *Facetiae*, 1499–1528: A New Listing." *Renaissance Quarterly* 39 (1986): 263–75.

Brett-Evans, David. *Von Hrotsvit bis Folz und Gengenbach: Eine Geschichte des mittelalterlichen deutschen Dramas*. 2 vols. Berlin: Erich Schmidt, 1975.

Brod, Max. *Johannes Reuchlin und sein Kampf*. Stuttgart: Kohlhammer, 1965.

Brown, Cheri. "The *Susanna* of Johannes Placentius: The First Latin Version of the Biblical Drama." *Humanistica Lovaniensia* 36 (1987): 239–51.

Conz, Carl Philipp. *Nikodem Frischlin: der unglückliche wirtembergische Gelehrte und Dichter*. Königsberg: Friedrich Nicolovius, 1792.

Coppel, Bernhard. "Jakob Locher und seine in Freiburg aufgeführten Dramen." In *Acta Conventus Neo-Latini Amstelodamensis*, edited by P. Tuynman, G. C. Kuiper, and E. Keßler, pp. 258–72. Munich: Fink, 1979.

Casey, Paul. *The Susanna Theme in German Literature*. Bonn: Bouvier, 1976.

Catholy, Eckehard. *Fastnachtspiel*. Stuttgart: Metzler, 1966.

Creizenach, Wilhelm. *Geschichte des neueren Dramas*. 5 vols. Halle: Niemeyer, 1893–1916.

Curtius, Ernst Robert. *Europäische Literatur und lateinisches Mittelalter*. Bern and Munich: Francke, 1978.

Dürrwächter, Anton. *Jakob Gretser und seine Dramen*. Freiburg i. Br: Herdersche Verlagsbuchhandlung, 1912.

Dyck, Joachim. *Athen und Jerusalem*. Munich: Beck, 1978.

Ellinger, Georg. *Philipp Melanchthon*. Berlin: Gaertners Verlagsbuchhandlung, 1902.

Elschenbroich, Adalbert. "Eine textkritische Nikodemus Frischlin-Ausgabe." *Jahrbuch für internationale Germanistik* 12, no. 1 (1980): 179–95.

————. "Imitatio und Disputatio in Nikodemus Frischlins Religionskomödie *Phasma*: Späthumanistisches Drama und akademische Unterrichtsmethode in Tübingen am Ausgang des 16. Jahrhunderts." In *Stadt-Schule-Universität-Buchwesen und die deutsche Literatur im 17. Jahrhundert*, edited by Albrecht Schöne, pp. 335–70. Munich: Beck, 1976.

Evans, R. J. W. *Rudolf II and His World*. Oxford: Clarendon Press, 1973.

Fink, Reinhard. "Studien zu den Dramen des Nikodemus Frischlin." Dissertation, Leipzig, 1920.

Francke, Otto. *Terenz und die lateinische Schulcomoedie in Deutschland*. Weimar: Hermann Böhlau, 1877.

Franz, Gunther. "Bücherzensur und Irenik." In *Theologen und Theologie an der Universität Tübingen*, edited by Martin Brecht, pp. 123–94. Tübingen: Mohr, 1977.

Friedländer, Paul. "Aristophanes in Deutschland." *Die Antike* 8 (1932): 229–53, and 9 (1933): 81–104.

Gerl, Hanna-Barbara. "*De imitatione* von Camerarius: Die Wichtigkeit der Nachahmung für humanistische Anthropologie und Sprachtheorie." In *Joachim Camerarius*, edited by Frank Baron, pp. 187–99. Munich: Fink, 1978.

Gmelin, Hermann. "Das Prinzip der Imitatio in den romanischen Literaturen der Renaissance." *Romanische Forschungen* 42 (1932): 83–360.

Goedeke, Karl. *Grundriß zur Geschichte der deutschen Dichtung aus den Quellen*. 16 vols. Dresden: Ehlermann, 1884–1984.

Hall, Vernon. *The Life of Julius Caesar Scaliger*. Transactions of the American Philosophical Society, 40. Philadelphia: American Philosophical Society, 1950.

Haller, Johannes. *Die Anfänge der Universität Tübingen, 1477–1537*. Stuttgart: Kohlhammer, 1927.

Helm, R. "Priscianus." In *Pauly Wissowa Realencyclopädia der classischen Altertumswissenschaft*, 22:2328–48. Stuttgart: Druckenmüller, 1954.

Hermelink, Heinrich. *Geschichte der evangelischen Kirche in Württemberg von der Reformation bis zur Gegenwart*. Stuttgart: Wunderlich, 1949.

Herrick, Marvin. *Comic Theory in the Sixteenth Century*. Urbana: University of Illinois Press, 1950.

Hess, Günter. *Deutsch-Lateinische Narrenzunft: Studien zum Verhältnis von Volkssprache und Latinität in der satirischen Literatur des 16. Jahrhunderts.* Munich: Beck, 1971.

Hille, Curt. *Die deutsche Komödie unter der Einwirkung des Aristophanes.* Leipzig: Quelle and Meyer, 1907.

Hofmann, Norbert. *Die Artistenfakultät an der Universität Tübingen 1534–1601.* Tübingen: Mohr, 1982.

Holstein, Hugo. *Die Reformation im Spiegelbilde der dramatischen Litteratur des sechzehnten Jahrhunderts.* Halle: Niemeyer, 1886.

Horawitz, Adalbert Heinrich. *Caspar Bruschius.* Leipzig: Brockhaus, 1874.

Kampschulte, Franz. *Die Universität Erfurt in ihrem Verhältnisse zu dem Humanismus und der Reformation.* 2 vols. Trier: Lintz, 1858–60.

Kiesel, Helmut. *Bei Hof, bei Höll.* Tübingen: Niemeyer, 1979.

Kohl, Josef. "Nikodemus Frischlin: Die Ständesatire in seinem Werke." Dissertation, Mainz, 1967.

Kolb, Robert. "Jakob Andreae." In *Shapers of Religious Traditions in Germany, Switzerland, and Poland, 1560–1600,* edited by Jill Raitt, pp. 53–68. New Haven: Yale University Press, 1981.

Könneker, Barbara. *Die deutsche Literatur der Reformationszeit.* Munich: Winkler, 1975.

———. *Hans Sachs.* Stuttgart: Metzler, 1971.

Krause, C. *Helius Eobanus Hessus: Sein Leben und seine Werke.* Gotha: Perthes, 1879.

Lange, Carl Heinrich. *Nicodemus Frischlin, vita, fama, scriptis ac vitae exitu memorabilis.* Braunschweig and Leipzig: Simon Jakob Renger, 1727.

Lausberg, Heinrich. *Handbuch der literarischen Rhetorik.* 2 vols. Munich: Max Hueber, 1973.

Lebeau, Jean. "De la comédie des humanistes a la 'divine comédie.' " In *L'Humanisme Allemand (1480–1540),* pp. 477–91. Munich: Fink, 1979.

———. "Sixt Bircks Judith (1539), Erasmus und der Türckenkrieg." *Daphnis* 9 (1980): 679–98.

Levinger, Helene. *Das Augsburger Schultheater.* Berlin: Otto Elsmer, 1931.

Ludwig, Walther. "Nicodemus Frischlin." In *Enzyklopädie des Märchens,* edited by Kurt Ranke, et al., 5:373–78. Berlin and New York: de Gruyter, 1977.

Magnien, Michel. "Erasme et Scaliger." In *Acta Conventus Neo-Latini Sanctandreani,* edited by I. D. McFarlane, pp. 253–61. Binghamton, N.Y.: Medieval and Renaissance Texts and Studies, 1986.

Michael, Wolfgang F. *Das deutsche Drama der Reformationszeit.* Bern: Peter Lang, 1984.

———. *Frühformen der deutschen Bühne.* Berlin: Selbstverlag der Gesellschaft für Theaterwissenschaft, 1963.

Muesel, Alfred. *Thomas Müntzer und seine Zeit.* Berlin: Aufbau Verlag, 1952.

Neumeyer, Erich. "Nicodemus Frischlin als Dramatiker." Dissertation, Rostock, 1924.

Oberman, Heiko A. *Werden und Wertung der Reformation.* Tübingen: Mohr, 1979.

Parente, James A. *Religious Drama and the Humanist Tradition*. Leiden: Brill, 1987.

Pigman, G. W. "Versions of Imitation in the Renaissance." *Renaissance Quarterly* 33 (1980): 1–32.

Pilger, Robert. "Die Dramatisierungen der Susanna im 16. Jahrhundert." *Zeitschrift für deutsche Philologie* 11 (1880): 129–217.

Price, David. "Nicodemus Frischlin and Sixteenth-Century Drama." Ph.D. dissertation, Yale University, 1985.

————. "Nicodemus Frischlin's Rhetoric." In *Acta Conventus Neo-Latini Guelpherbytani*, edited by Stella Revard, Fidel Rädle, and Mario Di Cesare, pp. 532–39. Binghamton, N.Y.: Medieval and Renaissance Texts and Studies, 1988.

————. "Politics, Poetry, and Whimsy: On the Humanist Dramaturgy of Jakob Locher (1471–1528)." *Yale University Library Gazette* 63 (1988): 23–31.

Reiff, Arno. *Interpretatio, Imitatio, Aemulatio*. Würzburg: Triltsch, 1959.

Ridé, Jacques. "Der Nationalgedanke im *Julius Redivivus* von Nicodemus Frischlin." *Daphnis* 9 (1980): 719–41.

————. *L'image du Germain dans la pensée et la littérature allemandes de la redécouverte de Tacite à la fin du XVIeme siècle*. 2 vols. Paris: Champion, 1976.

Ritter, Fr. "Zu den Strassburger Drucken des Nicodemus Frischlin." *Annuaire de la société historique littéraire et scientifique du Club Vosgien*, n.s. 4 (1936): 113–20.

Roethe, Gustav. "Nicodemus Frischlin als Dramatiker." In *Julius Redivivus*, edited by Walther Janell, pp. xxiv–lix. Berlin: Weidmannsche Buchhandlung, 1912.

Roloff, Hans-Gert. "Heilsgeschichte, Weltgeschichte und aktuelle Polemik: Thomas Naogeorgs *Tragoedia Nova Pammachius*." *Daphnis* 9 (1980): 743–67.

————. "Neulateinisches Drama." In *Reallexikon der deutschen Literaturgeschichte*, edited by Werner Kohlschmidt and Wolfgang Mohr, pp. 645–78. Berlin: de Gruyter, 1965.

Roth, P. Bartholomäus. *Franz von Mayronis O.F.M.* Werl: Franziskus-Druckerei, 1936.

Roth, R., ed. *Urkunden zur Geschichte der Universität Tübingen aus den Jahren 1476 bis 1550*. Tübingen: Laupp, 1877.

Roustan, L. "De N. Frischlini comoediis latine scriptis." Dissertation, University of Paris, 1898.

Sattler, Christian Friedrich. *Geschichte des Herzogthums Würtenberg*. 5 vols. Tübingen: Georg Heinrich Reiss, 1769–72.

Schade, Richard E. "*Julius Redivivus*: Entstehung und Stuttgarter Aufführung." In *Julius Redivivus*, translated by Jakob Frischlin and edited by Richard E. Schade, pp. 159–73. Stuttgart: Reclam, 1983.

————. "Nicodemus Frischlin und der Stuttgarter Hof: Zur Aufführung von *Julius Redivivus*." In *Europäische Hofkultur im 16. und 17. Jahrhundert*, edited by A. Buck and C. Wiedemann, 2:335–44. Hamburg: Hauswedell, 1981.

————. *Studies in Early German Comedy 1500–1650*. Columbia, S.C.: Camden House, 1988.

Scherer, Wilhelm. "Nicodemus Frischlin." *Allgemeine deutsche Biographie* 8:96–104. Leipzig: Duncker and Humblot, 1875–1912.

Schmidt, Charles. *Le vie et les travaux de Jean Sturm*. 1855. Reprint. Nieuwkoop: de Graaf, 1970.

Schmidt, P. Expeditius. *Die Bühnenverhältnisse des deutschen Schuldramas und seiner volkstümlichen Ableger im sechzehnten Jahrhundert*. Berlin: Duncker, 1903.

Schreiner, Klaus. "Frischlins 'Oration vom Landleben' und die Folgen." *Attempto* 43/44 (1972): 122–35.

Schulz-Behrend, George. "Nicodemus Frischlin and the Imperial Court: New Evidence from His Letters." *Germanic Review* 30 (1955): 172–80.

Seuffert, Bernhardt. "Frischlins Beziehung zu Graz und Laibach." *Euphorion* 5 (1898): 257–66.

Skopnik, Günter. *Das Straßburger Schultheater: Sein Spielplan und seine Bühne*. Frankfurt: Selbstverlag des Elsaß-Lothringen-Instituts, 1935.

Sohm, Walter. *Die Schule Johann Sturms und die Kirche Straßburgs in ihrem gegenseitigen Verhältnis, 1530–1581*. Munich: Oldenbourg, 1912.

Stahlecker, Reinhold. "Martin Crusius und Nicodemus Frischlin." *Zeitschrift für württembergische Landesgeschichte* 7 (1943): 323–66.

Strauß, David Friedrich. *Leben und Schriften des Dichters und Philologen Nicodemus Frischlin*. Frankfurt am Main: Literarische Anstalt, 1856.

Süß, Wilhelm. *Aristophanes und die Nachwelt*. Leipzig: Dieterich'sche Verlagsbuchhandlung, 1911.

Szarota, Elida Maria. *Das Jesuitendrama im deutschen Sprachgebiet*. 4 vols. Munich: Fink, 1979–87.

Tarot, Rolf. "Ideologie und Drama: zur Typologie der untragischen Dramatik in Deutschland." In *Typologia Litterarum: Festschrift für Max Wehrli*, edited by S. Sonderegger, A. Haas, and H. Burger, pp. 351–66. Zürich: Atlantis, 1969.

Telle, Emile V. *L'Erasmianus sive Ciceronianus d'Etienne Dolet*. Geneva: Librairie Droz, 1975.

Trometer, Christiane. "Die polemischen Züge in den Isaak-und-Rebekka-Dramen des sechzehnten Jahrhunderts (1539–1576)." *Daphnis* 9 (1980): 699–709.

Trunz, Erich. "Der deutsche Späthumanismus um 1600 als Standeskultur." In *Deutsche Barockforschung*, edited by Richard Alewyn, pp. 147–81. Cologne and Berlin: Kiepenheuer and Witsch, 1966.

Valentin, Jean-Marie. "Aux origines du théâtre néo-latin de la réforme catholique: *L'Euripus* (1549) de Livinus Brechtus." *Humanistica Lovaniensia* 21 (1972): 81–188.

———. "Die Moralität im 16. Jahrhundert: Konfessionelle Wandlungen einer dramatischen Struktur." *Daphnis* 9 (1980): 769–88.

———. *Le théâtre des Jésuites dans les pays de langue allemande (1554–1680)*. 3 vols. Bern: Peter Lang, 1978.

Verzeichnis der im deutschen Sprachbereich erschienenen Drucke des XVI. Jahrhunderts. Bayerische Staatsbibliothek and Herzog August Bibliothek. Stuttgart: Hiersemann, 1983– .

Vollert, Konrad. *Zur Geschichte der lateinischen Facetiensammlungen des 15. und 16. Jahrhunderts*. Berlin: Mayer and Müller, 1912.

Vormbaum, Reinhold. *Evangelische Schulordnungen*. 3 vols. Gütersloh: Bertelsmann, 1860–64.

Weinberg, Bernard. *A History of Literary Criticism in the Italian Renaissance*. 2 vols. Chicago: University of Chicago Press, 1961.

Wheelis, Samuel M. "Nicodemus Frischlin: Comedian and Humanist." Ph.D. dissertation, University of California, Berkeley, 1968.

———. "Nicodemus Frischlin's *Julius Redivivus* and Its Reflections on the Past." *Studies in the Renaissance* 20 (1973): 106–17.

———. "Publish and Perish: On the Martyrdom of Nicodemus Frischlin." *Neophilologus* 58, no. 1 (1974): 41–51.

Wiegand, Hermann. *Hodoeporica: Studien zur neulateinischen Reisedichtung des deutschen Kulturraumes im 16. Jahrhundert*. Baden-Baden: Koerner, 1984.

Zacher, J. "Nicodemus Frischlin." In *Allgemeine Encyklopädie der Wissenschaften und Künste*, edited by Johann Samuel Ersch and J. G. Gruber, 1:225–44. Leipzig: Brockhaus, 1849.

Zeydel, Edwin. "The Reception of Hrotsvitha by the German Humanists after 1493." *Journal of English and Germanic Philology* 44 (1945): 239–49.

Zielinski, Thaddaeus. *Cicero im Wandel der Jahrhunderte*. Darmstadt: Wissenschaftliche Buchgesellschaft, 1967.

Index

University of North Carolina
Studies in the Germanic Languages and Literatures

For other volumes in the "Studies" see p. ii.

Send orders to:
The University of North Carolina Press, P.O. Box 2288
Chapel Hill, NC 27515-2288

Several out-of-print titles are available in limited quantities through the UNCSGLL office. These include:

58 WALTER W. ARNDT, PAUL W. BROSMAN, JR., FREDERIC E. COENEN, AND WERNER P. FRIEDRICH, EDS. *Studies in Historical Linguistics in Honor of George Sherman Lane.* 1967. Pp. xx, 241.

68 JOHN NEUBAUER. *Bifocal Vision. Novalis' Philosophy of Nature and Disease.* 1971. Pp. x, 196.

70 DONALD F. NELSON. *Portrait of the Artist as Hermes. A Study of Myth and Psychology in Thomas Mann's "Felix Krull."* 1971. Pp. xvi, 146.

72 CHRISTINE OERTEL SJÖGREN. *The Marble Statue as Idea: Collected Essays on Adalbert Stifter's "Der Nachsommer."* 1972. Pp. xiv, 121.

73 DONALD G. DAVIAU AND JORUN B. JOHNS, EDS. *The Correspondence of Schnitzler and Auernheimer, with Raoul Auernheimer's Aphorisms.* 1972. Pp. xii, 161.

74 A. MARGARET ARENT MADELUNG. *"The Laxdoela Saga": Its Structural Patterns.* 1972. Pp. xiv, 261.

75 JEFFREY L. SAMMONS. *Six Essays on the Young German Novel.* 2nd ed. 1975. Pp. xiv, 187.

76 DONALD H. CROSBY AND GEORGE C. SCHOOLFIELD, EDS. *Studies in the German Drama. A Festschrift in Honor of Walter Silz.* 1974. Pp. xxvi, 255.

Orders for these titles only should be sent to Editor, UNCSGLL, CB# 3160 Dey Hall, Chapel Hill, NC 27599-3160.

Volumes 1–44, 46–50, 52, 60, and 79 of the "Studies" have been reprinted. They may be ordered from AMS Press, Inc., 56 E. 13th Street, New York, NY 10003.

For complete list of reprinted titles write to the Editor.